Research libraries and collections

in the

United Kingdom

a selective inventory and guide

Research libraries and collections

in the
United Kingdom

a selective inventory and guide

compiled by

STEPHEN ROBERTS
ALAN COOPER
LESLEY GILDER

CLIVE BINGLEY
LONDON

LINNET BOOKS
HAMDEN · CONN

FIRST PUBLISHED 1978
BY CLIVE BINGLEY LTD
16 PEMBRIDGE ROAD LONDON W11 UK
SIMULTANEOUSLY PUBLISHED IN THE USA
BY LINNET BOOKS
AN IMPRINT OF THE SHOE STRING PRESS INC
995 SHERMAN AVENUE HAMDEN CONNECTICUT 06514
SET IN 10 ON 10 POINT PRESS ROMAN BY ALLSET
PRINTED AND BOUND IN THE UK
BY REDWOOD BURN LTD
TROWBRIDGE AND ESHER
COPYRIGHT © 1978 STEPHEN ROBERTS,
ALAN COOPER, LESLEY GILDER
ALL RIGHTS RESERVED
BINGLEY ISBN: 0-85157-258-8
LINNET ISBN: 0-208-01667-8

Library of Congress Cataloging in Publication Data

Roberts, Stephen Andrew.
    Research libraries and collections in the United
Kingdom.

    Includes indexes.
        1. Research libraries—Great Britain—Directories.
2. Library resources—Great Britain—Directories.
I. Cooper, Alan, joint author. II. Gilder, Lesley,
joint author. III. Title.
Z791.A1R6 1978   026'.0025'41   78-11560
ISBN 0-208-01667-8

CONTENTS

PREFACE

TAKEN as a whole, a large number of lists and guides to libraries and collections have found their way onto library shelves. Nor will this present one be the last; so what is its justification?

The main impetus to produce this guide arose from the observation that there did not appear to be one publication holding in a convenient format a comprehensive list of British libraries and collections of interest and relevance to the researcher, whether specialist or not. A number of guides list more libraries than we do, and there are specialist guides and articles which provide more detailed information than is given here; there are also guides which give similar details about libraries and collections, but which are restricted to a particular geographical area.

The present volume does not attempt to supplement these, nor to oust them. What it does is to offer a useful general package of information about research libraries and collections in the United Kingdom, which can be used as a point of departure for more detailed exploration. At the same time it offers a conspectus of the rich resources available to potential users. In an age when cooperation between libraries has never been more important, this kind of 'tableau' assumes a new importance, perhaps helping to make clear what has appeared to be hidden, and giving prominence to things which deserve to be more widely known.

A practical belief in the interdependence of all kinds of library resources is shown by including a range of different kinds of research library, and giving the user a brief guide to further sources of information, which must necessarily be used if a maximum awareness of resources is desired.

We have consulted all the publications mentioned in the introductory section for inspiration, information and verification. Few guides can be produced without relying on those which have gone before.

We would also like to thank all librarians who answered correspondence and completed the entries and questionnaires sent to them for review. Responsibility for misquotation, and any errors of fact and interpretation, must remain the responsibility of the compilers, who would be more than glad to receive comments and information which could lead to improvement in future editions.

Stephen Roberts
Alan Cooper
Lesley Gilder

8

INTRODUCTION

A SELECTIVE GUIDE to libraries and collections must make clear its aims, and the grounds upon which selection is based. The purpose of this introduction is to deal with these points, and at the same time to direct the user to other sources of information which can provide additional and further guidance.

It has already been noted that there are a number of guides to libraries and collections available, and the question has been posed 'why produce another?' Apart from the fact that libraries and their collections change in character, and in the kind of services they offer, the main problem facing the relatively untutored user is how best to penetrate through the immense bibliographical jungle which already exists. The aim of the compilers of this volume has been to provide just such assistance. By definition a selective guide cannot be comprehensive either in coverage of institutions or contents, but if its entries are well-chosen and the scheme of choice logical, selectivity can be an asset. Selectivity is in fact no handicap if the materials discussed cover the principal resources in the field.

By and large, the guide is confined to libraries where the user can gain access relatively easily, subject to the usual courtesies and formalities (as listed here). Nevertheless, a number of libraries of more restricted access have been included, on the grounds that widespread knowledge of the existence of their special or unusually comprehensive collections is important. The term research library has been interpreted to mean one containing primary and secondary material of use to a wide range of scholars, researchers, and investigators.

National libraries and specialist libraries

At the hub of the library network in the United Kingdom is the British Library. Through the services of two of its main divisions—the Reference Division and the Lending Division—it fulfils the traditional functions of a National Library. There are in addition two specialist divisions classed as Bibliographical Services, and Research and Development. One important feature of the Reference Division is that under the copyright acts it has inherited the right to legal deposit of British material from the British Museum Library (although the administration of claims is exercised through the Copyright Receipt Office).

In addition to the British Library, important national collections are held by the National Library of Scotland and the National Library of Wales, which also have copyright privileges. The collections found in these three copyright libraries have to be considered in any guide such as this, although they are traditionally libraries of last resort, to which users go to consult items not available elsewhere.

The entries in this section (entries 1 to 89) are a selection of libraries, comprising the national collections just mentioned, together with a number of other libraries which can be considered to form comparable national collections in their own right. These include, for example, National Art Library, British Museum (Natural History) Library, National Maritime Museum, Public Record Office. Some are also listed because of the size of their holdings, particular subject strengths, range of formats of material held, and accessibility.

There are very many more specialist libraries in the UK (in library jargon usually referred to as special libraries, and located in industrial firms, specialist associations, and institutions) than could ever be listed in such a guide as this. Those chosen here may not even be the most important according to some criteria, but they are representative of non-industrial and non-commercial special libraries likely to be of use to researchers, and in the main provide a reasonable degree of public access. To get the selection into proper perspective, the specialist libraries listed should be thought of as complementary to the academic libraries which form the other main group of this guide.

The most readily available guide to special library resources is the *Aslib directory*, which enables users to extend their search to other libraries and collections; for example, to libraries belonging to a range of societies and specialist groups.

One major category of specialist library virtually excluded from this present guide is medical libraries, whether in clinical or teaching environments. For information on medical libraries the user is referred to the *Directory of medical libraries in the British Isles* published by the Library Association (Medical Section). Nevertheless, a certain amount of medical literature is to be found in some university libraries, and in the

10

Science Reference Library (Bayswater Division). No details are given of libraries in the London Postgraduate Medical Federation, or of the undergraduate medical and dental schools in London and elsewhere.

Public libraries

A number of the large public library collections are included in this inventory, both on grounds of wealth and specialisation of collections, and because they play an important regional function in the national library service network. The listing has been very selective indeed, and can be justified in two ways; firstly by the need to restrict the overall size of the book, but secondly, and more importantly, because the UK is fortunate in having a ubiquitous free public library service, within reasonable geographical range of the majority of users, and capable of serving a wide spectrum of basic requirements for books and information.

Users can locate their main public library system and service points by reference either to the Post Office telephone directory, or to one or other of the following: *Libraries in the United Kingdom and the Republic of Ireland*; the *Aslib directory*; the *Libraries, museums and art galleries yearbook*. The user of this guide should treat the public library as a source of ready reference, and as a point of referral to other points of the library network.

Academic libraries

Academic libraries in institutions of higher education account for nearly two-thirds of the entries in this inventory. There are two reasons for this emphasis in coverage. Firstly, the libraries serve institutions in which a large proportion of the UK research effort is carried out, particularly in the social sciences and the humanities, though they do not have a monopoly of scientific and technical research. Secondly, the libraries actively attempt to keep abreast of the relevant literature in the specialities of their institutions—at least in so far as their currently limited resources permit. In the course of serving teaching and research the libraries have often been able to build up collections of national and international importance.

The inventory lists libraries in all university and polytechnic institutions, and in a selection of Scottish central institutions. The entries for Oxford and Cambridge are not complete for all library facilities at those places, but a brief list and guides to further sources are mentioned (for example in individual colleges and departments, not all of which provide ready access to users without special arrangements.

Entries for London University are comprehensive with respect to colleges, schools and institutes, with the exception of those in the medical field. In other universities and polytechnics the main library institution and locations are given, but the listing is not complete with respect to exact details of all departmental and outlier collections. This is neither necessary nor particularly useful in an inventory of this kind.

GUIDES TO LIBRARIES AND COLLECTIONS

In order to become fully acquainted with relevant library resources the user must try and gain a working familiarity with some of the published guides and literature about collections and libraries. A number of the most wide-ranging and generally available guides are mentioned in this section, together with a number of less familiar and more specialised sources.

The user who finds the profusion of guides off-putting can always turn to a librarian for advice on sources to use for personal assistance and for referral. The guides listed here are classified broadly into three separate but not mutually exclusive categories: 1 general guides to national, regional and local resources; 2 guides covering specific subjects or forms of material; 3 guides to collections serving studies in special geographical areas (area studies, regional studies).

There are altogether a great many so called 'guides to the literature' available; many of these contain notes about library collections, although a surprising number do not do so in any detail. These are to be located in reference and bibliography sections in libraries (for instance in major public reference collections); consult a librarian for further details.

The place of publication is London unless otherwise indicated.

1 GENERAL GUIDES

Arts Libraries Society *ARLIS directory of members* Corsham, the
    Society, 1975.
*Aslib directory vol 1: Information sources in science, technology and
    commerce* 4th ed, Aslib, 1978. *Vol 2: Information sources in medi-
cine, the social sciences and the humanities* 3rd ed, Aslib, 1970. These
form one of the standard listings, with brief entries on subject scope.

British Council *Scientific and learned societies of Great Britain: a handbook compiled from official sources* Allen & Unwin, 1964. Provides brief notes on libraries and holdings.

British Library, Science Reference Library *Guide to government department and other libraries and information bureaux* BL/SRL, 1976. A useful short guide, but does not cover academic libraries in higher education, with a few exceptions.

Burkett, J *Special library and information services in the United Kingdom vol 1: Industrial and related library and information services in the United Kingdom* 3rd ed, LA, 1972. *Vol 2: Government and related library and information services in the United Kingdom* 3rd ed, LA, 1974. The standard narrative guide, describing in vol 2 many libraries to which there is no public access.

Department of Industry: Technical services for industry DOI, 1975. A specialised guide to sources, but with a very wide range of coverage, including some social science collections.

Fisher, R K *Libraries of university departments of adult education and extra-mural studies* 5th ed, LA, 1974.

Irwin, R and Staveley, R *The libraries of London* 2nd rev ed, LA, 1964. One of the classic guides to libraries, and still useful background reading. Consists of a series of individual essays.

Joint Committee on Learned Societies of the Royal Society and the British Academy *A survey of learned societies* The Society and the Academy, 1976. Not a guide to libraries in any sense, but useful to anyone wishing to set society libraries against their background.

Libraries, museums and art galleries yearbook 1976 Cambridge, James Clarke, 1976. A standard listing, useful in that it lists in detail public library service points down to branch level.

Library Association *Libraries in the United Kingdom and the Republic of Ireland: a complete list of public library services and a select list of academic and other library addresses* LA, 1971. A straightforward list; useful reference source of public library authorities and addresses of service points.

Library Association (Reference, Special and Information Section) *Library resources in* . . . One of the standard listings, with concise but brief details. Separate titles for London and South-east England, East Anglia, East Midlands, West Midlands, Merseyside, Yorkshire, Greater Manchester, Wales, South-west England and the Channel Islands.

McColvin, K R (ed) *Directory of London public libraries* 5th ed, Association of Chief Librarians, 1973. A useful source, more for the librarian than the general user.

Morgan, P (comp) *Oxford libraries outside the Bodleian: a guide* Oxford, Bibliographical Society and the Bodleian Library, 1974. A very thorough and comprehensive guide.

Newcombe, L *The university and college libraries of Great Britain and Ireland: a guide to the material available to the research student* Bumpus, 1927. Worth mentioning although historical by now. This present guide tries to fill the gap left unfilled by successors to this volume.

Scottish Health Services Centre Library *Library resources in the Scottish health service* Edinburgh, the Centre, 1976.

Smart, C R *Public reference services in England and Wales; a directory of key personnel* LA (Reference, Special and Information Section), 1976.

Stephenson, G R (ed) *Directory of northern libraries* Ashington, Northern Circle of College Librarians, 1972. Useful regional guide, similar in content to the LA (Reference, Special and Information Section) series.

Tait, J A and H F C (eds) *Library resources in Scotland 1976-77* Glasgow, Scottish LA, 1976. Companion guide to the LA (Reference, Special and Information Section) guides noted above.

University of Cambridge *First report of the General Board's Committee on Libraries. Cambridge University reporter* March 28 1969, no 4653. A very useful and detailed guide to supplement the other guides to Cambridge libraries.

2   GUIDES COVERING SPECIFIC SUBJECTS OR FORMS OF MATERIAL

Allum, D N, Bolton R V, Buchanan D S *Marine transport; a guide to libraries and sources of information in Great Britain* LA (Reference, Special and Information Section), 1975.

Armstrong, N E S *Local collections in Scotland* Glasgow, Scottish LA, 1977 (Scottish Library Studies no 5).

Barley, M W *A guide to British topographical collections* Council for British Archaeology, 1974.

Comfort, A F and Loveless, C *Guide to government data: a survey of unpublished social science material in libraries of government departments in London* Macmillan, for the British Library of Political and Economic Science, 1974.

Downs, R B and E C *British library resources; a bibliographical guide* Chicago, ALA; and Mansell Information Publishing, 1973. A guide to catalogues, lists and bibliographies describing the holding of research, academic and special libraries in the UK. Entries are arranged in a broad subject classification. Obviously an invaluable supplement to inventories and guides arranged by library and institution.

Hepworth, P (ed) *Select biographical sources: the Library Association manuscripts survey* LA, 1971. Arranged by person, with library locations.

Kitson Clark, G and Elton, G R *Guide to research facilities in history in the universities of Great Britain and Ireland* 2nd ed, Cambridge UP, 1965.

Library Association *Directory of medical libraries in the British Isles* 3rd ed, LA (Medical Section), 1969. The standard guide to medical libraries, with a very few exceptions.

Line, J *Archival collections of non-book materials: a preliminary list indicating policies for preservation and access* BL, 1977.

Long, M W *Music in British libraries: a directory of resources* 2nd ed, LA, 1974. Brief entries with wide range of coverage and notes on special collections.

Ottley, G *Railway history: a guide to sixty-one collections in libraries and archives in Great Britain* LA (Reference, Special and Information Section), 1973. A model of presentation, deserving emulation in other fields.

Percival, A C (ed) *English Association handbook of societies and collections* LA, 1977.

Salway, L (ed) *Special collections of children's literature: a guide to collections in libraries and other organisations in London and the Home Counties* Birmingham, LA (Youth Libraries Group), 1972 (pamphlet no 11).

3 GUIDES TO COLLECTIONS IN AREA AND REGIONAL STUDIES

Centre for South Asian Studies, University of Cambridge *Guide to South Asian material in the libraries of London, Oxford and Cambridge* Cambridge, the Centre.

Collison, R (comp) *Directory of libraries and special collections on Asia and North Africa* Crosby Lockwood, 1970.

Collison, R (comp) *The SCOLMA directory of libraries and special collections on Africa* 3rd rev ed by John Roe, Crosby Lockwood, 1973.

Commission of the European Communities *Liste des adresses des Centre de Documentation Européene et des bibliothèques dépositaires (universitaires et publiques)* Brussels, EEC, 1974. Address list for European Documentation Centres.

Dewar, A *Select list of Commonwealth history library resources in the Greater London area, Oxford and Manchester* Birkbeck College Library, 1976.

Hallewell, L (ed) *Latin-American bibliography: a guide to sources of information and research* Institute of Latin-American Studies and SCONUL Latin-America Group, 1978.

Hewitt, A R *Guide to resources for Commonwealth studies in London, Oxford and Cambridge* Athlone Press, 1957.

Mander-Jones, P (ed) *Manuscripts in the British Isles relating to Australia, New Zealand and the Pacific* Canberra, Australian National University Press, 1972.

Mathews, N and Wainwright M D *Guide to manuscripts and documents in the British Isles relating to Africa* Oxford UP, 1971.

Mathews, N and Wainwright M D (comps) and Pearson J D (ed) *Guide to manuscripts and documents in the British Isles relating to the Far East* Oxford UP, 1977.

Moon, B E (comp) *South-east Asia Library Group: survey of library resources* Hull, University Library, 1973. A worldwide survey with British material included.

Naylor, B et al *Directory of libraries and special collections on Latin America and the West Indies* Athlone Press, 1975.

University of London, Institute of Germanic Studies *An outline guide to resources for the study of German language and literature in national, university and other libraries in the United Kingdom* the Institute, 1978.

Wainwright M D and Mathews N *A guide to western manuscripts and documents in the British Isles relating to South and South-east Asia* Oxford UP, 1965.

Walker, G et al *Directory of libraries and special collections on Eastern Europe and the USSR* Crosby Lockwood, 1971.

Walne, P *A guide to manuscript sources for the history of Latin America and the Caribbean in the British Isles* Oxford UP and Institute of Latin American Studies, 1973.

Working party on library holdings of Commonwealth literature *A hand-hook of library holdings of Commonwealth literature: United Kingdom and Europe 1977* Boston Spa, BL Lending Division, 1977.

LIBRARIES AND ARCHIVES:
PRINTED AND MANUSCRIPT MATERIAL

This guide does not aim to be a source of information on archive and manuscript collections in a general sense, but where a library collection contains significant archive and manuscript holdings these are mentioned. The question of manuscripts and archives in libraries and elsewhere is best tackled through the specialist sources, such as those listed below. County record offices are major sources of material, and staff in them will act in a referral capacity. Diocesan record offices contain ecclesiastical records, although these may be jointly administered through county record offices, which themselves may have ecclesiastical holdings. Libraries have always held archives, manuscripts and non-book material, although it is only latterly that these have come to be thought of as library resources, and exploited in the same way as books and periodical holdings. In one or two cases it has been necessary to mention archive holdings and record collections in some detail, where these are closely connected to a library collection, eg Greater London Record Office, India Office Library and Records; or where they are an outstanding supplement to the printed sources, eg National Monuments Record, Public Record Office, Royal Commission on Historical Manuscripts.

The basic guide to the location of material is compiled by the Royal Commission on Historical Manuscripts: *Record repositories in Great Britain* (5th ed, HMSO, 1973). The main types of repository listed here are government and parliamentary archives; nationalised industries and public utilities; national and other libraries and museums; local record offices; religious archives and libraries; societies, colleges and institutions; university libraries and archives; banking and business archives. In the guide repositories are listed geographically, thus: London, English counties, Wales, Scotland, Northern Ireland, Isle of Man, and Channel Islands.

The following libraries listed in this present book are labelled as record repositories in the royal commission's guide: Public Record Office;

Office of Population Censuses and Surveys; India Office Records; British Library Reference Division Manuscripts Department; British Museum (Natural History); Imperial War Museum; National Army Museum; National Maritime Museum; National Monuments Record; Royal Botanic Gardens; Science Museum Library; Victoria and Albert Museum-National Art Library; Royal Commonwealth Society; Royal Institute of British Architects; Wellcome Institute for the History of Medicine; British Library of Political and Economic Science; Imperial College; King's College London; Royal Holloway College; School of Oriental and African Studies; University College London; University of London Library; Guildhall Library; Greater London Record Office; Reading University Library; Cambridge University Library; Scott Polar Research Institute; Exeter University Library; Durham University Library; Southampton University Library; Cambridge University Archives; Liverpool University and University Library; Manchester University Library; Newcastle upon Tyne University Library; Nottingham University Library; Bodleian Library; Oxford University Archives; Keele University Library; Keele University National Aerial Photographic Library; **Birmingham Reference Library**; Birmingham University Library; Hull University Library; Leeds Public Library; Leeds University Library; Sheffield City Library; Sheffield University Library; University College of North Wales Library; National Monuments Record for Wales; National Library of Wales; Swansea University Library; Scottish Record Office; General Register Office (Scotland); National Library of Scotland; Aberdeen University Library; Royal Botanic Gardens (Edinburgh); Edinburgh University Library; Strathclyde University Library; Mitchell Library (Glasgow Public Libraries). Glasgow University Library; Glasgow University Archives; St Andrews University Library; St Andrews University Archives.

Further information on archive collections can be obtained from the Royal Commission on Historical Manuscripts (incorporating the National Register of Archives) (see entry 72). The commission's publications are listed in HMSO sectional list no 17 *Publications of the Royal Commission on Historical Manuscripts*. For Scotland, users should consult the National Register of Archives (Scotland), General Register House, Edinburgh EH1 3YY; and for Northern Ireland, the Public Record Office of Northern Ireland, 66 Balmoral Avenue, Belfast BT9 6NY.

For business archives there are the Business Archives Council, Dominion House, 37-45 Tooley Street, London Bridge, London SE1 2PJ; and the Business Archives Council of Scotland, c/o The Secretary, R F Dell, City Archives Office, PO Box 27, City Chambers, Glasgow G2 1DU.

Material published by the Public Record Office is listed in HMSO sectional list no 24, *British national archives*. Other useful publications include those published by the Royal Historical Society, in the 'Guides and handbooks' series (various titles 1938-), for example, Mullins, E L C *Texts and calendars: an analytical guide to serial publications* Royal Historical Society, 1958. It is also worth consulting Hepworth, P *Archives and manuscripts in libraries* LA, 1964; Hepworth, P *How to find out in history* Oxford, Pergamon, 1966 (especially pages 211-238); and Hobbs, J L *Local history and the library* Deutsch, 1962.

FORMAT AND CONTENT OF ENTRIES

Entries for this inventory were selected after examination of a wide range of existing sources of information, guides to the literature, prospectuses, reference works, annual reports and material in the professional literature of librarianship. Existing information about each library and collection was noted. Libraries were contacted for the purposes of gathering information, verification and updating. The final entries reflect the extent to which this process has been successful. It has been necessary to rely on the voluntary cooperation of libraries; the completed returns reflect this, as well as the discretion of librarians in interpreting the guidelines supplied according to local circumstances.

Inevitably, entries vary in length for a variety of reasons, to the extent that length of entry and the nature of details supplied can only be a partial indicator of library and collection significance. It seemed wiser to the compilers not to edit entries down to a uniform length or texture, but to let richness and diversity (or otherwise) speak for themselves. A good deal of original wording has been retained to convey the precise meaning intended by the responding librarians. As this is a first attempt at such a user's guide (in terms of size, price, content and emphasis) it seems wise enough to allow any anomalies to be corrected in possible future editions. The main purpose has been to try and summarise scope, collections, principal services and availability, plus the essential information required for location and further contact. The compilers hope that the selection of libraries and the content of entries will provide the necessary utility for this enterprise.

The entries are grouped into four main categories: National, specialist, and public libraries; University libraries; Polytechnic libraries; and Scottish Central Institutions.

Within each section the entries are arranged by name of library and/ or parent institution. The British Library and the universities of Cambridge, London and Oxford have collective entries, but each institution and library follows the main number sequence. The number sequence of entries is continued throughout each section and subsection.

There are three indexes: the Name Index (collections, deposit libraries, libraries, persons); Subject Index (where possible the terms used conform to those in Sear's list of subject headings); and Geographical Index (listing library locations only, other geographical names being entered in the Subject Index).

The format of each entry is as follows. (Note that some entries contain only a selection of applicable headings, and in others it has been necessary to depart from the standard order of elements to take account of and to best present local variations in provision.)

1a) The official name of the library (together with the most usual form of reference, if different) is shown preceded by its inventory number.

1b) Name of parent institution or organisation

2a) Postal address of main library and of subsidiary locations which have distinct postal addresses

2b) Telephone number(s)

2c) Telex number and telegraphic address if available

3) Name of librarian

4a) Date of foundation of library, and brief historical details if relevant.

4b) Brief description of present aims and purpose of library service, and the principal and notable facilities

5a) Subject coverage—in general

5b) Subject coverage—special subject coverage, including participation in cooperative schemes where applicable. Note on departmental and sectional organisation

6a) Stock—brief statistical details
Bookstock either in total (monographs and bound serials), or as a count of monographs or bound serials separately. Pamphlet and offprint collections often listed separately.
Current serials received—number of titles (periodicals and other serials)
Serials retained—number of titles current and dead together
Other materials—listed according to the form of original return submitted.

6b) Special collections, strengths and resources
Named special collections of bibliographical materials, and manuscripts and archives. Manuscript and archive collections are not

fully listed or described, but those of major note are worthy of mention in connection with holdings of books and serials.
Other collections where systematic stock building to some level, is being, or has been maintained. This section sought and provides information on any areas of the collection in which the library would regard itself as having strength

7a) Arrangement of materials
Classification used, and open and/or closed access arrangements

7b) Library catalogues maintained

8a) Availability to users and admissions policy. Procedure to follow in order to gain access

8b) Opening hours
Although information on opening hours was sought on the questionnaire the arrangements have been reported selectively. Details have been given more often for the national and specialist libraries; in some cases universities provide compendia of opening hours, which are updated regularly, and these are mentioned where appropriate.

8c) Services to users
The main reader, bibliographic and information services provided for users. This excludes the listing of secondary bibliographical tools held by the library

9) Publications
Current publications, guides, pamphlets and bibliographical material produced by the library (either independently or in conjunction with other bodies), and details of major publications produced in the past

10) Bibliography
Publications in the literature describing the library and its collections

NATIONAL LIBRARIES, SPECIALIST LIBRARIES AND PUBLIC LIBRARIES

1   ANIMAL BREEDING LIBRARY
1b) Commonwealth Agricultural Bureau/Animal Breeding Research
     Organisation
2a) West Mains Road, Edinburgh EH9 3JX; 2b) 031-667-6901
3)   Mrs Victoria S Graham
4a) 1964; 4b) To provide library and information services for the ab-
     stracting needs of CBABG and research needs of ABRO
5a) Animal breeding, genetics and production; 5b) General livestock—
     cattle, sheep, horses, pigs, some poultry, other mammals
6a) Monographs: 4480. Current serials received: 327. Some photo-
     graphs; 6b) Reprint collection; fair-size collection of Eastern
     European journals in the field
7a) Specialised classification for use in this library only. By author
     within specific subject fields; 7b) Dictionary catalogue
8a) Members of staff, other research workers, and postgraduate stu-
     dents of Edinburgh University; 8b) M-F 0900-1700; 8c) Biblio-
     graphies prepared on a cost basis. Translation service (on appli-
     cation)
9)   Accessions list (produced every month for books, reports and
     reprints); half-yearly lists produced for books only

2   AUSTRALIAN REFERENCE LIBRARY
1b) Australian High Commission
2a) Australia House, The Strand, London WC2B 4LA; 2b) 01-836-2435;
     2c) 21143
3)   Ivan Page (also acts as liaison officer for National Library of
     Australia)
4a) 1944; 4b) The library provides a service to the High Commission,
     as well as acting as a public reference collection on Australia
5a) Australia; 5b) Australian history, law, literature, and social as-
     pects. Australian Federal Government publications
6a) Bookstock: 15,000 volumes. Current serials received: 1500
     titles; 6b) Press cuttings, pamphlets
7a) Dewey Decimal Classification; 7b) Dictionary catalogue
8a) Open to the general public for reference purposes; 8b) M-F 0900-
     1715; 8c) Australian News and Information Bureau

3   BIRMINGHAM REFERENCE LIBRARY
1b) Birmingham Public Libraries
2a) Central Library, Paradise Circus, Birmingham B3 3HQ; 2b)
     021-235-4511; 2c) 337655
3)   B H Baumfield FLA, FRSA, MBIM
4a) 1866. Reorganised into subject departments prior to move to
     new building in 1973; 4b) Stock divided into the following
     subject departments: quick reference and commercial information;
     social sciences and music; fine arts, history and geography, philo-
     sophy and religion; science and technology; language and litera-
     ture and local studies.

3   BIRMINGHAM REFERENCE LIBRARY (continued)

5a)   General range of subjects; 5b) Member of Birmingham Libraries
      Cooperative Mechanisation Project (BLCMP) and West Midlands
      Library and Information Network (WESLINK)

6a)   Bookstock: 910,000 volumes.
      Current serials received: 3084 titles. Large collection of defunct
      titles.
      Maps: c315,000 items.
      Photographs and prints: c142,000 items.
      Manuscripts: c170,000 items.
      Microforms: c97,000 items.

6b)   Social sciences department: stock of c255,000 volumes and 650
      current serials; original sources on trade unions and labour his-
      tory; comprehensive collection of British parliamentary papers and
      government publications; European Communities publications;
      publications of international organisations; yearbooks, directories
      and statistical publications
          Fine arts, history and geography, philosophy and religion:
      stock of c160,000 volumes; Sir Benjamin Stone collection of
      Victorian and Edwardian photographs, lantern slides and other
      illustrations (worldwide and European coverage); E Marston
      Rudland collection (engraved portraits of historical personages);
      British and foreign postcard collection; collection of printed
      parish registers; family history index; heraldry index; British-
      Israel World Federation collection; Societas Rosicruciana in
      Anglis collection; Swedenborg Society collection; Catholic
      Truth Society collection; newspaper cuttings collection; organ-
      isations index (philosophy and religion); patron saints index
          Science and technology department: complete set of British
      patent specifications since 1864; 50-year file of American
      patents; large collection of Atomic Energy Reports; collection
      of school's science literature
          Language and literature department: Shakespeare Library;
      War poetry collection (c2500 items); Cervantes collection (c1000
      volumes donated by William Bragg of Birmingham in 1873);
      Samuel Johnson collection (c1700 volumes); Milton collection
      (presented by Frank Wright in 1881; c1200 volumes); Parker collectio
      of early children's books (c4600 volumes); early and fine printing colle
      tion (pre-1701 works, c12,000 volumes); illustrated books collection;
      fine bindings collection
          Local studies department and archives: About 90,000 printed
      items relating to Birmingham and to Staffordshire, Warwickshire
      and Worcestershire; collections of watercolours, engravings and
      photographs; local map collection; special collections on John
      Baskerville, Joseph Priestley, Thomas Bray and Thomas Hall.
          Archive collection contains over 100,000 items dating from
      the twelfth century (manorial documents, diocesan records,
      family estate papers, probate records, rate books, tithe plans
      and awards, industrial records, Boulton and Watt collection,

3   **BIRMINGHAM REFERENCE LIBRARY** (continued)
William Murdoch collection, Galton records, business archives of
Hardmans (metal and stained glass work) and Metro-Cammell Ltd).

Other named special collections: Kings Norton and Sheldon
parish libraries; Oberammergau Passion Play collection; Richard
Williams collection of computer manuals and software

Other special strengths: Civil War tracts; art exhibition catalogues; index of trade marks (1934-).

7a)   Dewey Decimal Classification, with special schemes for local
studies and Shakespeare Library. All departments except local
studies have a proportion of their stock on open access, with
remainder shelved in stack (stack service); 7b) Each department
has its own name and classified catalogues, 1879-1973 on cards,
1974 onwards on microfilm cassettes. BLCMP union name and
serials catalogue on microfilm

8a)   All services available to the general public for reference. Requi-
sition slips to be completed for stack material, and proof of
identity and address is required for certain areas of the stock.
Seating for 1230 readers, including study carrels on most floors;
8b) M-F 0900-1800, Tues, Wed, Thurs 0900-2000, Sat 0900-1700;
8c) Complete photographic service, information services, microreading facilities

9)   Guides to the Reference Library and the following departments
and collections: Quick reference and commercial information;
Social sciences; History and geography; Stone collection of
photographs; Fine arts; Philosophy and religion; Science and
technology; Language and literature; Shakespeare Library;
Milton collection

Business news sheet (weekly); *Statistics and market research*
(monthly); *Guide to religious periodical literature* (bi-monthly);
Shakespeare library: a brief description; technical bibliographies
(various); Fine arts department bibliographies (various)

*A Shakespeare bibliography: catalogue of the Birmingham
Shakespeare Library*. 7 volumes, Mansell, 1971

10)   Berriman, S G 'A view of Paradise: Birmingham Central Libraries'
Library Association record 76(3), 1974, pp37-41; Library
Association (Reference, Special and Information Section) *The
new Birmingham Central Libraries*. LA, 1975 (building only);
Birmingham Public Libraries *Notes on the history of Birmingham
Public Libraries 1861-1961*. Birmingham, the Library, 1962.

4   **BRITISH ARCHITECTURAL LIBRARY** (Sir Banister Fletcher
Library)
1b)   Royal Institute of British Architects
2a)   66 Portland Place, London W1N 4AD; and 21 Portman Square,
London W1H 9HF (drawings collection); 2b) 01-580-5533
(Portland Place); 01-580-5533 ext 245 or 01-487-5441 (Portman
Square)

(continued)

4   BRITISH ARCHITECTURAL LIBRARY (continued)

3)   David E Dean MA, DipEd, ALA (librarian); John Harris (curator of drawings collection)

4a)   1834; 4b) One of the most comprehensive collections on architecture in the world. The bulk of the collection is for reference only.

5a)   Architecture; building; town and country planning; topography

6a)   Bookstock: c100,000 volumes (monographs and bound serials). Current serials received: c650 titles. Serials retained: c1050 titles. Photographic collection: c40,000 items. Drawings: over 250,000 items. Manuscripts: c12,000 items; 6b) East European materials collection esp since 1934; Handley-Read collection (Victorian decorative arts). The drawings collection is probably the largest single group of architectural drawings in existence

7a)   Majority of collection on open access. Universal Decimal Classification; 7b) Author/title catalogue; preparation of *Architectural periodicals index*

8a)   Available to general public for reference purposes only; 8b) M-F 1000-2000 (Mon to 1700, Sat to 1330). Closed for 4 weeks prior to August bank holiday; 8c) Small loan collection for members only; photocopying and photographic service.

9)   *Architectural periodicals index* (4 pa on subscription); Drawings catalogue (21 volumes when complete); List of books (annual); Technical reference list; Current information on library in *RIBA directory of members* (annual); Current book accessions list (as insert to *API*); *Catalogue of the Royal Institute of British Architects Library*: vol 1 Author catalogue of books and manuscripts, vol 2 Classified index and alphabetical subject index of books and manuscripts. RIBA, 1937 and 38.

10)   Dean, D 'A great library in need' *Architectural review*, 157 (940) 1975, pp324-326.

THE BRITISH LIBRARY

The British Library was formed in July 1973 from four major institutions: the British Museum Library, the National Central Library, the National Lending Library for Science and Technology, and the British National Bibliography. The British Library is not part of the British Museum; it is directed by a board of management under a chairman, and it is organised into three main divisions: Reference, Lending, and Bibliographic Services.

In this guide the main sections of the Reference and Lending Divisions are listed separately. The full structure of the British Library is illustrated in the organisation chart.

THE REFERENCE DIVISION (BLRD)

The function of the Reference Division is to keep books on the premises so that they can be made available in the shortest possible time to readers who come to consult them, and indeed to others who cannot visit the library through the medium of photographic copies and micro-

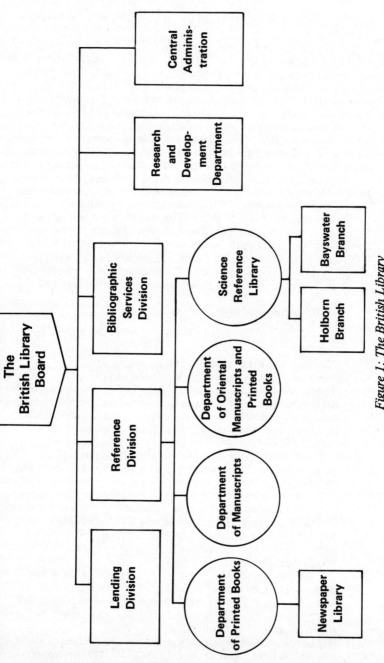

Figure 1: The British Library

film. The Reference Division is also a centre for exhibitions based on the collections.

The Reference Division was formed in 1973 from the Library Department of the British Museum and is one of the finest research libraries in the world. At its nucleus are the collection of books and manuscripts which were brought together on the foundation of the British Museum in 1753, since when many more collections have been acquired. The old Royal Library was given to the British Museum in 1757 and the right to a deposit copy of every book published in the United Kingdom was transferred with it. Since then it has been obligatory for every publisher in the United Kingdom to deposit one copy of every book, periodical and newspaper in the library and this has assured a continuous and comprehensive supply of indigenous material ever since. Foreign material is obtained by purchase or exchange from most countries of the world. The total number of books is now nearly 10 million.

The Reference Division in Bloomsbury (in the same building as the British Museum) comprises: the Department of Printed Books, the Department of Manuscripts, and the Department of Oriental Manuscripts and Printed Books. The Science Reference Library (SRL), at present divided between Holborn and Bayswater, is also a department of the Reference Division, and houses modern scientific literature.

5   BLRD Department of Printed Books
1b) The British Library
2a) Great Russell Street, London WC1B 3DG; 2b) 01-636-1544;
     2) 21462
3)   J L Wood and R J Fulford (keepers)
4a) The present library collection dates back to 1753. The present
     reading room was opened in 1857; 4b) The library services of the
     Reference Division are tailored to meet the requirements of those
     conducting research, usually of a long-term nature and which
     cannot be carried out elsewhere, in fields other than current
     science and technology.
         The collections are on closed access and readers look up shelf-
     marks in the catalogues and apply on application slips for items to
     be brought to them
         The Department of Printed Books includes the following sec-
     tions: The reading room (to which the bulk of this entry applies);
     Official Publications Library (formerly the State Paper Room);
     Map Library (see separate entry); Music Library (see separate
     entry); Newspaper Library (see separate entry); Library Association Library (see separate entry).
5a) The Department of Printed Books is the largest of the library
     departments, containing works in all languages except those of
     Asia. All subject fields covered except for modern science and
     technology; 5b) Particular collection strength in history, biography
     art, languages and literature
6a) Bookstock: c10 million volumes. Annual acquisitions of about
     one million items of all kinds, including 105,000 monographs

5   BLRD Department of Printed Books (continued)

6b)   The collections of early printed books, of old English books and of books in all European languages make for one of the finest libraries in the world. As well as being a working collection of older books, it is with the continuous accession of modern publications, a rapidly growing modern library.

The department receives a copy of every work published in the United Kingdom, and the Republic of Ireland. There is an annual grant for the purchase of foreign books. The department is also a repository for the publications of foreign governments acquired by exchange through HMSO.

7a)   Own classification scheme. Apart from the reading room collection of bibliographies, catalogues and reference works material is kept on closed access. Material is fetched from the stacks and the usual delivery time is one and a half to two hours. Less-frequently consulted material and certain classes of material are kept at Woolwich, with delivery normally on the day after request.

Current British government publications, maps and works in oriental languages can be made available more quickly in the appropriate reading room.

Apart from the main reading room there are others. Rare books are available in the North Library; British and foreign government publications in the Official Publications Library; maps in the Map Library. There are reading rooms in the Department of Oriental Manuscripts and Printed Books and at the Newspaper Library at Colindale.

Music is made available to readers in the reading room.

7b)   *General catalogue of printed books* and *Supplements*

8a)   Readers tickets are issued by the Library Board only to persons needing to use the library for research or reference that cannot be carried out elsewhere. Admission is not granted to students reading for first degrees at British or overseas universities, nor are persons normally admitted who are under 21 years of age. Admission may be refused if the reader's requirements can be more conveniently met in another type of library.

8b)   M, F, Sat 0900-1700; T, W, Th 0900-2100. Closed on Sundays and public holidays, and for the whole of the first week in May.

8c)   Book fetching services; reader inquiry desk

9)   *The Reading Room; a brief account of the services in the Great Russell Street (British Museum) building; Publications of the British Library Reference Division.*

10)   Esdaile, A *The British Museum Library: a short history and survey* London, Allen and Unwin, 1948; Articles in *Encyclopedia Britannica* and *Chambers Encyclopedia*

6   BLRD Department of Printed Books—Map Library

1b)   The British Library

2a)   Great Russell Street, London WC1B 3DG; 2b) 01-636-1544

3)   Miss H M Wallis

6   BLRD Department of Printed Books—Map Library (continued)

4a   In present location from c1914; 4b) The Map Library is on the mezzanine floor of the King Edward Building on the north side of the British Museum. As a sub-department of the Reference Division it provides its own reader services and has a separate student's room, with an open-access reference library and appropriate equipment for the use of maps.

5a)   Modern and historical maps; 5b) Atlases, topographical views

6a)   Bookstock: 40,000 volumes; Maps and plans: over 700,000 items; 6b) The Map Library is one of the world's major historical collections of maps, charts, plans and topographical views. Special collections include the King George III Topographical Collection and the largest extant collection of Ordnance Survey material

7a)   Open-access reference collection. Bulk of map stock on closed access with fetching arrangements

7b)   *Catalogue of printed maps. Photolithographic edition to 1964 plus later accession parts* (available in reading room and Map Library). Accessions from 1965 are incorporated in a cumulative card index in the Map Library. Map catalogue contains entries for all maps, atlases, views, globes and other materials preserved in the Map Library and for the more important maps contained in books of the General Library. All books in the Map Library which contain a substantial portion of text are entered in the *General catalogue of printed books.* Manuscript maps in the Map Library and the Department of Manuscripts are entered in the *Catalogue of manuscript maps . . . in the British Museum* (3 volumes 1844-1861 repr 1962)

8a)   Admission to the Map Library and the use of its facilities are governed by the regulations for admission to the reading room, with a number of differences (see Map Library leaflet for full details); 8b) M-Sat 0930-1630, including bank holidays, but excluding Good Friday, Christmas Eve, Christmas Day, Boxing Day, New Year's Day, and the week beginning with the first Monday in May; 8c) Photographic service

7   BLRD Department of Printed Books—Music Library

1b)   The British Library

2a)   Great Russell Street, London WC1B 3DG; 2b) 01-636-1544

3)   O W Neighbour

4a)   The nucleus of the Music Library was created in the early nineteenth century. Systematic acquisition of material began in the middle of last century; 4b) Specialist section of the Department of Printed Books

5a)   Printed music and books about music; 5b) Material in the collection covers the whole range of musical activity, including religious, domestic, concert, folk and popular of all countries and periods

6a)   The printed music collection contains c1,250,000 items. Some 6000 to 7000 items acquired per year

(continued)

BLRD Department of Printed Books—Music Library (continued)

6b) The collections are particularly strong in music published in all European countries from the beginning of the sixteenth century to the present time. There are important collections of English and other music deposited from the late eighteenth century under the various copyright acts.

The collections of English printed books about music are virtually comprehensive, and there are extensive collections of foreign books.

In the present century, copyright deposit has become more comprehensive for British music, but less so for foreign. Deficiencies are made good by an extensive acquisition programme. In the antiquarian sphere the aim is to build up as complete as possible an archive of music published in the United Kingdom, including popular and ephemeral; foreign music is acquired more selectively.

Paul Hirsch Music Library contains 20,000 items from all periods and is strong in musical theory, opera full scores, and first editions of Viennese classics. Royal Music Library, while predominantly a collection of early printed music, includes a unique collection of Handel autographs in 97 volumes.

The majority of manuscript music is kept in the Department of Manuscripts.

7a) Own scheme for arrangement of material; 7b) The British Library publishes the *British catalogue of music* (3 pa). Produced by the Bibliographic Services Division it is based on music published in the United Kingdom deposited in the Reference Division under the copyright act. Excluding most popular music, it includes both scores and books. Working catalogue in book form.

8a) Similar regulations apply as for the Department of Printed Books and the reading room. Printed music and books are made available in the reading room; 8b) Hours as the reading room; 8c) Photographic services

9) Squire, W B *Catalogue of printed music published between 1487 and 1800 now in the British Museum* (incl first supplement) 2 volumes, 1912, second supplement 1940. Squire, W B *Catalogue of the King's Music Library*, 3 volumes 1927-1929. Meyer, K and Hirsch, P *Katalog der Musikbibliothek Paul Hirsch* 4 volumes, 1928-1947. *Mozart in the British Museum* reprint of 1956 ed, British Museum Publications for the British Library, 1976.

10) Blom, E (ed) *Grove's dictionary of music and musicians 5th edition* Macmillan, 1954. Volume 5 pp183-185.

8 BLRD Department of Printed Books—Newspaper Library
1b) The British Library
2a) Newspaper Library, Colindale Avenue, London NW9 5HE; 2b) 01-200-5515; 2c) 21462
4a) Established 1905 as a storage library for post-1800 newspapers; reading room facilities added 1932; 4b) The major national repository of newspapers.

8   BLRD Dept. of Printed Books—Newspaper Library (continued)

5a)   Newspapers; 5b) Newspapers published after 1800 from all countries, and also British provincial papers published before 1800

6a)   Stock: 502,000 volumes and parcels; Microfilm: 93,000 reels; Number of titles: c35,000;6b) The collection at Colindale also holds many weekly and larger sized periodicals

7b)   Holdings listed by title and geographically

9   BLRD Department of Manuscripts

1b)   The British Library

2a)   Great Russell Street, London WC1B 3DG; 2b) 01-636-1544

3)   D P Waley, BA, PhD, FRHistS

4a)   1753; 4b) The main location for Western manuscripts in the British Library Reference Division

5a)   The Department of Manuscripts covers Western history, art and literature including manuscript maps and music from the earliest times to the present day in the forms of books and documents; 5b) Material in classical and European languages

6a)   Stock: 81,100 volumes of manuscripts; 6b) By the nature of the material covered the department contains unique and valuable collections. A selection of outstanding items is displayed to the public in the exhibition galleries (Grenville Library and Manuscripts Saloon). Categories of material include charters and rolls, detached seals, manuscript music, maps, plans, topographical drawings, literary and historic autographs.

7a)   Own classification schemes; 7b) Numerous catalogues and finding lists. For a survey see British Museum, Department of Manuscripts *The catalogues of the manuscript collections* rev ed (by T C Skeat), British Museum, 1962.

8a)   Facilities for readers are provided in a student's room, for which a ticket is required; 8b) M-Sat 1000-1645. Closed Sundays, Good Friday, Christmas Eve, Christmas Day, Boxing Day and the last complete week in October.

10   BLRD Department of Oriental Manuscripts and Printed Books

1b)   The British Library

2a)   Great Russell Street, London WC1B 3DG; 2b) 01-636-1544

3)   G E Marrison BA, PhD

4a)   The foundation collections of manuscripts and printed books of the British Museum (1753) contained some oriental material. This expanded rapidly in the nineteenth century, and a special oriental sub-department in the Department of Manuscripts was formed in 1867. By taking over the collections of oriental material in the Department of Printed Books this was enlarged to become the Department of Oriental Printed Books and Manuscripts in 1892. When the British Library was created in 1973 it was renamed the Department of Oriental Manuscripts and Printed Books.

10 BLRD Dept. of MSS and Printed Books (continued)
In 1975 the Oriental Exchange Unit, which acquires government publications from Asian countries, was transferred from the Department of Printed Books to this department.

4b) The department covers the literature of the oriental world and North Africa. It is one of the world's principal research collections of oriental material. The department acquires all significant material in the humanities and social sciences in the languages concerned.

5a) Oriental printed books and manuscripts; 5b) The character of the collections and specialisation of staff make it convenient to consider the department in five linguistic/geographical groups: 1 Hebrew, with Coptic, Syriac, Georgian, Armenian and the languages of Ethiopia; 2 Islamic, including Arabic, Persian, Turkish, and the Iranian and Turkic languages of Central Asia; 3 South Asian, including Sanskrit, Hindi, Urdu, Bengali, Tamil, Sinhalese, Tibetan etc; 4 South-east Asian, including Burmese, Thai, Vietnamese, Malay, Indonesian and Javanese; 5 Far East, mainly Chinese, Japanese, Korean, Mongol and Manchu

6a) Printed books: c400,000. Current serials: c4,000 plus further 10,000 dealt with by the Oriental Exchange Unit. Manuscripts: c40,000;

6b) The manuscript and book collections include fine illustrated manuscripts from Persia and India; Hebrew and Arabic religious texts; and early block printed books from the Far East

The printed book collections have been developed to provide a representative coverage of the literature of the countries concerned, not only in their classical aspects but also, increasingly, modern literature, as well as official documentary publications and other materials required for the study of contemporary Asia and North Africa in all its aspects.

The department has a reference collection of bibliographical works and other studies in western languages relating to Asia and North Africa, but the main collections in European languages are located in the Department of Printed Books.

7a) Mainly a closed access collection; 7b) A major feature of the department is the high standard of its printed catalogues. More than one hundred languages are involved covering a large variety of scripts. Separate catalogues for individual languages or groups of languages are printed and published from time to time. Current cataloguing is on cards which are accessible to readers in the department's reading room.

8a) Reader's ticket required for use of department reading room. Same general conditions as for Department of Printed Books; 8b) M-F 1000-1700, Sat 1000-1300. Closed on Sundays, Good Friday, Christmas Day, Boxing Day, and the week preceding the last complete week in October; 8c) All senior staff are language specialists and experts in the culture of the people whose literature

10   BLRD Dept. of Oriental MSS and Printed Books (continued)
      is in their care. In addition to dealing with bibliographical queries
      they may be consulted on matters relating to the religion, history,
      sociology, art, politics and economics of the literature concerned.
      The reading room has open-access reference collection. Enquiries
      from scholars and the general public dealt with personally, by
      telephone and post. Photographic services available

9)   In addition to a wide publication programme concerning the col-
      lections and their contents, there is a short *Guide to the depart-
      ment* giving basic information on catalogues, services and collec-
      tions

11   BL SCIENCE REFERENCE LIBRARY Holborn Branch
1b)   The British Library
2a)   25 Southampton Buildings, London WC2A 1AW; 2b) 01-405-8721;
      2c) 266959
3)   M W Hill (Director)
4a)   The Science Reference Library was known until 1973 as the
      National Reference Library of Science and Invention, which was
      founded in 1960 by the British Museum, and to which was added
      in 1966 the Patent Office Library (founded in 1855), now the
      Holborn Branch of the Science Reference Library.
4b)   The Science Reference Library is the national library for modern
      science and technology, and as such, has the most comprehensive
      reference collection in Western Europe of such literature from the
      whole world. The Holborn branch houses the national library for
      patents, trade marks and designs.
5a)   The Holborn branch contains most of the literature of the chemi-
      cal and physical sciences and technologies, including engineering
      and industry related literature.
6a)   Total stock (Holborn and Bayswater)—Bookstock: 138,000 mono-
      graphs. Current serial titles: 32,600 titles. Patent specifications:
      18 million. Microforms: c1,400,000 items
6b)   The collections at Holborn include the following: 23,000 periodi-
      cals with issues since 1950 available on open-access (pre-1950 ma-
      terial available at the Kean Street annexe nearby); 80,000 mono-
      graphs on open-access (pre-1956 material readily available);
      19 million patents mostly on open-access; worldwide collection
      of official journals, books on law and on design, trade directories
      with non-official lists of marks and other supporting literature;
      collection of recent report literature mainly on microfiche;
      current and archival collections of trade literature at the Kean
      Street annexe; about 1000 science and technology abstracting
      journals; collection of foreign language dictionaries
7a)   Substantial portion of the collection available on open access,
      classified by Universal Decimal Classification; 7b) Author/title,
      and classified catalogues

11 SCIENCE REFERENCE LIBRARY Holborn Branch (continued)
8a) Generally available. No reader's ticket required; 8b) M-F 0930-
2100; Sat 1000-1300 (main library). Closed on public holidays;
8c) Photocopying; inquiry service; bibliographical assistance;
linguistic aid service; courses of instruction for users. Bibliographical searches undertaken (apply Deputy Director (Services)).
Access to computer data bases on-line
9) *Guide to the Science Reference Library; Aids to readers; Periodical
publications in the SRL; Occasional publications; Notes to readers;
SRL news; List of publications*

12 BL SCIENCE REFERENCE LIBRARY Bayswater Branch
1b) The British Library
2a) 10 Porchester Gardens, London W2 4DE; 2b) 01-727-3022;
2c) 22717
3) M W Hill (Director)
4a) The Science Reference Library was known until 1973 as the
National Reference Library for Science and Invention, which was
founded in 1960 by the British Museum, and to which was added
in 1965 the Patent Office Library (founded in 1855), now the
Holborn Branch of the Science Reference Library.
4b) The Science Reference Library is the national library for modern
science and technology, and as such has the most comprehensive
reference collection in Western Europe of such literature from the
whole world. The Bayswater branch complements the Holborn
branch collections of scientific literature, and specialises in the
life sciences
5a) Life, earth and space sciences. Also strong in material on any
science in Slavonic and Oriental languages; 5b) Medicine, pure
mathematics
6a) Serials: 24,000 titles current. Monographs and pamphlets: 60,000;
6b) About 400 abstracting journals
7a) Substantial proportion of the collection available on open-access,
Universal Decimal Classification used; 7b) Author/title, and classified catalogues
8a) Generally available. No reader's ticket required; 8b) M-F 0930-
1730; Closed on public holidays; 8c) Photocopying; inquiry service; courses of instruction for users. Bibliographical searches
undertaken—apply Deputy Director (Services) at Holborn. Access
to computer data bases on-line
9) As for Holborn branch

13 BRITISH LIBRARY LENDING DIVISION
1b) The British Library
2a) Boston Spa, Wetherby, West Yorkshire LS23 7BQ; 2b) 0937-843434;
2c) 557381
3) Maurice B Line MA, FLA (Director General Lending Division)

13   BRITISH LIBRARY LENDING DIVISION (continued)

4a)   The Lending Division is one of the three sections of the British Library which was set up in July 1973. The Lending Division (BLLD) was formed by merging the former National Central Library and the former National Lending Library for Science and Technology

4b)   The Lending Division is the largest library in the world concerned specifically with interlending. As well as its main function of providing a loan/photocopy service, the Lending Division has several supplementary functions. These include a translating service which, subject to certain conditions, will arrange for the translation into English of articles and books in other languages

5a)   Science and technology; social sciences; and humanities

5b)   The current purchasing programme includes: all significant serials, irrespective of subject and language; all significant English language monographs; monographs in other languages—Russian science as comprehensively as possible—other languages selectively or on demand; report literature as comprehensively as possible; conference proceedings in all subject fields; all British official publications since 1962, all Unesco publications since 1954, all OECD publications since 1960, and all EEC publications since 1973, plus considerable stocks before these dates; printed music of all types, excluding popular music, sets of orchestral parts and multiple copies of vocal scores

6a)   Serials currently received: 49,000. English language monographs: c75,000 per year acquired. Reports: 1.5 million documents mainly on microfiche. Conference proceedings: over 89,000.
      Total stock comprises about 2.5 million volumes of books and periodicals and over 1.5 million items on microform. Monograph holdings, about 1.7 million items

6b)   Extensive holdings of Russian and Slavonic material. Specific categories of material for lending through registered users include trade directories; general directories; trade journals; house journals; manufacturer's catalogues and leaflets of historical importance. abstracts of patent literature; British standards; industry surveys; bank reports

7a)   No conventional subject classification. Material mostly filed by title. No public access to the main bookstock; 7b) Various catalogues available for internal purposes for interlending

8a)   The Lending Division provides a document supply service for institutions (not individuals) who are registered borrowers and who use prepaid forms.
      Individuals needing to use the service may do so only through an organisation which is a registered borrower. Most of those industrial companies which have libraries are in this category as are the majority of university, polytechnic and major public libraries.
      The reading room at Boston Spa is available to the public and comprises an open-access collection of reference books, with

13   BRITISH LIBRARY LENDING DIVISION (continued)
      current runs of all important indexing and abstracting services.
      Any item from the main collection can be made available to
      readers for use in the reading room. Supplies of reading room
      forms will be sent by post on request to intending readers.
8b)   Reading room: M-F 0900 to 1700. Not public holidays; 8c) Loan
      and photocopy services; translating service; MEDLARS: (The
      BLLD is the UK centre for MEDLARS—Medical Literature Anal-
      ysis and Retrieval System—further information available from the
      MEDLARS office.) Courses for librarians and users. Individual
      enquiries should be directed to the Director General.
9)   *The British Library Lending Division: a brief guide to its services;
      The British Library Lending Division: a brief guide for overseas
      users; Current serials received by the Lending Division; Index of
      conference proceedings; Interlending review* (4 pa); guides to new
      accessions and translations; *Lending Division publications and
      other publications distributed by the Lending Division*
10)   Numerous articles in the professional literature. For a history see
      Houghton, B *Out of the dinosaurs: the evolution of the National
      Lending Library for Science and Technology*. Bingley; Linnet,
      Hamden (Conn), 1972.

14   BRITISH MUSEUM (NATURAL HISTORY) LIBRARY
1b)   British Museum (Natural History)
2a)   Cromwell Road, South Kensington, London SW7 5BD;
      2b) 01-589-6323
3)   M J Rowlands (Head of Library Services)
4a)   The development of the museum libraries belongs almost exclus-
      ively to the period from 1880, when the natural history collections
      were moved from the British Museum in Bloomsbury to a new site
      at South Kensington, to form the British Museum (Natural History).
      Before this the various scientific departments had slowly built up
      small collections of reference books, periodicals and other ma-
      terials.
4b)   A centralised Department of Library Services under the direct
      control of the museum librarian was created in October 1975. It
      comprises the General Library, together with the Botany, Ento-
      mology, Mineralogy, Palaeontology and Zoology libraries, which
      hold specialist literature relevant to the museum's scientific depart-
      ments. In addition, the Zoological Museum at Tring contains the
      Rothschild Library and a comprehensive collection of ornitho-
      logical publications.
         These constituent libraries are treated individually here.

GENERAL LIBRARY
3)   R E R Banks
5a)   General science and natural history, scientific voyages and ex-
      peditions, biography, history of natural history

6a)   Total bookstock: 163,000 monograph and serial volumes. Current
serials received 2900 titles. Maps: 16,000; 6b) Linnaeus collection,
Owen collection, manuscripts and drawings, handwriting specimen
collection

7a)   Shelf arrangement by own scheme (B B Woodward); subject catalogue UDC; 7b) Author and title, classified subject catalogue,
portrait index, manuscripts and drawings index

8a)   Generally available for reference to research workers, students,
and the general public; 8b) M-Sat 1000-1700, closed on recognised public holidays;

8c)   It is important to stress the role played by the subject and
language specialists within the Department of Library Services in
dealing with inquiries from the museum and from other users.
Inquiries are accepted by post and telephone. There are photo-
copy and microform reading services available.

9/10) *The history of the collections contained in the Natural History
Departments of the British Museum* Volume 1, the Trustees,
1904. (Libraries, pp3-76); *Catalogue of the books, manuscript,
maps and drawings in the British Museum (Natural History)* the
Trustees, 1903-1940. 8 vols; *List of serial publications in the
British Museum (Natural History)*, the Trustees, 1975. 3 vols;
*A catalogue of the works of Linnaeus (and publications more
immediately relating thereto) preserved in the libraries of the
British Museum (Bloomsbury) and the British Museum (Natural
History) (South Kensington)* 2nd edition, the Trustees, 1933;
Sawyer, F C 'A short history of the libraries and list of manu-
scripts and original drawings in the British Museum (Natural
History)' *Bulletin of the British Museum (Natural History)*
Historical series 4, 1971; Gilbert, P *A compendium of the bio-
graphical literature on deceased entomologists* the Museum, 1977.
      Many important papers relating to the library collections have
been issued in the Bulletin of the British Museum (Natural
History) historical series (1953-   ), eg: Lysaght, A 'Some eighteenth century bird paintings in the library of Sir Joseph Banks
(1743-1820) Series I 1959, pp 251-371; de Beer, Sir Gavin
'Darwin's notebooks on transmutation of species, parts I-VI'
Series 2 1960-61: pp23-200, Series 3 1967: pp129-176; White-
head, P J P 'The Reeves Collection of Chinese fish drawings'
Series 3 1969; pp191-233

BOTANY LIBRARY

3)   Miss S A Gasteen

5a)   Taxonomy, general botany, plant physiology and anatomy, evol-
ution, ecology, medical botany and poisonous plants, economic
plants, gardening and botanic gardens, history of gardening,
plant pathology, biography of natural history. Strong collections
of older botanical literature

14   BM (NATURAL HISTORY)—BOTANY LIBRARY (continued)

6a)   Total bookstock: 70,000 monograph and serial volumes. Current serials received: 700 titles. Maps: 2000. Plates: 250,000.

6b)   Linnaeus collection (fine collection of herbals and folios); Manuscript collection of great importance for the history of botany and taxonomy (Sir Joseph Banks, and his three curator/librarians Solander, Dryander and Robert Brown); Major collections of original drawings and paintings (Sydney Parkinson, J G A Forster, Franz and Ferdinand Bauer, G D Ehret, and anonymous Chinese and Japanese artists). Plate collection in the general herbarium; mounted and published illustrations arranged by family and genus

7a)   UDC classification; 7b) Author and title, subject catalogues, manuscripts, drawings, biographies, portraits, microform

8a)   Generally available for reference; 8b) M-F1000-1630; Sat by special arrangement. Closed on recognised public holidays

ENTOMOLOGY LIBRARY

3)   Miss P Gilbert

5a)   Systematic and economic entomology

6a)   Total bookstock: 76,000 monograph and serial volumes. Current serials received: 650 titles; 6b) Manuscript collections and drawings; Walsingham entomological collection; scientific collectors' notebooks

7a)   Shelf arrangement by own scheme (Woodward); UDC subject catalogue; 7b) Author and title, classified subject catalogue, manuscripts, biographies, portraits

8a)   Generally available for reference; 8b) M-F 1000-1630; Sat by special arrangement. Closed on recognised public holidays

MINERALOGY LIBRARY

3)   R T W Atkins

5a)   Mineralogy, crystallography, gemmology, oceanography, physical sciences (selected), mining, topographical mineralogy and petrology, geophysics, tectonics

6a)   Total bookstock: 40,000 monograph and serial volumes. Current serials received: 500 titles; 6b) Photographs (monochrome); minerals; crystals; rocks; meteorites; reprints on minerals, rocks and meteorites; translations

7a)   UDC; 7b) Author and title, classified subject catalogue

8a)   Generally available for reference; 8b) M-F 1000-1630; Sat by special arrangment. Closed on recognised public holidays

PALAEONTOLOGY LIBRARY

3)   A P Harvey

5a)   Geology, palaeontology, stratigraphy, regional geology, structural geology, history and biography of geology, geomorphology, palaeoecology, sedimentology, documentation of geology, geological techniques and geological maps. Includes the library of

14   BM (NAT. HIST.)–PALAEONTOLOGY LIBRARY (continued)
      the sub-department of anthropology which covers physical anthro-
      pology, palaeoanthropology, serology and biochemical genetics
6a)   Total bookstock: 78,000 monograph and serial volumes. Current
      serials received: 1500. Maps: 40,000; 6b) Prints, drawings, plates,
      photographs relevant to the scope of the library, manuscripts,
      portraits, translations, collection of geology books for children
7a)   Shelf arrangement by own scheme (Woodward); subject catalogue
      by UDC; 7b) Author, title and subject catalogues; individual cata-
      logues of translations, microforms, portraits, archives, special
      books and manuscripts, and maps. Biographical index
8a)   Generally available for reference; 8b) M-F 1000-1630; Sat by
      special arrangement. Closed on recognised public holidays

ZOOLOGICAL MUSEUM
2a)   Akeman Street, Tring HP23 6AP; 2b) 044282-4181
3)   Mrs D A Vale
5a)   Ornithology; early general zoology and travel
6a)   Total bookstock: 50,000 monograph and serial volumes. Current
      serials received: 400 titles; 6b) Rothschild Library of ornitho-
      logical and general natural history works.
7a)   Shelf arrangement by own scheme; 7b) Author catalogue, list of
      periodicals
8a)   Generally available for reference; 8b) M-F 1000-1630; Sat by
      special arrangement. Closed on recognised public holidays

15   BRITISH STANDARDS INSTITUTION LIBRARY
1b)   British Standards Institution
2a)   2 Park Street, London W1Y 4AA; 2b) 01-629-9000; 2c) 266933
      BSI LONDON
4b)   The BSI is the national centre for all matters relating to standards
5a)   Standards and material relating to standards theory and practice
6b)   Complete sets of British, international and overseas standards;
      current journals issued by standards bodies
7b)   Indexes and catalogues
8a)   Open to the general public for reference purposes; 8b) M-F
      0900-1730; 8c) Borrowing by members only; information service;
      translation section
9)   Worldwide list of published standards (available to subscribing
      members, 12 issues per year); *BSI yearbook* provides list of li-
      braries holding complete sets of British standards for reference

16   BUSINESS STATISTICS OFFICE LIBRARY
1b)   Department of Industry
2a)   Cardiff Road, Newport, Gwent NPT 1XG; 2b) 0633-56111
      ext 2973; 2c) 497121 BSONPT G
3)   Vacant
4a)   Established in its present form in 1972; 4b) Acts as referral centre
      to officially produced sources of information in the UK Govern-
      ment Statistical Service

16   BUSINESS STATISTICS OFFICE LIBRARY (continued)
5a)   Statistical methodology and UK official statistics; 5b) Particularly
      strong in the field of production and distribution statistics.
6b)   The library also houses the Royal Statistical Society's 'G R Porter'
      collection, which comprises official UK and foreign statistics of
      the nineteenth and early twentieth centuries.
7a)   Dictionary catalogue
8a)   The library provides an enquiry service for anyone wanting infor-
      mation on UK statistics and it is open to the public for reference.
      Copies of the statistical publications produced by the office can be
      purchased from the library; 8b) M-Th 0900-1700, F 0900-1630;
      8c) Photocopying facilities are available
9)   *List of G R Porter collection material* £0.50 from the library;
      Business Statistics Office Reference Library: a government stat-
      istical inquiry point on your doorstep.
10)   This library is mentioned in many guides and directories including:
      Burkett, J *Government and related library and information ser-*
      vices in the United Kingdom LA, 3rd rev ed, 1974; Vernon, K D C
      (ed) *Use of management and business literature,* Butterworths,
      1975; Campbell, M J (ed) *Manual of business library practice*
      Bingley; Hamden (Conn), Linnet, 1975; *Guide to government de-*
      partment and other libraries and information bureaux, British Li-
      brary (Science Reference Library), 1976.

17   CANADA HOUSE LIBRARY
1b)   Office of the High Commission for Canada
2a)   Canada House, Trafalgar Square, London SWlY 5BJ; 2b) 01-930-
      9741
4a)   Library founded 1946; 4b) Centre for reference, information and
      referral about Canada and Canadian affairs
5a)   Canada and Canadian life; 5b) Acts as a depository for Canadian
      government documents in the non-scientific and technical field.
      Specialised collections of Canadian statistical material
7a)   Dewey Decimal Classification; 7b) Divided dictionary catalogue
8a)   Primarily for Canada House staff, but available to the general
      public for reference purposes; 8c) Information provided by phone
      and post. Restricted loan service
9)   *Bibliography of selected Canadian books*

18   CENTRAL ASIAN RESEARCH CENTRE
1b)   Central Asian Research Centre
2a)   18 Parkfield Street, London N1 OPR; 2b) 01-226-5371
3)   David Morison
4a)   Library founded in 1953 to further the study of Kazakhstan and
      the Soviet Central Asian Republics. The centre is now involved in
      the study of Soviet and Chinese relations with the Third World
5a)   Soviet Central Asia and adjacent countries; Soviet and Chinese
      relations with Asian countries; 5b) Large collections of Russian
      materials; Soviet periodicals on Central Asia and Soviet foreign
      relations; material on history, politics, religion, education, arts,
      45

18   CENTRAL ASIAN RESEARCH CENTRE (continued)
      living conditions, demography, ethnography, economic develop-
      ment, transport
6b)   Special strength is in Russian language material
7a)   All stock on open-access; 7b) Author and subject catalogues; in-
      dex of Soviet journal articles
8a)   Open to researchers with an interest in the field for reference
      purposes; 8c) No borrowing permitted
9)   *USSR and the Third World* (8 pa); *The USSR and Arabia* (1971);
      Soviet-Third World relations 3 vols (1973); *The Hazaragi dialect
      of Afghan Persian* (1973); Microfilm edition of *Central Asian Re-
      view* (1953-1971)

19   CENTRAL MUSIC LIBRARY
1b)   Westminster City Libraries
2a)   Victoria Library, Buckingham Palace Road, London SW1W 9UD;
      2b) 01-730-8921
4a)   Established in 1946 as the Central Music Library Ltd, and de-
      posited with the Westminster City Council in 1947, but retaining
      independent status and character within Westminster City Libraries'
      main music library; 4b) With the Westminster City collection this
      forms the largest truly public music collection in the southern half
      of England
5a)   All aspects of musical knowledge and production
6b)   The contents of the library fall into three main sections: books
      about music (lending and reference collection); music (divided
      into composers, sheet music, miniature scores, instrumental collec-
      tions and tutors, orchestral parts); periodicals (including the
      principal titles in English, German, French and Italian)
7a)   Own classification. Open-access and closed-access reserve collec-
      tion; 7b) Author/composer, classified, and alphabetical subject
      catalogues. Title index to song collections; index to music period-
      icals; index of analyses of musical works; index of illustrations of
      opera productions
8a)   Generally available for reference, and for lending to holders of
      Westminster City and current British public library tickets from
      other systems; 8b) M-F 0930-1900, Sat 0930-1700; 8c) Infor-
      mation and guidance services. Borrowing for personal visitors
      only
9)   Guide pamphlet

20   CENTRE FOR ENVIRONMENTAL STUDIES LIBRARY
1b)   Centre for Environmental Studies
2a)   62 Chandos Place, London WC2N 4HH; 2b) 01-240-3424
3)   Susan Anketell
5a)   Urban and regional planning; 5b) Housing, planning education,
      population studies, social policy, urban economics

46

20   CENTRE FOR ENVIRON. STUDIES LIBRARY (continued)
6a)   8000 indexed items, including government publications, local
       authority documents, and working papers of university depart-
       ments and research centres. Current periodicals received:
       200 titles
8a)   Open to researchers and others for reference purposes; 8c) No
       loans to visiting readers; photocopying facilities usually available
9)   Library guide; List of periodical holdings

21   CHEMICAL SOCIETY LIBRARY
1b)   The Chemical Society
2a)   Burlington House, London W1V OEN; 2b) 01-734-0675;
       2c) 268001
3)   R G Griffin FLA
4a)   1841; 4b) The purpose of the library is to provide lending, refer-
       ence, photocopying and information services over the whole field
       of chemistry
5a)   Chemistry in all aspects
6a)   Monographs: 15,000 volumes. Bound serial volumes: 50,000 vol-
       umes. Current serials received: 600 titles. Serial titles retained:
       1000 titles; 6b) Collection of early chemical and alchemical
       books; Nathan collection on explosives; collection of portraits of
       chemists
7a)   UDC; 7b) Classified catalogue
8a)   Unrestricted access to members of the Chemical Society and Bio-
       chemical Society. Other research workers may be admitted with
       a letter of introduction to use the library for reference purposes.
       Corporate bodies subscription available. Library visits can be ar-
       ranged; 8b) M-F 0930-1800; 8c) Information given by phone and
       post. Borrowing for fellows and corporate subscribers
9)   List of periodicals held by the library; additions to the library

22   CHETHAM'S LIBRARY
1b)   Chetham's School of Music
2a)   Long Millgate, Manchester M3 1SB; 2b) 061-834-7961
3)   Miss A C Swape MA
4a)   1653; 4b) The present aim of the library service is to provide
       access to the library's stock, and provide research and photographic
       services to scholars and to the general public
5a)   A general collection of material up to c1850. Acquisitions since
       then have mainly been related to the local history of North-west
       England plus general bibliographical and reference material;
       5b) History and topography of the North-west
6a)   Bookstock: c100,000 monograph and serial volumes. Current
       serials received and retained: 54. A quantity of slides, maps and
       plans; 6b) Incunabula and early printed books; printed and manu-
       script local material relating to Chetham's hospital and library;

22 CHETHAM'S LIBRARY (continued)
    collections of deeds; John Byrom library; Halliwell-Phillipps col-
    lection of broadsides; Popery tracts; Radcliffe collection (gen-
    ealogy and heraldry); illustrations; photographic slides
7a) Conyers Middleton and Dewey classifications used; 7b) Printed
    catalogue to 1883
8a) Open to any member of the general public over the age of 18
    years; 8b) M-F 0900-1700; Sat by appointment only; 8c) General
    range of services
9) Catalogues to special collections
10) Whatton, W R *A history of the Chetham Hospital and Library*
    1833; *Chethams Hospital and Library* Manchester, CHL, 1956;
    Nicholson, A *Chethams Hospital and Library* Sherratt and Hughes,
    1910

23 CITY BUSINESS LIBRARY
1b) Corporation of London
2a) Gillett House, Basinghall Street, London EC2V 5BX;
    2b) 01-638-8215/8216; 2c) 887955
3) M J Campbell ALA
4a) A free service of information for the businessman was established
    by the City Corporation at the Guildhall Library in 1872. From
    this developed the Commercial Reference Room. The present
    premises were occupied as a specialist business library in 1970;
    4b) The purpose of the library is to supply the day-to-day infor-
    mation needs of the business community
5a) Business, commerce, economics, management
6b) UK town, county and telephone directories; trade directories,
    overseas directories; company data (annual reports, Moodies
    cards, McCarthy services, periodical indexes, stock market prices);
    market data; management and business monographs; official pub-
    lications; town guides of UK; periodicals; newspapers; maps,
    atlases
7a) Open-access collection; 7b) Author/title catalogue
8a) Generally available for reference; 8b) M-F 0930-1730; 8c) Photo-
    copying
9) *City business courier* (2 pa additions to stock); reading lists; lists
    of periodicals and newspapers

24 COMMONWEALTH BUREAU OF HORTICULTURE AND PLAN-
    TATION CROPS LIBRARY (Joint library with the East Malling
    Research Station)
1b) Commonwealth Agricultural Bureau
2a) East Malling, Maidstone, Kent; 2b) 0732-83-3033
4a) East Malling Research Station established 1913. Commonwealth
    Bureau of Horticulture and Plantation Crops established 1929
5a) East Malling Research Station specialises in deciduous fruit and
    hops whilst the Commonwealth Bureau of Horticulture and

24   COMMONWEALTH BUREAU OF HORTICULTURE (continued)
      Plantation Crops covers a wider field; 5b) Horticulture; applied
      entomology; applied mycology; plant physiology; plant breeding;
      plant protection; biochemistry; horticultural meteorology; soils and
      fertilizers
6b)   Collection of over 70,000 pamphlets
7a)   UDC; 7b) Author/title and classified catalogue

25   COMMONWEALTH INSTITUTE LIBRARY AND RESOURCE
      CENTRE
1b)   Commonwealth Institute
2a)   Kensington High Street, London W8 6NQ; 2b) 01-602-3252;
      2c) COMWEL INST LONDON
3)   Michael Foster FLA
4a)   Library founded 1959. Originally intended only for teachers and
      student teachers, the general public was encouraged to use all its
      facilities, including the loan service from 1972 onwards. Moved to
      new premises within the institute in 1978 where printed and audio-
      visual materials are interfiled on the shelves
4b)   The library and resource centre is a multi-media library open to the
      general public. Its stock aims to describe the people and the way
      of life of all present day Commonwealth countries.
5a)   The Commonwealth. Particularly strong on cultural activities,
      politics, economics, education and geography
5b)   The territories of the contemporary Commonwealth are the
      following: Antigua, Ascension Island, Australia, Australian
      Antarctic Territory, Bahamas, Bangladesh, Barbados, Belize,
      Bermuda, Botswana, Britain, British Antarctic Territory, British
      Indian Ocean Territory, British Virgin Islands, Brunei, Canada,
      Cayman Islands, Christmas Island, Cocos Islands, Cook Islands,
      Cyprus, Dominica, Falkland Islands, Fiji, The Gambia, Ghana,
      Gibraltar, Gilbert Islands, Grenada, Guernsey/Alderney/Sark,
      Guyana, Hong Kong, India, Isle of Man, Jamaica, Jersey, Kenya,
      Lesotho, Malawi, Malaysia, Malta, Mauritius, Montserrat, Nauru,
      New Hebrides, New Zealand, Nigeria, Niue, Norfolk Islands, Papua
      New Guinea, Pitcairn Island, Rhodesia, St Helena, St Kitts/Nevis/
      Anguilla, St Lucia, St Vincent, Seychelles, Sierra Leone, Singapore,
      Solomon Islands, Sri Lanka, Swaziland, Tanzania, Tonga, Trinidad
      and Tobago, Tristan da Cunha, Turks and Caicos Islands, Tuvalu,
      Uganda, Western Samoa, Zambia
6a)   Monographs: c55,000 volumes. Current serials received: 700 titles.
      Serials retained: c500 titles. Non-book materials: c15,000-20,000
      items; 6b) Bibliographical coverage of all Commonwealth countries;
      Commonwealth literature collection; children's literature collection;
      Commonwealth telephone directories. Recordings of traditional,
      folk, popular and composed music from all Commonwealth countries;
      slide and film strip collection.

(continued)

25   COMMONWEALTH INSTITUTE LIBRARY (continued)
7a)   Modified Bliss Classification. Stock arranged in following sections:
      bibliographies, quick reference, general and United Kingdom,
      Commonwealth literature, Commonwealth children's literature,
      the Commonwealth, separate collections for each country; 7b)
      Card catalogues: author/title, classified subject index. Publish
      selective bibliographies of stock at the library/resource centre
8a)   Open to all for reference purposes; open to residents in the UK
      for loan purposes; 8b) M-Sat 1000-1730; 8c) Information given
      by phone and post to all
9)   Publications list gives full details of material on services, stock
      and bibliography

26   EDINBURGH CENTRAL LIBRARY
1b)   Edinburgh Public Libraries
2a)   George IV Bridge, Edinburgh EH1 1EG; 2b) 031-225-5584
3)   A P Shearman FLA BA
4a)   1890; 4b) The Central Library houses the main reference and
      special collections
5a)   General range of subjects, but strong in history and the social
      sciences; 5b) Art library; Edinburgh Library and Scottish Library
      are sub-divisions of the Reference Library
6a)   Bookstock: c1,250,000 volumes. Current serials received: c1200
      titles. Serials retained: c770 titles. Slides: c25,000 items. Prints:
      c45,000 items; 6b) Cowan collection and Boog-Watson collection
      (Edinburgh); Sanderson bequest (art); British Cartographic Society
      Library; Scottish Beekeepers' Association (Moir) Library; Scottish
      Mountaineering Club Library; technical books service for firms;
      Open University books
7a)   Library of Congress Classification; some of stock on closed-access;
      7b) Dictionary catalogue to Reference Library
8a)   Open to the general public for reference and lending (separate
      lending department at Central Library); 8b) M-F 0900-2100; Sat
      0900-1300; 8c) General reference and information services.
      Photocopying facilities
9)   Annual report; various publications on local, historical and biblio-
      graphic topics

27   EUROPEAN COMMUNITIES INFORMATION OFFICE
1b)   Commission of the European Communities
2a)   20 Kensington Palace Gardens, London W8 4QQ; 2b) 01-727-8090;
      2c) 23208 EUROPA LDN
3)   Miss Emma Harte
4a)   1964; 4b) The office provides an official information service for the
      European Communities
5a)   European Communities
6b)   All EEC publications
7a)   Open-access

27   EUROPEAN COMMUNITIES INFORMATION OFFICE (continued)
8a)   Open to the general public for reference and information; 8b) M-F
      1000-1300, 1430-1800

28   FOREIGN AND COMMONWEALTH OFFICE and
      MINISTRY OF OVERSEAS DEVELOPMENT LIBRARY
1b)   Foreign and Commonwealth Office and Ministry of Overseas
      Development
2a)   FCO Library: Sanctuary Buildings, Great Smith Street, London
      SW1P 3BZ; MOD Library: Eland House, Stag Place, London SW1E
      5DH; 2b) FCO: 01-212-6568/0732/0663; MOD: 01-834-2377
3)   H Hannam ALA
4a)   The collection dates from about 1782. The libraries of the former
      Colonial Office and Foreign Office form the basis of the collection;
      4b) The FCO Library is administered by the Library and Records
      Department, and forms part of a library system which provides
      services to the FCO and the MOD. Besides serving the needs of
      personnel from these departments, the libraries are available to
      researchers for reference purposes.
5a)   International relations, diplomacy, and the history, politics, law
      and economics of foreign and Commonwealth countries; aid, over-
      seas development, and technical cooperation; 5b) The main library
      is housed in Sanctuary Buildings, and there are additional service
      points in Downing Street, East Building (legal and statistical collec-
      tions) and Eland House (MOD collections, including collection of
      statistical serials from developing countries)
6b)   Comprehensive indexed collection of Commonwealth legislation;
      several hundred volumes of photographs of Commonwealth
      countries and UK dependent territories, c1850-c1950; published
      treaty collections; early works on travel; Commonwealth official
      publications and diplomatic lists
7a)   Library of Congress Classification; 7b) Divided dictionary catalogue
8a)   Open for reference purposes without formality; 8b) M-F 0930-1730;
      8c) Routine enquiries dealt with by phone and post. Limited photo-
      copying service available
9   *Technical cooperation* (monthly bibliography of Commonwealth
      official publications); *British aid: a select bibliography; Public
      administration: a select bibliography; Development index* (fort-
      nightly list of articles in periodicals). Published catalogues: *Cata-
      logue of printed books in the library of the Foreign Office* HMSO,
      1926 (reprint in preparation); *Catalogue of the Colonial Office
      Library* Boston (Mass), G K Hall, 1966; *First supplement 1963-67;
      Second supplement 1968-71; Catalogue of the Foreign Office
      Library 1926-68* Boston (Mass), G K Hall, 1973.

29   GENERAL REGISTER OFFICE (SCOTLAND) LIBRARY
1b)   Department of the Registrar General for Scotland
2a)   New Register House, Edinburgh, EH1 3YT; 2b) 031-556-3952

29 GENERAL REGISTER OFFICE (SCOTLAND) (continued)
4a) 1962; 4b) Reference facilities for persons using the record collections of the General Register Office
5a) Population statistics; vital and health statistics; 5b) Local history
6a) Bookstock: c3,000 volumes. Current serials received: 30 titles; 6b) Collections of genealogical material: c1,000 vols associated with old parish registers
7a) Own classification based on UDC; 7b) Author and classified catalogues
8a) Available to members of the public consulting records; 8b) M-Th 0900-1630 (F 1600)

30 GLASGOW PUBLIC LIBRARIES Commercial Library
1b) The Mitchell Library (Glasgow Public Libraries)
2a) Royal Exchange Square, Glasgow G1 3AZ; 2b) 041-221-1872 and 041-204-1202; 2c) 778732
3) C F Rice ALA
4a) 1916; 4b) A public commercial reference library
5a) Economics and commerce
6a) Monographs: 6000 volumes. Current serials received: 470 titles; 6b) Newspapers; town, trade and telephone directories; government statistical publications; map collection; manufacturers trade catalogues; trade marks (British, since 1959); Scottish company registrations 1972- ; research index; incomes data; patent specifications—Great Britain (1617-   ), USA (1893-   ), Australia (1904-   ), Eire (1928-); abridged patent specifications—Canada (1879-), New Zealand (1914-); abstracts of patents—West Germany and USSR from 1960-.
7a) Dewey Decimal Classification; 7b) Classified catalogue
8a) Generally available to the public; 8b) M-F 0930-1700; 8c) Extel services

31 GLASGOW PUBLIC LIBRARIES Mitchell Library
1b) City of Glasgow Corporation
2a) North Street, Glasgow, G3 7DN; 2b) 041-248-7121/8; 2c) 778732 LIBRARIO GLW
3) A G Alison FLA (Director of Libraries)
4a) 1874; 4b) The largest public reference library in Scotland, containing a number of important collections of research value. A new extension to the present Mitchell Library building of 1911 opened at the end of 1978, bringing a change in character from general reference to more departmentalised organisation, with a greater proportion of stock on open access
5a) General range of subjects; 5b) Special departments include Glasgow local history, Science and technology, Music. Subject strengths in Scottish history and literature.
6a) Bookstock: c1 million items. Current serials received: c1300 titles. Serials retained: c6000. Maps: 14,000; 6b) Amour donation
52

31 GLASGOW PUBLIC LIBRARIES Mitchell Library (continued)
    (German literature); Donald purchase (shorthand); Clem Edwards
    donation (Labour movement c1890 to 1915); Glasgow Collection;
    Moncrieff Mitchell Collection; Early Glasgow Printing Collection;
    Andrew Bain Memorial Collection; Henderson purchase (Celtic
    languages); Hillhouse purchase (draughts); McClelland donation
    (phrenology); Morgan Collection (pure and applied science); Mori-
    son Collection (theology); music collections including Moody
    Manners Collection (vocal and orchestral opera scores); North
    British Locomotive Company collection; private press collection
    (including complete sets of Kelmscott Vale and Nonsuch Press
    books); Reid Collection (angling); Reynolds Donation (rationalist
    literature); Scottish Collection; Scouler Collection (philosophy);
    Slains Castle Collection; R L Stevenson Collection; E J Thomson
    Donation (Scottish topography); J H Thomson Collection (Coven-
    anting history); trades unions Collection (West of Scotland trades
    union activity); United Nations Document Collection; Gourlay
    Collection (Books on India published 1790-1810); Secretary of
    State for India Collection (gazetteers and statistics 1905-1935);
    collections of old and current local and national newspapers; un-
    restricted Unesco, UN and FAO publications in English; manu-
    scripts; print and slide collection.
7a) Dewey Decimal Classification; 7b) Dictionary catalogue (1877-1914);
    classified catalogue (1915-1949); dictionary catalogue (1950-1969);
    classified catalogue (1970-)
8a) Generally available to the public; 8b) M-F 0930-2100. Closed Sat
    until further notice; 8c) Reference only. Information given by
    phone and post to all; photocopying service; audio-visual and micro-
    form equipment
9) Annual reports; annual programme of lectures; catalogue of incuna-
    bula and STC books; catalogue of periodicals; catalogue of Burns
    collection; classified catalogue of additions to the library, 1915-
    1949, 2 volumes.
10) *Glasgow Public Libraries 1874-1966; The Mitchell Library 1877-
    1977*

32 GOETHE INSTITUT LIBRARY (GERMAN INSTITUTE LIBRARY)
1b) Goethe Institut München
2a) 50/51 Princes Gate, Exhibition Road, London SW7 2PG; 2b)
    01-581-3344/7
3) Mrs Inge Niemöller Dipl-Bibl
4a) 1958; 4b) Promotion of German language and culture abroad
5a) Mainly German books, some English translations and English works
    on Germany covering all fields in the humanities and social sciences;
    5b) Main emphasis on German literature, history, art and language.
    Linked to German interlending service.
6a) Monographs: 23,000 volumes. Current serials received: 125 perio-
    dicals, 25 leading daily and weekly newspapers (back numbers of

32   GOETHE INSTITUT LIBRARY (continued)
      most periodicals and of *Frankfurter Allgemeine Zeitung, Die Welt*
      and *Die Zeit* are kept; 6b) German literature—primary and secondary
7a)   Open-access. Classification: Amerika Gedenkbibliothek; 7b) Cata-
      logues: index of periodicals and newspapers held in GI Libraries,
      London, Manchester, York, Glasgow, Dublin. Catalogue of German
      literature and fiction in stock (loose leaf collection, updated an-
      nually)
8a)   Open to the general public free of charge; 8b) M, T, Th, F: 1500-
      1800; W, Sat: 1000-1300; 8c) Readers may borrow 3 books at a
      time for 3 weeks. Postal lending service to readers living outside
      London. Interlending service. Photocopying facilities. Information
      service, by phone and post to all on any aspect.
9)   Pamphlet: 'The Goethe-Institut in the United Kingdom'. Leaflet:
      'Facilities offered by the Goethe Institut Library'. A-Level set
      book list (listing primary and secondary literature for all examina-
      tion boards apart from Joint Matriculation Board)

33   GRASSLAND RESEARCH INSTITUTE LIBRARY
1b)   Grassland Research Institute
2a)   Hurley, near Maidenhead, Berkshire SL6 5LR; 2b) 062-882-3631
4a)   The Grassland Research Institute was established in 1953 and is
      grant-aided by the Agricultural Research Council; 4b) The library
      serves the needs of the staffs of the Grassland Research Institute,
      and provides library services to the Commonwealth Bureau of
      Pastures and Field Crops
5a)   Production and utilisation of herbage, and related subjects; 5b)
      Ecology, animal nutrition, biochemistry, crop conservation, ley
      agronomy, plant physiology, biometrics
6a)   Bookstock: over 6500 volumes. Pamphlets: c35,000 items.
      Current serials received: c1000 titles.
7a)   UDC; 7b) Dictionary catalogue
8a)   Bona-fide researchers admitted on application; 8c) Information
      services

34   GREATER LONDON HISTORY LIBRARY
1b)   Greater London Council
2a)   Room 114, County Hall, London, SE1 7PB; 2b) 01-633-7132/6759
      (books and periodicals), 01-633-7193 (maps and prints),
      01-633-3255 (photographs)
3)   H O Wilson ALA
4a)   1889; 4b) To provide material and information on all aspects of
      London history and topography and on the history of local govern-
      ment together with such general reference sources as are necessary
      for research in these fields.
5a)   London, local government, historical research generally
6a)   90,000 books and pamphlets. 180 periodicals received currently.
      289 periodicals retained. 10,000 maps. 40,000 prints and drawings

34 GREATER LONDON HISTORY LIBRARY (continued)
    250,000 photographs. 6b) John Burns Collection—books and
    prints of London
7a) Some material on open-access, remainder available on application.
    Own classification; 7b) Author and classified catalogues.
8a) Available to members and officers of GLC and ILEA (reference
    and loan). Available to public (reference *only*); 8b) 0915-1700
    M to F; 8c) Enquiries by post or telephone, Books and periodicals
    lent to members, officers and on inter-library loan basis, Photographs
    lent to all. But, prints and maps for reference only, Photocopies
    subject to suitability of originals and provisions of copyright act,
    and a microfilm reader available.
9) *Annual report of Greater London Record Office and Library.*
    Accessions list. LCC Members' Library Catalogue vol 1. London
    history and topography, 1939. Reproductions of historical maps
    and prints.
10) The library functions in conjunction with the Greater London
    Record Office which is open to all for reference purposes. It con-
    tains the official records of the GLC and its predecessors and other
    types of records including parish, diocesan, manorial, estate, business,
    etc.
        Because of the close link with the Record and Archive sections
    reference entries are given to the following: the Greater London
    Record Office, Middlesex Records, the Greater London Record
    Office map, print and photograph collection

35 GREATER LONDON RECORD OFFICE London Section
1b) Greater London Council
2a) The County Hall, London SE1 7PB; 2b) 01-633-6851
3) W J Smith MA FR Hist S (Head Archivist, GLC)
4a) From 1889; 4b) The section is responsible for the official records
    of the London County Council and its predecessors, dating from
    1570, as well as for those of the Greater London Council
5a) London records
6b) Official records: eg Commissioners of Sewers (1570-1847), Metro-
    politan Commission of Sewers (1847-1855), Metropolitan Build-
    ings Office (1845-1855), Metropolitan Board of Works (1855-1889),
    London County Council (1889-1965), School Board for London
    (1870-1904), Technical Education Board (1893-1904), Boards of
    Guardians (1834-1930), Metropolitan Asylums Board (1867-1930);
    Ecclesiastical Records: eg Diocesan Records of London and South-
    wark (former London County Council area excluding the pre-1965
    City of Westminster, and the City of London; Congregational Church
    records; Methodist archives; manorial, family, estate, business and
    other private records; material deposited since 1946 relating to the
    former London County Council area

36 **GREATER LONDON RECORD OFFICE** Middlesex Section
1b) Greater London Council
2a) 1 Queen Anne's Gate Buildings, Dartmouth Street, London SW1H 9BS; 2b) 01-633-4431
3) Miss J Coburn (Deputy Head Archivist)
4a) From 1889; 4b) The section has custody of the records of the Middlesex County Council and the Middlesex Sessions dating from 1549
5a) Middlesex records
6b) Official records: eg Middlesex Deeds Registry (1709-1837), Metropolis Roads Commission (1826-1872), turnpike trusts (1726-c1870), petty sessions records (from c1880), Middlesex County Council (1889-1965); ecclesiastical records eg Parochial records of the Middlesex area of the Diocese of London; manorial, family, estate, business and private records: private records received on deposit or gift from c1928; records of some sixty manors; business archives include those of the predecessors of London Transport and the North Thames, and Eastern Gas Boards; maps and illustrations: extensive collections relating to Middlesex

37 **GREATER LONDON RECORD OFFICE** Maps, Prints and Photographs Section
1b) Greater London Council
2a) The County Hall, Room B66, London SE1 7PB; 2b) 01-633-7193/3255
5a) Graphic and cartographic materials relating to the history of London
6b) Map collection: over 10,000 maps and plans dating from the early sixteenth century onwards; large scale Ordnance Survey plans. Prints and drawings collection: although covering all centuries the collection is particularly rich in material relating to the eighteenth and nineteenth century; also much ephemeral material relating to London life. Some 40,000 items. Photograph Library: a collection of some 250,000 photographs taken for official purposes from about 1900 onwards, together with earlier material from private sources
8c) Photographic service

38 **GUILDHALL LIBRARY**
1b) Corporation of London
2a) Guildhall, London EC2P 2EJ; 2b) 01-606-3030; 2c) 887955
3) G Thompson FLA
4a) Established 1824 by the corporation to contain a reference library on the history and development of London. Gradual broadening of scope and coverage throughout nineteenth century; 4b) The public library of the City of London. Consists of four main sections: The Guildhall Library, four lending libraries, St Bride

38   GUILDHALL LIBRARY (continued)
      Printing Library (see entry 80), and the City Business Library (see
      entry 23). The Guildhall Library is arranged in three main sec-
      tions: printed books; maps, prints and drawings; manuscripts.
      Each section has its own reading room and enquiry desk.

5a)   General range of subjects; 5b) History and development of the
      City of London and the London area together with its economic,
      social and cultural life

6a)   Monographs: 150,000 items. Current serials received: 1180 titles.
      Serials retained: 980. Dead serials retained: 4700 titles. Maps:
      25,000 items. Prints and drawings: 30,000 items. Photographs:
      18,000 items. Playbills and theatre programmes: 15,000 items.
      Manuscripts: 80,000 items.

6b)   Printed books: comprehensive range of basic reference works,
      mainly in humanities and social sciences (excluding modern
      fiction and literary criticism); London collections (monographs,
      official publications, etc); English county history; printed parish
      registers; seventeenth and eighteenth century law reports;
      Gardeners' Company Library; Glaziers' Company Library;
      Fletchers' Company Library; Gresham College collection of early
      music; Cock collection of Sir Thomas More and Erasmus; Horo-
      logy collection; wine and spirit collection; eighteenth century
      non-conformist tracts
      Maps, prints and drawings: mainly but not entirely material relating
      to London; T C Noble collection of London material; Willshire
      collection of early prints; Company of Makers of Playing Cards
      collection
      Manuscripts: The Guildhall Library is the official repository for
      deposited records relating to the City of London. Extensive
      holdings of parish, ward and livery company records. Business
      and commercial records including those of the London stock
      exchange. Records of Christ's Hospital School, New England
      Company, Metropolitan District Nursing Association. Serves as
      one of the London diocesan record offices and holds the adminis-
      trative and estate archives and the probate and other records of
      the London Archdeaconry Court and the Bishop of London's
      Commissary Court.
      Genealogical and topographical collections. Note: Corporation
      of London municipal archives are separately administered in the
      Corporation of London Record Office which adjoins the library.

7a)   Although some of the material is on open access most of it is not.
      Books are fetched by staff for consultation in the reading rooms.
      Dewey Decimal Classification; own classification for London
      collection; 7b) Name, general subject and London subject catalogue
      for printed books. Separate lists for directories, poll books, play-
      bills and most British parliamentary papers. Separate catalogues
      and lists for maps, plans, drawings and manuscripts

8a)   Generally available to the public; 8b) M-Sat 0930-1700;

38   GUILDHALL LIBRARY (continued)
8c) Photographic and copying facilities; facilities for use of type-
writers and tape recorders in carrels; facilities for disabled readers

9)   'Guildhall Library: a brief guide'; List of publications for sale
(includes bibliographies, books and pamphlets, etc)

10)   Spence, K '550 years of Guildhall Library' *Country life* 156,
1974. Corporation of London *The Corporation of London: its
origin, constitution and powers* Oxford, OUP, 1950. pp164-6.
Welch, C *The Guildhall Library and its work*, 1893.

39   HISPANIC AND LUSO-BRAZILIAN COUNCIL Canning House
Library

1b)   Hispanic and Luso-Brazilian Council Economic Affairs Council

2a)   2 Belgrave Square, London, SW1X 8PJ; 2b) 01-235-2303/7

3)   G H Green MBE BA

4a)   1947; 4b) The library operates as a free public reference library,
although special permission is required to borrow material

5a)   Latin America and the British connection with countries in that
area; 5b) Spain and Portugal

6a)   About 50,000 items; 6b) Reference collection of modern technical
dictionaries in Spanish and Portuguese; current material on invest-
ment situation in Latin America; works of and on R B Cunning-
hame-Graham, W H Hudson, A F Tschiffely

7a)   Library of Congress Classification; 7b) Classified catalogue

8a)   Generally available to the public for reference; 8b) M-F 0930-1730

9)   'British bulletin of publications on Latin America, West Indies,
Portugal and Spain'; *Diamante* (Booklet reprinting annual lectures);
*Author and subject catalogue of the Canning House Library, the
Hispanic Council—the Luso-Brazilian Council (London)* Boston
(Mass) G K Hall. *Hispanic catalogues* (1967) 4 volumes, and *First
supplement* (1973); *Luso-Brazilian catalogues* (1967) 1 volume, and
First supplement (1973), 1 volume.

40   IMPERIAL WAR MUSEUM Department of Printed Books

1b)   Imperial War Museum

2a)   Lambeth Road, London SE1 6HZ; 2b) 01-735-8922

3)   G M Bayliss ALA (Keeper of the Department of Printed Books)

4a)   1917; 4b) Acts as a major reference library on all aspects of war
and military affairs since the First World War. Besides the Department of Printed Books there are important sources of research
material in the other departments as well as in the public exhibition
galleries.
    Department of Art: over 9000 works of art carried out by
official war artists; poster collection of 50,000 items, medallions,
coins, currency, postage stamps and ephemera
    Department of Documents: collections of German documents
relating to the Second World War; war crimes trials papers; private
papers of serving officers and men. Acts as referral centre to

40   IMPERIAL WAR MUSEUM (continued)
British, European and American archives in the field of contemporary history

Department of Film: some 37 million feet of film from the two world wars plus a growing collection of material on major post-1945 conflicts

Department of Photographs: four million photographs and negatives covering every theatre of operations in the two world wars.

Department of Sound Records: a growing collection of material collected since the department was established in 1972. The department is currently conducting its own oral history programme

5a)   Detailed coverage of the two world wars and major conflicts since that time; 5b) Social, economic and political background to warfare. Weapons, equipment, uniforms, medals, insignia, war poetry, propaganda, pacifism, trade and industry

6a)   Bookstock: 140,000 volumes of all types. Current serials received: 350 titles. Maps and drawings: 15,000 items; 6b) Outstanding collection of British, French, German and American unit histories; technical manuals and handbooks; pamphlet collection with many items of propaganda, ephemera, army forms etc; newscuttings files from the Ministry of Information and transcripts of BBC monitoring reports from September 1939. Specialist periodicals relating to the armed services produced at home and in various theatres of war. Maps and technical drawings including trench maps and battle maps (limited access at present due to current cataloguing programme)

7a)   Own classification scheme; 7b) Author and subject catalogues; detailed index to periodical articles

8a)   Generally available to the public, but 24 hours notice of visit required; 8b) M-F 1000-1700. Department closed for annual stocktaking during last two full weeks of October; 8c) Full information and advice service to personal visitors; limited postal service as far as resources permit. Reading room facilities; microfilm and typing facilities; photocopying services

9)   Accession lists (12 pa); Bibliographies and booklists on various topics available on request. Descriptive pamphlets on services of the main departments.

41   INDIA OFFICE LIBRARY AND RECORDS
1b)   Foreign and Commonwealth Office
2a)   197 Blackfriars Road, London SE1 8NG. Newspaper Reading Room at Bush House, Aldwych, London WC2; 2b) 01-928-9531
3)   Miss J C Lancaster CBE, MA, FSA, FR Hist S (Director)
4a)   The library was founded in 1801 by the East India Company and continued from 1858 as the official library of the Secretary of State for India. It is now the official reference library for South Asian affairs of the Secretary of State for Foreign and Commonwealth Affairs. The Record Office, founded in 1771, holds the

41   INDIA OFFICE LIBRARY AND RECORDS (continued)
      extant archives (from 1600) of the East India Company and the
      Board of Control and of their legal successor, the India Office,
      supplemented by relevant private papers.

4b)   The major research collection in the west for South Asian studies,
      it is available for consultation by members of the public with
      limited lending facilities for certain library materials. Photo-
      copying services available.

5a)   Classical and modern South Asian studies in western and oriental
      languages: history, literature, language, religion, the arts, social
      studies, anthropology (science and technology and law excluded).
      The archives are strongest on British India, but also cover the
      Middle East and other large areas of Asia. These interests are
      also reflected in the library's stock.

5b)   See 5a. Cooperation with other orientalist libraries, eg South
      Asia Library Group. Each section of the Library and the Record
      Office has its own specialist staff. The Common Services Section
      provides reading room services and conservation.

6a)   Library: 100,000 books in western languages. 200,000 books in
      oriental languages. 642 current periodicals in western languages.
      91 current periodicals in oriental languages. 3840 serial titles
      retained. 25,000 European and oriental drawings and paintings.
      160,000 photographs. 30,000 maps (Record Office); 6b) 20,000
      Oriental manuscripts (Library). 20,000 private papers. 200,000
      volumes of archives. 100,000 official publications.

7a)   Closed-access. No classification scheme for printed books. Ar-
      chival arrangement for the records. Local classified arrangement
      for official publications; 7b) Catalogues for western languages:
      printed catalogues; card catalogue for post-1936 accessions; older
      stock being recatalogued. G K Hall reprints of sheaf and card
      catalogues. Oriental languages: published and card catalogues.
      Prints and drawings: published catalogues. Archives: Guide (in
      preparation); typed lists in catalogue hall

8a)   Open to all persons who have obtained a readers' ticket; 8b) M-F
      0930-1800, Sat to 1300. Closed the first fortnight in October;
      8c) Professional members of the staff always on duty at the staff
      counter to assist readers in their research. Photocopying facilities
      available

9)   A detailed list of publications is to be found in S C Sutton's guide
      (see below). Appendix III lists publications of the library (cata-
      logues of printed books; catalogues of manuscripts; other publica-
      tions) and Appendix IV publications of the India Office Records
      (Guides and catalogues; lists and indexes; calendars; calendars not
      published by the India Office; reports; selections from the records).
      List of publications in print; monthly list of accessions in European
      languages; irregularly published lists of accessions in Sanskrit and
      Prakrit, and in selected modern Indian or Pakistan languages;
      Rules; *Notes for readers*

41   INDIA OFFICE LIBRARY AND RECORDS (continued)
10) Sutton, S C *A guide to the India Office Library* HMSO, 1967.
     Arberry, A J *The India Office Library: a historical sketch*,
     1967. Lancaster, J C 'The India Office Records' *Archives* vol 9
     no 43, April 1970, pp130-41. Lancaster, J C 'The scope and uses
     of the India Office library and records with particular reference
     to the period 1600-1947' *Asian affairs* vol 9 no 1, February 1978,
     pp31-43.

42   INSTITUTE OF GEOLOGICAL SCIENCES LIBRARY
     Reference Library of Geology
1b) National Environment Research Council
2a) Main library: Geological Museum, Exhibition Road, South
     Kensington, London SW7 2DE (Phone 01-589-3444)
     Other libraries: i) Institute of Geological Sciences, Murchison
     House, West Mains Road, Edinburgh EH9 3LA (Phone 031-667-
     1000); ii) Institute of Geological Sciences, Ring Road, Halton,
     Leeds LS15 8TQ (Phone 0532-605343); iii) Institute of Geological
     Sciences, Keyworth, Nottingham NG12 5NG (Phone 06077-5261);
     iv) Institute of Geological Sciences, Exeter (Full address will be
     available from mid-summer 1978)
3)   K J Spencer FLA (Chief Librarian and Archivist)
4a) Main library established 1840. The present library is the result of
     the amalgamation in 1968 of the Geological Survey and Museum
     Library with the library of the former Overseas Geological Surveys;
     4b) The library, apart from providing a full service to the staff of
     the institute, provides reference and photocopying services to the
     public.
5a) Geological sciences—worldwide coverage; 5b) Geology of the British
     Isles. The branch libraries contain mainly duplicate stock; both
     Edinburgh and Leeds provide a public reference service
6a) Main library only: Bookstock: c250,000 volumes (monographs and
     bound serials). Current serials received: c3000 titles. Serial titles
     retained: c8600 titles. Maps: c100,000 sheets. Pamphlets: c40,000
     items. Photographs: c25,000 items. Microforms: c2000. Archives:
     c20,000 items; 6b) Map library; photographic collection illustrating
     British scenery and geology; Ramsay pamphlets; Murchison pamph-
     lets
7a) UDC (more recent pamphlets and bookstock); maps classified by
     Geosaurus; serials classified by Geosaurus (but not for shelf arrange-
     ment). At main library only a small proportion of the stock is on
     open-access (mainly bookstock post 1960; less than five per cent of
     serials; most of photographs). Maps, microforms, archives, special
     collections and older pamphlets are on closed-access
7b) i) Bookstock/pamphlet catalogue—UDC and AACR in three se-
     quences of cards: title; subject (classified); ii) Map catalogue—
     computer printout (not yet available to the public); iii) Serials
     holdings list—computer printout (various sequences produced);

42 INSTITUTE OF GEOLOGICAL SCIENCES (continued)
    iv) Photographs—printed book catalogue (1963); v) Archives—
    register and alphabetical name index on cards
8a) See 4b). Available to the public for reference only; 8b) Opening
    hours to the public (main library): M-F 1000-1600 (closed on
    public holidays, Christmas Eve and for three weeks in January).
    Other libraries: M-F opening hours and closing days vary; 8c) The
    library provides enquiry and bibliographical services available by
    post and telephone as well as to visitors.
9) 'Regulations for public use'
10) A brief description of the library is contained in the booklet des-
    cribing the Geological Museum (new edition in press)

43 INSTITUTE OF OCEANOGRAPHIC SCIENCES LIBRARY
1b) National Environment Research Council
2a) Wormley, Godalming, Surrey GU8 5UB; 2b) 048279-4141
3) D W Privett MSc AIInfSc
4a) 1953; 4b) There are two associated libraries: Bidston, Birkenhead
    L43 7RA (Phone 051-653-8633); and Crossway, Taunton TA1
    2DW (Phone 0832-86211). (Details not reported in this entry)
5a) Oceanography; 5b) Range of subjects related to oceanography
6a) Monographs: 4600. Current serial titles: 760. Serial titles retained
    1300 titles. Reprints: 46,000. Reports: 17,000. Charts: 5000.
    Atlases: 160; 6b) Challenger Society card catalogue of 'Bibliograph
    of the Marine Fauna', which lists works published between 1758
    and 1907 under author, region and systematic names
7a) No classification. Open-access; 7b) Card catalogue comprising
    sections for authors, subjects (oceanography and marine biology),
    regions (including named currents and topographic features),
    ships, expeditions and charts
8a) Library available for the use of bona-fide researchers by arrange-
    ment with the librarian; 8c) Information service
9) Annual report; 'Discovery reports' (irregular); Collected reprints
    (annual) LIbrary accession list; Reports

44 INSTITUT FRANÇAIS (FRENCH INSTITUTE LIBRARY)
1b) Institut Français
2a) 15 Queensberry Place, London SW7 2DT; 2b) 01-589-6211 ext 33
3) M Troulay
4a) 1910; 4b) Serves as a general reference library for the public.
    Lending service available on subscription
5a) A collection of materials on contemporary French life and culture
    5b) French literature, history and civilisation, languages, philosoph
    and the arts
6a) Bookstock: 65,000 volumes. Current and retained serials: 250
    titles; 6b) The collection formerly housed a scientific library, the
    material from which is now shared between the Science Museum
    Library and Marylebone Public Library (medical literature)

44　INSTITUT FRANCAIS (continued)
7a)　Dewey Decimal Classification. Much material on closed-access;
　　7b) Author and subject catalogues
8a)　Generally available to the public for reference purposes; 8b)
　　M and T 1000-2000; W-F 1000-1800. Closed ten days at Easter
　　and for six weeks during the summer; 8c) Information given by
　　phone and post to inquirers. Borrowing permitted on payment of
　　an annual subscription
9)　Accessions list (2 pa)

45　INSTITUTION OF MINING AND METALLURGY LIBRARY
1b)　Institution of Mining and Metallurgy
2a)　44 Portland Place, London W1N 4BR; 2b) 01-580-3802; 2c)
　　261410 MINANMET LONDON W1
3)　Mrs J A Edkins (Librarian and Information Officer)
4a)　1892; 4b) The Institution of Mining and Metallurgy is a professional
　　body whose members are practising in one or more branches of the
　　minerals industry. The institution houses the most important col-
　　lection in the Commonwealth in its field.
5a)　Economic geology, mining, mineral processing, extractive metallurgy
6)　Monographs: c5000 volumes. Bound serials: c70,000 volumes.
　　Current serials received: c1400 titles. Serial titles retained: c2000
　　titles. Maps: c5000 items; 6b) Historical and manuscript collections;
　　descriptions of old mines; records of early surveys
7a)　UDC Classification (books only); serials arranged geographically
　　under country of origin (UDC); open-access collection; 7b) Author
　　and title catalogue; classified catalogue; map catalogue; geographical
　　index
8a)　Full range of services available to institution members, but reference
　　facilities available to serious enquirers; 8b) M-F 1000-1700 (W to
　　1900); 8c) Bibliographic assistance given by phone and post. Infor-
　　mation service available for which a fee applies, to members and non-
　　members; specialises in technical and economic matters. Photo-
　　copying services
9)　*IMM abstracts* (6 pa)

46　LANGUAGE TEACHING LIBRARY
1b)　English Teaching Information Centre, the British Council and
　　Centre for Information on Language Teaching and Research
2a)　20 Carlton House Terrace, London, SW1Y 5AP; 2b) 01-839-2626
　　ext 13 and 01-930-8466 ext 2782
3)　Miss J E A Price BA ALA and R B Furner BA ALA, joint librarians
4)　1961
5a)　Language teaching. Linguistics; 5b) Linguistics. Principles and
　　methods of language-teaching with particular reference to English
　　as a foreign language. French, German, Italian, Russian, Spanish.
　　Collection of teaching materials for each language.

(continued)

LANGUAGE TEACHING LIBRARY (continued)

6a) Monographs: 24,000 vols. Current serials: 400. Audiotapes. Discs
Filmstrips. Slides. OHP transparencies. Videotapes. Microfilms.
Microfiche. Videocassettes. Wallcharts; 6b) Theses and disserta-
tions on language teaching. Foreign ELT textbooks.

7a) Open-access. ETIC Classification; 7b) Author/title, classified and
subject catalogues

8a) Available for reference to all those concerned with the study,
learning and teaching of languages. Some duplicate copies available
for loan to members. Membership available to all; 8b) M-Th 0930-
1730, Fri to 1700; 8c) Enquiries answered by phone and post.
Photocopying machine available. Collection of audiovisual equipment for use by readers. Specialist advice on materials available
from both centres, by appointment.

9) Over sixty specialised bibliographies. Monthly accessions list.

47   LEEDS CITY LIBRARIES Central Library
1b) Leeds City Council
2a) Central Library, Municipal Buildings, Leeds LS1 3AB; 2b) 0532-31
3)   A B Craven FLA (Director of Library Services), R G Benjamin ALA
(Librarian)
4b) The library provides a central reference and information service for
Leeds and the surrounding region
5a) General subject coverage; 5b) The reference section is divided as
follows: humanities, local history, commerce, science, technology
and information services, music, art, law (located at the Town Hall,
Leeds LS1 3AD), archives (Sheepscar Library, Chapeltown Road,
Leeds LS7 3AP)
6a) Bookstock: c500,000 volumes. Current serials received: c1900
titles; 6b) Local history collection; Gott Bequest (early gardening
and flora); Yorkshire Ramblers' Club Library (mountaineering and
caving); Leeds Philatelic Society Library; Jewish and Hebrew
books (Porton Room), Civil War tracts
7a) Dewey Decimal Classification; 7b) Author/title and classified
catalogues
8a) Generally available to the public for reference; open and closed-
access; 8b) M-F 0900-2000; Sat to 1600

48   LIBRARY ASSOCIATION LIBRARY
1b) British Library Reference Division, Department of Printed Books
2a) 7 Ridgmount Street, London WC1E 7AE; 2b) 01-636-1544; 2c)
21897 LALDN G
3)   L J Taylor
4a) The Library Association was founded in 1877. Since 1933 the
association has maintained a fully staffed library and information
service on the subject of libraries and librarianship, and in April
1974 the British Library took over responsibility for it. 4b) The
library is intended to serve the book and other document needs
of librarians in their professional capacity

48   LIBRARY ASSOCIATION LIBRARY (continued)
5a) Librarianship; 5b) Documentation and information science; bibliography; enumerative and subject bibliographies; guides to the literature; library catalogues; book trade
6a) Monographs: 45,000 items. Current serials: 950. Number of serials retained: 1250 titles; 6b) Research reports; annual reports of libraries; theses and dissertations in librarianship; samples and publicity material prepared by libraries; audiovisual materials relevant to librarianship; plans and photographs of libraries
7a) Dewey Decimal Classification (18th edition); 7b) Author/title and classified catalogues on microfiche. Earlier card catalogue in process of conversion. Detailed leaflets on the current state of the catalogues are available
8a) Full range of services available to members of the Library Association and staff of the British Library. Generally available to the public for reference; 8b) M-F 0900-1800 (Tue and Th to 2000 except mid-July to mid-September). Full service 0900-1700 only; 8c) Details of lending arrangements in library guide; photocopying; information services provided through Information Department of the Library Association and the British Library
9) Library guide; CABLIS (Current Awareness for British Library Staff) available on subscription (10 pa)

49   LIVERPOOL CITY LIBRARIES
1b) Liverpool City Council
2a) William Brown Street, Liverpool L3 8EW; 2b) 051-207-2147; 2c) 62500
3) Ralph Malbon FLA (City Librarian)
4a) 1850; 4b) Acts as a major regional reference library
5a) General subject coverage; 5b) The central libraries are divided into the following main sections: General information and bibliographical services; Music and gramophone records; International (world language, literature, history and topography); Commercial and social sciences; Science and technology; Arts and recreation; General, religion and philosophy; Archives and local studies; Hornby Library and Oak Room; Print collection; LADSIRLAC (Liverpool and District Scientific, Industrial and Research Library Advisory Council); Municipal Resources Library Service (an information service for councillors and senior officials); Microfilm unit (provides photocopying and associated services); General and popular lending; Central junior services. The library is a repository of government and EEC publications, and patents.
6a) Monographs (reference and lending): c1,250,000 volumes. Current serials received: Periodicals 1929, Abstracts 189, Newspapers 111 (figures include multiple copies). Serials retained: Periodicals 1622, Abstracts 178; 6b) Hornby Library; Oak Library; print and autograph collections; archives collections include family papers (eg Roscoe, Norris, Derby, etc), business records, municipal archives, ecclesiastical records; patent collection (second in size in UK after

65

49   LIVERPOOL CITY LIBRARIES (continued)
      Science Reference Library, London); Carl Rosa Library (in music
      library—scores and orchestral parts belonging to the Carl Rosa Oper
      Company); bookplate collection; microfilm collection of English an
      American plays from 16th to 18th century.
7a)   Dewey Decimal Classification; 7b) Dictionary catalogue in sheaf
      form
8a)   Generally available to the public for reference and lending; 8b) M-F
      0900-2100, Sat to 1700; 8c) as 5b above
9)   Current publications: *Catalogue of non-fiction* 10 vols, 1925-71;
      Catalogue of fiction 4 vols, 1951-71; *Children's books* 3 vols, 1958
      71; *Music catalogue* 1954 (supplement in preparation). Past
      publications: Chandler, G *Liverpool*, 1957; *Liverpool under
      James I* 1960; *Liverpool under Charles I*, 1965. Cowell, P *Liver-
      pool public libraries: a history of fifty years*, 1903. *Catalogue of
      the Hornby Library*, 1906. *Liverpool prints and documents*, 1908.
10)   Chandler, G 'Public libraries of the Liverpool Metropolitan Area'
      Library trends 14 1965-6, pp60-7; Evans, J T 'Liverpool public
      libraries: a historical survey' *Library world* 41, 1939, pp 227-9,
      251-4; *Encyclopedia of library and information science*, ed A Kent
      et al, vol 16, New York, 1975, pp220-6; Reynolds, J D 'Editorial
      excursions: Liverpool' *Library Association record* 63, 1961, pp
      293-9; Steele, C *Major libraries of the world: a selective guide*,
      London and New York, 1976.

50   LONDON LIBRARY
1b)   The London Library
2a)   14 St James Square, London SW1Y 4LG; 2b) 01-930-7705/6
3)   S Gillam B Litt MA
4a)   Established 1841, as a subscription circulating and reference
      library; 4b) The London Library is one of the major independent
      collections in the country; it exists as an educational charity under
      Royal Charter. Subscribing members number about 6000 persons
5a)   The arts and humanities; 5b) Russian literature and history; nine-
      teenth and twentieth century material on Africa, including exten-
      sive collection of parliamentary papers; philosophy, history, archae
      ology, art, theology
6a)   Bookstock: c750,000 volumes; 6b) Heron-Allen collection (Omar
      Kháyyám); Higginson collection (Hunting and field sports); Record
      of Cape Colony 1793-1831; back runs of periodicals of learned
      societies
7a)   Own classification scheme; 7b) Dictionary catalogue; Printed
      catalogue (to 1950) in 5 volumes (including 3 supplements);
      Subject index to the London Library to 1955 in 4 volumes
8a)   Persons wishing to use the library pay an annual subscription
9)   Annual report
10)   Purnell, C J 'The London Library' in Irwin, R and Staveley, R
      The libraries of London 2nd ed, LA, 1964, pp231-41.

51 MANCHESTER PUBLIC LIBRARIES Central Library
1b) Manchester City Council
2a) Central Library, St Peter's Square, Manchester M2 5PD
    2b) 061-236-9422; 2c) 667149 and 669475
3) K D King BA ALA (Director of Libraries)
4a) 1852; 4b) Provides a regional reference and information service.
    The collections are arranged in a number of subject departments:
    social sciences, commercial, technical, arts, music, language and
    literature, local history, archives, Jewish.
5a) General subject coverage; 5b) British official publications; United
    Nations documents
6a) Bookstock: c800,000 volumes. Current serials received: c4500
    titles
6b) Anti-Corn Law League papers; ballad collection; Bataillard collec-
    tion (gypsies); Bellot collection (Chinese); broadside collection
    (mostly local); Bronte collection; Burton manuscripts (Manches-
    ter local history); Coleridge collection; Crossley papers (literature
    and bookselling in the nineteenth century); De Quincey collection;
    Edward Edwards collection (library history); English Dialect
    Society collection; Farrer deeds and manuscripts (Lancashire
    local history); Gaskell collection (literary); Thomas Greenwood
    (library for librarians); John Greswell collection (literary); Hamp-
    den Club papers (local political); Hibbert-Ware manuscripts
    (literary); James Lansdale Hodson papers (literary); Alexander
    Ireland collection (literary); Stanley Jast papers (library history);
    Jewish collections; Lancashire Parish Register Society collections;
    Neville Laski collection (World War I); Manchester and Salford
    sanitary collection; Manchester cathedral transcripts; Manchester
    Chamber of Commerce archives; Manchester collection (cuttings,
    drawings etc); Manchester Dante Society; Manchester Esperanto
    Society; Manchester General Defence Accounts; Manchester
    Literary and Philosophical Society collections; Manchester Pitt
    Club records; Manchester Regiment Records; Manchester sessions
    records; Manchester Statistical Society collections; Manchester
    theatres collection; National Union of Women's Suffrage Manches-
    ter collection; Nazi collection (propaganda); Charles Nowell collec-
    tion (library history); Owen manuscripts (local genealogy); Photo-
    graphic Survey Record of Manchester (1898 to date); Manchester
    and Salford collection, and other local collections (local history
    etc); Royal Lancashire Regiment material; Royal Manchester Insti-
    tution collection; shorthand collection; Simon papers (Lord Simon
    of Wythenshawe); Oliver J Sutton collection (witchcraft); John
    Hibbert Swann collection (literary); Vegetarian Society collection;
    Wilmslow Turnpike Trust documents.
        A number of society libraries are retained on deposit including:
    Ancient Monuments Society; Anthroposophical Society; Chartered
    Institute of Secretaries; Dicken's Fellowship Manchester branch;
    Institute of Cost and Works Accountants; Insurance Institute

51 MANCHESTER PUBLIC LIBRARIES (continued)
    of Manchester; Lancashire and Cheshire Antiquarian Society;
    Lancashire Author's Association; Manchester Actuarial Society;
    Manchester Chess Club; Manchester Law Student's Society;
    Manchester Literary Club; Manchester Astronomical Society;
    Modern Language Association; Peak District and Northern
    Counties Footpath Preservation Society; Philatelic Societies
    of Manchester; Rucksack Club
7a) Dewey Decimal Classification; 7b) Author/title and classified
    catalogues
8a) Collections generally available to the public for reference;
    8b) M-F 0900-2100; Sat to 1700; 8c) Information and advice to
    readers; photocopying
9) Library guide; Annual report; 'Manchester review' (2 pa)

52 MINISTRY OF AGRICULTURE, FISHERIES AND FOOD
    Main Library
1b) Ministry of Agriculture, Fisheries and Food
2a) 3 Whitehall Place, London SW1A 2HH; 2b) 01-839-7711; 2c)
    22124
3) F C Hirst FLA
4a) 1889; 4b) The library exists primarily to serve the needs of the
    ministry and other government departments, but is available to
    other bona-fide users for reference
5a) Agriculture; 5b) Related subjects—scientific and economic. There
    are branch libraries at Great Westminster House, Horseferry Road,
    London SW1P 2AE, and at Government Buildings, Hook Rise
    South, Tolworth, Surrey KT6 7NF
6a) Bookstock: c160,000 volumes. Current serials received: c2000
    titles; 6b) Cowan and Cottons collection (apiculture); Punnett
    collection (poultry genetics); food and nutrition collections con-
    centrated at Great Westminster House
7a) Dewey Decimal Classification; 7b) Classified catalogue
8a) Available for reference purposes to research workers
9) HMSO sectional list no 1 (2 pa); catalogue of departmental publica-
    tions (2 pa); ADAS quarterly review; Domestic food consumption an
    expenditure (annual); Experimental horticulture and experimental
    husbandry (2 pa); Library accessions list and selective index to
    current periodicals (12 pa); Plant pathology (4 pa); Plant varieties
    and seeds gazette (12 pa). Various bulletins, leaflets and pamphlets
    are produced irregularly.

53 NATIONAL ARMY MUSEUM LIBRARY
1b) National Army Museum
2a) Royal Hospital Road, London SW3 4HT; 2b) 01-730-0717
4a) 1959; museum originally opened at the Royal Military Academy,
    Sandhurst; 4b) reading room

(continued)

53   NATIONAL ARMY MUSEUM LIBRARY (continued)
5a)   History of the British Army 1550-1914; 5b) History of the Indian
      Army to 1947; history of colonial armies to independence
6a)   Bookstock: c25,000 volumes. Current serials received: over 200
      titles; 6b) Collections of manuscripts, photographs and prints; regi-
      mental histories; army lists
7a)   Some material on closed-access
8a)   Reference collection only. Readers ticket available on application
      to the director in writing; 8b) M-Sat 1000-1730; 8c) Photocopying
      and microreading facilities

54   NATIONAL BOOK LEAGUE Mark Longman Library
1b)   National Book League
2a)   7 Albemarle Street, London W1X 4BB; 2b) 01-493-9001
3)   Mrs S A Clarke ALA
4a)   Established 1924 as a small nucleus of books belonging to the
      National Book Council, later renamed the National Book League;
      4b) Central book trade library with unbiased interest in the history
      and current status of books in Britain
5a)   The book in all its aspects; 5b) Authorship, publishing, printing,
      bookselling, collecting, bibliography, reading techniques, children's
      books, librarianship, history and critical studies of literature, author
      and national bibliographies. Book Information Service for tracing
      bibliographical details of books published in English
6a)   Bookstock: c10,000 volumes. Current serials received: 42 titles.
      Serial titles retained: 42 titles; 6b) Linder collection (Beatrix
      Potter); collections of drawings by Beatrix Potter; Perez collection
      (British ex-libris); the Children's Reference Library of current
      books (excluding textbooks)—under the care of the Children's
      Books Officer
7a)   Modified Bliss Classification; 7b) Author catalogue only
8a)   Full range of services available to members. Open to others for
      reference purposes; 8b) M-F 0930-1730. Closed Saturdays, public
      and bank holidays; 8c) Information service to members. Charges
      for Book Information Service research available on request (for
      searching for titles and compiling selective book lists)
9)   Library guide (30p by post); 101 books on the book trade (£1.05);
      Linder collection catalogue (65p)
10)   Clarke, A in *Bookseller* 21 August 1976; Myers, R *British book
      trade* Deutsch, 1973

55   NATIONAL FARMERS' UNION LIBRARY
1b)   National Farmers' Union
2a)   Agriculture House, 25/31 Knightsbridge, London SW1X 7NJ;
      2b) 01-235-5077; 2c) 919669
3)   Mrs V Beale
4a)   1945; 4b) Serves the National Farmers' Union as part of the Infor-
      mation Division

55   NATIONAL FARMERS' UNION LIBRARY (continued)

5a)   Agriculture and horticulture; 5b) Political, economic and marketing aspects of agriculture; general and technical aspects of agriculture; land use; agricultural trade

6a)   Bookstock: 2000 items. Current serials received: 100 titles. Small photograph collection; 6b) National Farmers' Union history collection

7a)   Dewey Decimal Classification; 7b) Classified catalogue

8a)   Open to the public for reference purposes; 8b) M-F 0930-1700; 8c) Information service to users

9)   Monthly accessions list

56   NATIONAL INSTITUTE FOR RESEARCH IN DAIRYING
       Stenhouse Williams Memorial Library

1b)   National Institute for Research in Dairying, University of Reading

2a)   Church Lane, Shinfield, Reading RG2 9AT; 2b) 0734-883103

3)   B F Bone BA ALA

4a)   1923; 4b) Literature is acquired appropriate to the needs of the research staff. Information officers prepare weekly SDI bulletins for researchers using the ICI ASSASSIN system. Literature searches carried out by Lockheed DIALOG system

5a)   Dairy science and dairying; 5b) Agriculture, biochemistry, microbiology, nutrition, physiology, statistical analysis

6a)   Bookstock: 19,000 volumes. Pamphlets and reports: 32,000. Current serials received: 450 titles. Serial titles retained: 700; 6b) Houses the collection of the Commonwealth Bureau of Dairy Science and Technology

7a)   Modified UDC. Open-access; 7b) Author and subject catalogues for books; strip index to report series

8a)   Open to the public for reference purposes; 8b) M-Th 0900-1730, F 0900-1700; 8c) Photocopying; linguistic aid service

9)   Weekly SDI bulletin

57   NATIONAL LIBRARY FOR THE BLIND

2a)   Cromwell Road, Bredbury, Stockport SK6 2SG; 2b) 061-494-0217/8/9

3)   W A Munford MBE NSc PhD FLA (Librarian and Director General)

4a)   Established 1882, known as the Incorporated National Lending Library for the Blind from 1898; and from 1916 as National Library for the Blind. The NLB is a registered charity and limited company; 4b) The principal national collection of literature for the blind and partially sighted

5a)   General range of subjects

6a)   Bookstock: over 400,000 volumes (braille and moon types). In addition there is a collection of letterpress works (including many large typeface items for partially sighted readers); 6b) Collection of speech records; reference library of works on blindness

7a)   Dewey Decimal Classification; 7b) Classified catalogue

57   NATIONAL LIBRARY FOR THE BLIND (continued)
8a)   Generally available to the blind and partially sighted; 8c) Lending
      service (material in braille, and in large type faces)
9)   Annual report; Braille library bulletin (6 pa)
10)   Schaunder, D E and Cram, M D *Libraries for the blind: an inter-
      national study of policies and practices* Stevenage, Peter Peregrinus,
      1977.

58   NATIONAL LIBRARY OF SCOTLAND
2a)   George IV Bridge, Edinburgh EH1 1EW; 2b) 031-226-4531; 2c)
      72638 NLSEDI G
3)   Professor E F D Roberts MA PhD
4a)   Established originally in 1682 as the Library of the Faculty of Advocates.
      Acquired the copyright privilege in 1710. The library, with the excep-
      tion of the legal collections, was transferred to the state in 1925,
      becoming the National Library of Scotland. A new building,
      started before the Second World War, was opened in 1956. In 1974
      the Scottish Central Library merged with the National Library to
      become the National Library of Scotland Lending Services, respon-
      sible for inter-library lending in Scotland.
4b)   A large non-specialist library, the National Library of Scotland is a
      centre for reference and research of any kind undertaken through
      the medium of the printed book. As a national library its collections
      of Scottish manuscripts and books printed in or relating to Scotland
      make it pre-eminently a centre of research in all aspects of Scottish
      literature, history and culture. It has a special responsibility for
      Scottish bibliography, both historical and current, and for inter-
      library lending. As a British copyright library, and because many
      of its manuscripts are of British rather than purely Scottish signifi-
      cance, it can provide material for research in the wider context of
      Great Britain. Deposit also ensures much popular or ephemeral ma-
      terial not found in other libraries. Finally, it is well-provided with
      the literature of foreign countries, although most of the foreign
      material is limited to European languages and the humanities.
5a)   Full range of subjects. Almost complete coverage of British (and
      Irish) publications.
5b)   The great bulk of the manuscript collection is Scottish, but the
      collection has a wider significance since many eminent Scotsmen
      whose papers are in the library have been concerned in British
      literary, social or political life, imperial administration or military
      service. Consequently much of the subject matter is of interest
      for English literature, British history, and the history and culture
      of other countries. In particular there is important material relating
      to India, Africa and America. The library has three departments—
      administration, manuscripts and printed books. The Department
      of Printed Books also contains the Map Room, the Music Room,
      the Periodicals Room, and the Official Papers Unit.

(continued)

6a)   3 million volumes of books and bound periodicals. 10,119 current
      periodicals received. All serial titles retained. Over 1 million maps.
      A wide collection of music; 6b) Allhusen collection (20th century
      French); Astorga (Spanish material); Balfour (Handel); Birkbeck
      (printing); Blaikie (Jacobite); Blairs College, Dowden, Cowan, Gray
      and Jolly (theology and associated subjects); Bute (17th and 18th
      century English plays); Combe (phrenology); Crawford and Diete-
      richs (Lutheran tracts); Durdans (sport, travel and politics); Glen
      and Inglis (Scottish music); Hopkinson (Berlioz and Verdi);
      Keiller (witchcraft); Lauriston Castle (Scottish books, pamphlets
      and chapbooks); Lloyd and Brown (mountaineering); Macadam
      (baking and confectionery); McDonald (town-planning slides);
      Morrison, Blair, Campbell and Ossian (Celtic languages); New-
      battle (16th-18th century European literature and history); Rose-
      bery and Ferguson (early and rare Scottish books and pamphlets);
      Sharp (English and American first editions); Smith (16th-18th
      century English and French literature); Thorkelin (Scandinavian
      history, literature and law); Warden (shorthand); Weir (Scottish
      theatre posters and playbills); Wordie (Polar exploration); Wood-
      burn (Russian revolutionary posters); Mason (children's books);
      Townley (railway postcards). The major foreign language collec-
      tions are supplemented by purchase. East European material has
      been acquired since 1950. Alpine and mountaineering literature
      in the Graham Brown collection is supplemented by a substantial
      fund to maintain and add to the collection.

7a)   Closed-access; 7b) Catalogue 1—author catalogue following British
      Museum rules for all books published before 1968 catalogued befor
      1974. Catalogue 2—author catalogue following AACR rules for
      all books published in or after 1968 and all books catalogued in
      or after 1974. Title catalogue—entries for all books in catalogue 2.

8a)   Six-monthly and three-day tickets for research and reference not
      easily carried on elsewhere. Special conditions for admission of
      undergraduates. Enquiries should be addressed to the Superin-
      tendent of the Reading Room; 8b) Reading Rooms M-F 0930-
      2030, Sat to 1300. Map Room and Exhibition Room M-F 0930-
      1730, Sat to 1300. Exhibition Room also open Sunday 1400-
      1700, but not from October to March. Closed on New Year's Day,
      the following week-day, Good Friday, Christmas Day and Boxing
      Day; 8c) The library can supply xerox copies, microfilms, enlarge-
      ments of microfilms, tone photographs of printed or manuscript
      materials in the collections. There are also facilities for infra-red
      and ultra-violet photography and beta radiography of watermarks.

9)   Guide to the National Library of Scotland; Annual report; Current
      periodicals; catalogues of exhibitions; catalogues of national exhi-
      bitions; commemorative publications; *A short title catalogue of
      foreign books printed up to 1601* (1970); H C Aldis *A list of books
      printed in Scotland before 1700* (1970); Summary catalogue of

58   NATIONAL LIBRARY OF SCOTLAND (continued)
      the advocates' manuscripts (1970); Catalogue of manuscripts
      acquired since 1925, 3 volumes (1938, 1966, 1968); Accessions of
      manuscripts 1954-1960 (1964); Accessions of manuscripts 1965-
      1970 (1971); Ferguson, J P S *Scottish family histories held in
      Scottish libraries* (1960)

59   NATIONAL LIBRARY OF WALES/LLYFRGELL GENEDLAETHOL
      CYMRU
2a)   Aberystwyth, Dyfed SY23 3BU; 2b) 0970-3816/9; 2c) 35165
3)   D Jenkins CBE MA JP
4a)   Established 1907 by Royal Charter, came into existence on
      1 January 1909. One of the six libraries in the British Isles en-
      titled to certain privileges under the copyright acts.
4b)   Main objects of the library: collection, preservation and mainten-
      ance of manuscripts, printed books, periodical publications,
      newspapers, maps, photographs, paintings, pictures, engravings,
      drawings and prints, musical publications and works of all kinds
      especially manuscripts, records, printed books and other works
      which have been or shall be composed in Welsh or any other Celtic
      language or which relate or shall relate to the Welsh and other
      Celtic peoples; works including audiovisual material whether con-
      nected or not with Welsh subjects in whatsoever language, subject
      or wheresoever published.
5a)   Full range of subjects. The library is entitled to claim material
      under the Copyright Act. The library specialises in subjects re-
      lating to Wales and the Welsh people, their history, language and
      literature; 5b) The library contains the world's largest collection
      of books in Welsh and relating to Wales and other Celtic countries.
      Headquarters for the Wales Regional Libraries Bureau and pro-
      vides a back-up service for the BLLD at Boston Spa. Three
      main departments—Printed books; Manuscripts and records;
      Prints, drawings and maps.
6a)   2 million volumes and bound periodicals. 31,000 archives.
      3,500,000 MSS. 12,000 photographs. 150 gramophone
      records. 170,000 maps. 2500 microforms. 2000 slides.
      200 filmstrips. 250 wallcharts. 6000 current serials received.
      Every item—monograph or serial part—is retained. The present
      number of serial titles received is approximately 6000. It is
      estimated that in all there are about 10,000 titles of serials, ie
      periodicals.
6b)   Celtic subjects; Witton Davies Semitic collection (Oriental books);
      Hartland collection (African anthropology and folklore); publi-
      cations of the Egypt Exploration Fund and the British School
      of Archaeology in Egypt; Sir John Williams collection (books,
      manuscripts and graphic material); Collection of Gregynog Press
      books; Hengwrt-Peniarth collection (fine collection of Welsh
      manuscripts).

59   NATIONAL LIBRARY OF WALES (continued)

7a)   Library of Congress Classification; 7b) Author catalogue

8a)   Open to members of the public in possession of a reader's ticket; 8b) M-F 0930-1800, Sat to 1700. Closed Christmas, New Year and Easter bank holidays; 8c) Information given by phone, telex and post to inquirers. Every assistance is given to readers by the staff about sources, as and when required in the library. A varied photographic reproduction service is available.

9)   Regular publications: Annual report; *Bibliotheca Celtica; National Library of Wales journal* (2 pa); Handlist of Manuscripts; The National Library of Wales—a brief summary of its history and its activities. Major publications in the past: Sir William Ll Davies *The National Library of Wales*, Aberystwyth, 1937; *A Bibliography of Robert Owen, the socialist, 1771-1858*. 2nd edition, revised and enlarged. 1925. Recent major publications: *George Owen of Henllys—A Welsh Elizabethan; The Cartulary of Shrewsbury Abbey; Giraldus Cambrensis—The Growth of the Welsh Nation.*

60   NATIONAL MARITIME MUSEUM LIBRARY

1b)   National Maritime Museum

2a)   Romney Road, Greenwich, London SE10 9NF; 2b) 01-858-4422

3)   D T Bradley MA BSc Dip Lib ALA

4a)   Established 1934 with the creation of the museum; 4b) the aims of the library are as follows: to collect literature in the fields of maritime art, science, technology, history and archaeology. Particular attention is paid to the areas of exploration, the administrative history of the Royal Navy, strategical and tactical developments, the economics of transportation and the management of merchant shipping in peace and war.

5a)   Maritime art, science, technology, history and archaeology; 5b) The museum authority responsible for library matters is the Department of Printed Books and Manuscripts. The department consists of two sections: The Printed Books Section is responsible for all printed books, journals and related material, covering all aspects of the maritime field. The Manuscripts Section is responsible for all manuscripts and related material, covering all aspects of the maritime field. Both sections work together in maintaining a service to the public and the staff through the reading room.

    As of March 1978 the senior staff of the Department of Printed Books and Manuscripts is as follows: Head of Department— D V Proctor MA DIC, Head of Printed Book Section and Librarian —D T Bradley MA BSc Dip Lib ALA, Head of Manuscript Section and Deputy Head of Department—R J B Knight MA PhD

6a)   Monographs (books and pamphlets): 76,000. Current serials: 350. Total number of serial titles retained: 820. Microfilm: 1400 reels; 6b) Since the museum's establishment the library has acquired several important collections of material dealing with maritime affairs.

60 NATIONAL MARITIME MUSEUM LIBRARY (continued)
These include the libraries of R C Anderson (naval history and architecture especially that of the sailing ships era), Brindley, Gosse
(piracy and privateering) and Reynolds (polar exploration).

7a) At present (March 1978) a system of broad subject groupings is
employed. This is being replaced by the introduction of UDC;
7b) An author card catalogue is maintained in the reading room.
Five volumes of the library's printed catalogue have been produced
to date. Details are as follows: vol 1 Voyages and travel, vol 2 Biography (in two parts), vol 3 Atlases and cartography (in two parts),
vol 4 Piracy and privateering, vol 5 Naval history part one: from
early times to 1815. This programme in its existing form has now
been terminated. At the moment the library is beginning an
extensive recataloguing programme in which data processing
equipment is being utilised wherever possible. This programme
will take at least seven years to complete. It is hoped that the
final output of this programme will be produced on microfilm.

8a) Admission to the library is by reader's ticket only; 8b) M-F 1000-
1700, Sat to 1300 and 1400-1700 by prior appointment.
The library is closed on Sundays, bank holidays, Good Friday,
Christmas Eve and Christmas Day, and also throughout the
third week of February; 8c) A reading room is provided for
library users. Catalogues and other readers' aids are available
for consultation by users.

9) In addition to the catalogues described at 7b the Manuscripts
Section of the Department of Printed Books and Manuscripts
has just published Knight, R J B (ed) *Guide to the manuscripts
in the National Maritime Museum vol I: The personal collections* Mansell, 1978.

61 NATIONAL METEOROLOGICAL LIBRARY
1b) Meteorological Office, Ministry of Defence (Air)
2a) London Road, Bracknell, Berks RG12 2SZ; 2b) 0344-20242.
Librarian ext 2250; Information Officer ext 2252 and 2712;
visual aids ext 2253; loans desk ext 2251; 2c) 848160 and
847010
3) E W C Harris
4a) 1870; 4b) Support to the Meteorological Office in particular
but as the National Meteorological Library available to anyone
with a genuine interest.
5a) Meteorology and associated disciplines; 5b) All available worldwide meteorological and climatological published data and literature. More limited coverage in the related disciplines such as
fluid dynamics, hydrology and oceanography. General information available for a wide range of other scientific and technical
topics.
6a) 125,000 volumes are held. Data, reports and journals predomi-
nate, while books represent a fairly small proportion. There

61   NATIONAL METEOROLOGICAL LIBRARY (continued)
      are also 28,000 pamphlets. There is a large collection of daily
      weather reports from many countries of the world, some records
      being continuous for over a century. Over 300 periodical titles
      are received excluding data series; 6b) Several thousands of
      photographs and slides of meteorological interest (particularly
      of clouds). A videotape collection is being formed.

7a)   Open-access. All articles are individually classified by UDC;
      7b) Author card catalogue; subject bibliographies.

8a)   May be used by anyone with a genuine interest; 8b) M-Th 0830-
      1645, Fri to 1615; 8c) Full service to users, but preferably by
      appointment.

9)   Monthly accessions list (generally containing some 700 references).

62   NATIONAL MONUMENTS RECORD
1b)   Royal Commission on Historical Monuments (England)
2a)   Fortress House, 23 Savile Row, London W1X 1AB; 2b) 01-734-601C
3)   E Mercer MA FSA
4a)   1941; 4b) The major record archive for historical buildings and
      architecture, and archaeological sites
5a)   Building and architecture
6a)   Approximately 1 million photographs, 20,000 measured drawings,
      15,000 slides; 6b) Photographs, plans and other records of archae-
      ological sites in England. Aerial photographs of sites
7a)   Own classification scheme
8a)   Open to all for reference, and in particular for architectural students
9)   Annual report

63   NATIONAL MONUMENTS RECORD FOR WALES
1b)   Royal Commission on Ancient Monuments in Wales
2a)   Edleston House, Queens Road, Aberystwyth, Dyfed SY23; 2b)
      0970-2256
4a)   1908; 4b) The major record archive for historical buildings and
      architecture, and archaeological sites
5a)   Building and architecture
6b)   Collection of photographs and drawings relevant to buildings and
      archaeological sites
7a)   Own classification scheme; 7b) Dictionary catalogue
8a)   Open to bona fide research students for reference only; 8c) Infor-
      mation given by phone and post to inquirers

64   OFFICE OF POPULATION CENSUSES AND SURVEYS
      LIBRARY
1b)   Office of Population Censuses and Surveys (OPCS)
2a)   St Catherine's House, 10 Kingsway, London WC2B 6JP; 2b)
      01-242-0262
3)   Miss P Beskow
4a)   The original library service dates back to the early 19th century.
      It provided a reference service for medical statistics, demography

64   OFFICE OF POPULATION CENSUSES (continued)
      and censuses. Coverage broadened to include survey work in the
      last decade. The OPCS was formed in 1970 by merger of the
      General Register Office and the Government Social Survey Depart-
      ment. 4b) To provide staff of OPCS with a reference library; to
      give access to a wide range of foreign material on censuses and
      surveys to members of the general public
5a)   Medical and vital statistics, demography, census data, survey re-
      ports, methodology of surveys; 5b) Extensive exchange arrange-
      ments with overseas countries based on OPCS publications
6a)   Bookstock: c75,000 volumes (includes c8000 monographs).
      Current serials received: c300 titles; 6b) Overseas census reports
      and other official publications (eg WHO, UN, EEC). The library
      is building-up a collection of material and studies using census
      statistics as part of the Census Use Study, and is based on the use
      and integration of primary data and secondary sources
7a)   Own classification scheme. Open-access; 7b) Author index; Census
      Use Study card index
8a)   Generally available to the public for reference. Working space
      limited and prior notification of visit may be helpful to user and
      library; 8b) M-F 0900-1600; 8c) Photocopying, bibliographical
      assistance, telephone enquiries
9)   OPCS library guide

65   OVERSEAS DEVELOPMENT INSTITUTE LIBRARY
2a)   10-11 Percy Street, London W1P 0JB; 2b) 01-637-3622
3)   Miss C Mortier
4a)   1961; 4b) Catering for ODI research staff
5a)   Aid and development; 5b) Interested specifically in agriculture
      and rural development, trade, Africa and Asia. One separate
      documentation unit specialising in agricultural administration
6a)   About 10,000 books; and 200 periodicals currently received; 6b)
      Newspaper cutting files by subject and by countries. Documents
      and reports on agricultural administration (irrigation management
      and management of arid zones)
7a)   Own classification. Open-access arrangement; 7b) Classified cata-
      logue by authors and subjects
8a)   Available for reference—open to anyone doing research; 8b) M-F
      1000-1800; 8c) Information given by phone and post to inquirers
9)   'Periodicals reference bulletin' (6 pa), available under subscription
      —lists articles appearing on aid and development, classified according
      to subject and/or country

66   THE POLISH LIBRARY
1b)   Polish Social and Cultural Association
2a)   238-246 King Street, London W6 0RF; 2b) 01-741-0474
3)   Dr Z K Jagodziński
4a)   Established 1942 by the Ministry of Education of the Polish
      government in exile; between 1948 and 1953 attached to the

THE POLISH LIBRARY (continued)

Polish University College in London; later taken over by the Interim Treasury Committee for Polish Questions, and subsequently by the Committee for the Education of Poles in the United Kingdom Since 1967 owned by the Polish Social and Cultural Association on behalf of the Polish community in Britain

4b) Apart from catering for the needs of the Polish community, the library supplies information regarding various aspects of Polish affairs, biographical and bibliographical queries. It provides a free service for students, scholars and researchers. It compiles and publishes bibliographies, organises exhibitions, lectures and discussions. The library has concentrated on a comprehensive expansion in the field of Polish studies, and collects both Polish and non-Polish material extensively. Since the end of 1976 the library has been housed in new premises at the Polish Centre where there is a full range of other facilities.

5a) Poland and Polish life, culture and history; 5b) Polish culture, history, literature, language, geography, law, economics, politics, folklore, sociology, military science, philosophy, religious life, music, art

6a) Monographs and pamphlets: c100,000 items. Serial titles retained: 2468. Maps and atlases: 210. Photographs: 38,000. Bookplates: 11,500. Manuscripts: 530 items; 6b) Collection of Conradiana (Joseph Conrad); collections of bookplates; Polish emigré publications

7a) Dewey Decimal Classification. Mostly closed-access; 7b) Author catalogue only

8a) Open for reference to all interested in Poland and Polish studies; 8b) M and W 1000-2000; Tu and F 1000-1700; Th and Sat 1000-1300. During July and August, M-F 1000-1700 and Sat 1000-1300; 8c) Reference and information services; reading room with general access collection of reference material

9) 'Books in Polish or relating to Poland, added to the Collections of the Polish Library: a quarterly list of new accessions 1950- ' Current XXIX, 1978. 'Bibliography of books in Polish or relating to Poland, published outside Poland since September 1st 1939' by J Zabielska and others 3 vols, 1953, 1959, 1966. Vols 4 and 5 in preparation. 'Bibliography of works by Polish scholars and scientists, published outside Poland in languages other than Polish' by M L Danilewicz and J Nowak. vol 1, 1964. vol 2 in preparation. 'Catalogue of periodicals in Polish or relating to Poland and other Slavonic countries, published outside Poland since September 1st 1939' Compiled by M L Danilewicz and G Sadowska. 1st ed 1964. 2nd ed, compiled by M L Danilewicz and B Jabłońska, 1971. 'Katalog Wystawy Zbiorów Historycznych/Catalogue of the exhibition of historical collection in the Polish Library in London' by M L Danilewicz and Z Jagodziński, 1970. 'Jacek Malczewski in Asia Minor and in Rozdól' by M Paszkiewicz, 1972. Also in

66   THE POLISH LIBRARY (continued)
      Polish: 'Jacek Malczewski w Azji Mniejszej i w Rozdole'. 'Polska
      prasa podziemna w zbiorach londyńskich 1939-1945' by Józef
      Garlińsky/Polish Underground Press in the London Collections,
      1962. 'The Katyn bibliography: books and pamphlets' by Z
      Jagodziński, 1976. 'Dorobek gospodarczy odrodzonej Rzeczypos-
      politej 1918-1939'/Economic achievement of the restored Poland
      1918-1939' by W Zaleski, 1975. Annual reports: in Polish.
      Mimeographed, some printed.
10)   Nowak, J (comp) 'The Joseph Conrad Collection in the Polish
      Library in London catalogue, nos 1-399', 1970.

67   PUBLIC RECORD OFFICE
1b)   Public Record Office
2a)   i) Ruskin Avenue, Kew, Richmond, Surrey TW9 4DU; ii) Chancery
      Lane, London WC2A 1LR; 2b) i) 01-876-3444; ii) 01-405-0741
3)   J R Ede (Keeper of the Public Records)
4a)   Established in 1838, bringing together records formerly widely dis-
      persed
4b)   The Public Record Office contains many millions of documents re-
      lating to the actions of central government and the courts of law of
      England and Wales, of Great Britain from 1707, and of the United
      Kingdom from 1801 to the present day. With few exceptions public
      records more than thirty years old can be seen by holders of a valid
      reader's ticket.
          Records are stored in two buildings: the new headquarters build-
      ing at Kew and at the original building in Chancery Lane. Records
      are available for consultation only in the building in which they are
      stored.
5a)   The Public Records. These are described in the guide mentioned at 9.
      The first volume deals principally with the records of the Chancery,
      the Exchequer and other courts of law; the second with the records
      of the State Paper Office and the public departments; the third with
      accessions between 1960 and 1968. Information about accessions
      since 1966 is published in the Annual Report of the Keeper of Public
      Records
5b)   Chancery Lane: Records described in volume 1 of the *Guide* con-
      sisting of records from the Norman Conquest onwards, of the
      King's Court and the divergent branches and offshoots through
      which it discharged its administrative, financial and judicial func-
      tions. Also included are records of the Palatinates of Lancaster,
      Chester and Durham, of special jurisdictions, of the High Courts
      of Admiralty and of Delegates, and of the Judicial Committee of
      the Privy Council. Records of some departments with quasi-legal
      functions or whose records are relevant to the records described
      above; Crown Estate Commissioners, Land Revenue Record Office,
      Law Officer's Department, Privy Council Office, Privy Purse Office,
      Privy Seal Office, Director of Public Prosecutions, Queen Anne's
                                    79

67   PUBLIC RECORD OFFICE (continued)
Bounty, Signet Office and Treasury Solicitor, and Records of the
Lord Chamberlain's Office and the Lord Steward's Office. There
are also certain special collections (artificially made classes of
documents brought together from various sources) relevant to the
main records described above, including Ancient Correspondence,
Ancient Petitions, Court Rolls, Hundred Rolls, Minister's and
Receivers Accounts, Papal Bull, Rentals and Surveys, etc. Records
of the State Paper Office (papers of the Secretaries of State from
the sixteenth to the late eighteenth centuries). Census returns
for 1841, 1851, 1861 and 1871; non-parochial registers held by
the office; probate records of the Prerogative Court of Canterbury. Estate Duty Registers.

Kew: Records of present and defunct government departments,
public offices, etc, which are described in the *Guide* volumes 2 and
3. These records include those of the Cabinet, the Treasury (back
to the sixteenth century), the Admiralty (and the Navy Board),
the Foreign Office, the War Office (including the papers of the
Board of Ordnance going back to the sixteenth century), and the
Copyright Office.

It is important to remember that certain official records are not
in the Public Record Office. The Lord Chancellor has appointed
local repositories as places of deposit (see: *Record depositories in
Great Britain*, HMSO, 1976). Certain government departments
maintain their own records, in particular the Principal Probate
Registry (Somerset House, London WC2R 1LP) and the India
Office Library and Records (197 Blackfriars Road, London SE1
8NG). The following are the chief places where official documents not covered by the Public Records Act of 1958 are preserved:
The Record Office, House of Lords, London SW1A 0PW (records
of Parliament); The Office of Population Censuses and Surveys
(General Register Office), St Catherine's House, Kingsway, London,
WC2B 6JP (registrations of births, marriages and deaths in England
and Wales since 1837; earlier registers kept in parish churches are
mainly retained locally); The Scottish Record Office, HM General
Register House, Edinburgh EH1 3YY (registration of births,
marriages and deaths in Scotland); The Public Record Office of
Northern Ireland, 66 Balmoral Avenue, Belfast, BT9 6NY (the
records of Northern Ireland courts and departments); The General
Register Office, Chichester Street, Belfast BT1 4HL (registrations
of births, marriages and deaths in Northern Ireland).

A number of collections remain in private hands, or have been
given, sold or lent to institutions, notably the British Library.
Further information can be obtained from the Historical Manuscripts Commission, Quality Court, Chancery Lane, London
WC2A 1HP.

7a)   The classification of records reflects the arrangement which they
were given for administrative purposes within the departments

67   PUBLIC RECORD OFFICE (continued)
      or courts; 7b) There is no general index to the records, but the
      Guide in its old and new (computer produced) forms is the basic
      tool for searching for items about a specific subject, person or
      place. More detailed class lists are available to readers at the
      office; some of these are officially printed (see Sectional List no
      24, British National Archives), and others have been published by
      the List and Index Society.
8a)   Readers' tickets are issued at Kew and Chancery Lane to applicants
      who have written recommendation from a person of recognised
      position or who can otherwise satisfy the Keeper of Public Records
      of their identity. Tickets are valid for one year; 8b) M-F 0930-
      1700. Closed for stocktaking usually last week in September and
      first week in October. Closed on public holidays; 8c) All photo-
      graphic reproduction of documents undertaken by the office.
9)   Information for readers; *Guide to the contents of the Public
      Record Office* 3 volumes HMSO, 1963-1968.
10)   Galbraith, V H *An introduction to the use of the public records*
      Oxford, OUP, 1971 (1st ed 1934).

68   PUBLIC RECORD OFFICE LIBRARY
1b)   Public Record Office
2a)   and b) As previous entry
3)   Dr A Prochaska
4a)   Established 1838 as the successor to the Library of the Record
      Commission 1801-1838; 4b) Reference collection concerning the
      growth, content and use of the public records
5a)   Records and archives; history of England, the British Empire and
      British foreign relations; 5b) Publications of and about the public
      records; all aspects of English history in particular local and medie-
      val aspects; French medieval history; archives and records manage-
      ment. Material is divided between the two sites of the Record
      Office
6a)   Bookstock: c100,000 volumes. Current serials received: c200
      titles; 6b) George Watson collection (French genealogy); large
      collection of topographical items; library of the former British
      Transport Historical Record Office.
7a)   Own classification scheme; 7b) Dictionary catalogue
8a)   The library is used almost exclusively by the staff of the Record
      Office and the Historical Manuscripts Commission, and is not on
      open-access to readers of the public records. However readers of
      the public records may obtain volumes of parliamentary papers
      on request. A small selection of reference works are on open-
      access in the reference room at Kew and the search room at
      Chancery Lane. The library of the former British Transport
      Historical Record Office is available to users of the BTHR subject
      index

81

69   ROTHAMSTEAD EXPERIMENTAL STATION LIBRARY

1b) Rothamstead Experimental Station

2a) Rothamstead Experimental Station, Harpenden, Herts; 2b) 058-27-4671

4a) Established in 1843, Rothamstead is the oldest and one of the most noted agricultural experimental stations in the world; 4b) The library serves the needs of staff at the Rothamstead station and at other local experimental stations, and also provides a service to the Commonwealth Bureau of Soils and the Soil Survey of England and Wales

5a) Agriculture and related topics; 5b) Botany, plant pathology, soil science, pedology, nematology, entomology, apiculture, fungicides

6a) Bookstock: over 80,000 volumes. Current serials received: c2000 titles. Serials retained: c5000 titles; 6b) Historical collection on agriculture 1471-1840; reports of the US Department of Agriculture and Experimental Station reports; collection of Russian agricultural and soil science journals; manuscripts collection; small print collection

7a) UDC Classification (except for historical collection); 7b) Author and subject catalogues; Commonwealth Bureau of Soils card index 1930-1972 (continued as computer database 1972 onwards— CABS Abstracts)

8a) Primarily for the use of Rothamstead and related staff; 8b) M-F 0900-1730 (Fri 1700); 8c) Photocopying facilities; information services based on Commonwealth Bureau of Soils

9)   List of current serials; Commonwealth Bureau of Soils produces abstracts journals: *Soils & fertilizers* (monthly), *Irrigation and drainage abstracts* (4 pa), and about 200 annotated bibliographies a year.

10) Catalogue of early printed books on agriculture 1471-1840 2nd ed 1940, Supplement 1949

70   ROYAL BOTANIC GARDEN LIBRARY (EDINBURGH)

1b) Royal Botanic Garden Edinburgh

2a) Inverleith Row, Edinburgh EH3 5LR; 2b) 031-552-7171

3)   M V Mathews BA DLSc ALA

4a) The garden was established in 1670; 4b) A working research library, under the Scottish Office

5a) Botany, horticulture, agriculture, forestry, early medicine, medical botany; 5b) Taxonomic botany and amenity horticulture

6a) Bookstock: 75,000 monographs and bound serials. Pamphlets and reprints: 65,000. Current serials received: 1300 titles. Retained serials: 3500 titles. Slides: 20,000. Photographs: 10,000. Maps and plans: 1200 items. Paintings, prints, drawings: 2000. Cuttings: 200,000; 6b) Incorporates the library of the Royal Botanical Society of Edinburgh, 1872; vast collections of archival materials, including correspondence of early eminent scientists, documents relating to the history of the garden, accounts

70   ROYAL BOTANIC GARDEN LIBRARY (EDINBURGH) (cont'd)
      of botanical expeditions. Approximately 15,000 volumes of pre-
      Linnaean literature
7a)   Modified Bliss Classification; 5b) Classified catalogue
8a)   Bona-fide visitors by appointment only; 8b) M-Th 0830-1700,
      Fri 0830-1630. Closed for lunch on all days; 8c) Information
      given by phone and post to inquirers wherever possible
9)   List of periodical holdings; exchange arrangements for *Notes from
      the Royal Botanic Garden Edinburgh, Transactions of the Botanical
      Society of Edinburgh, British fungus flora*

71   ROYAL BOTANIC GARDENS LIBRARY (KEW)
1b)   Royal Botanic Gardens Kew
2a)   Kew, Richmond, Surrey; 2b) 01-940-1171
3)   V T H Parry MA FLA (Chief Librarian & Archivist)
4a)   Established 1852, from the amalgamation of the collections of
      W A Broomfield, G Bentham, and Sir W Hooker in the period
      1852-1867. Dr D Oliver appointed first Keeper of Library in
      1860; 4b) Working research library and important national collec-
      tion of botanical and related material
5a)   Botany and related subjects; 5b) Anatomy; cyto-genetics, econo-
      mic botany, horticulture, physiology; plant taxonomy; plant geo-
      graphy. Stock held in main library and five branch libraries.
6a)   125,000 vols. 2000 current periodicals. 140,000 pamphlets.
      170,000 plant illustrations. 10,000 sheet maps. 17,500 micro-
      forms; 6b) The library has been designated a statutory place of
      deposit under the Public Records Act. Holds registered files and
      over 250,000 letters and manuscripts covering botanical subjects
      dating back some 200 years. Also portraits of botanists, collec-
      tion of materials relating to the history of Kew Gardens, Linnean
      Collection, Darlington reprint collection, pre-Linnean collection.
7a)   Own classification and UDC. Open and closed access; 7b) Author
      and classified catalogues
8a)   Admission to approved visitors on application; 8b) M-F 0900-
      1700, Sat to 1630, public holidays to 1600. Closed Good Friday,
      Christmas Day, Boxing Day, New Year's Day; 8c) Enquiry service
      for visitors, by telephone and by letter for Library and Archives.
9)   Current awareness list (monthly, internal); *Kew record of taxono-
      mic literature* (annually from HMSO); Guide to the library;
      Gardens' library guide; *Author and classified catalogues of the
      library* 9 vols, Boston (Mass), G K Hall, 1974; Catalogue of perio-
      dicals, 1978.

72   THE ROYAL COMMISSION ON HISTORICAL MANUSCRIPTS
2a)   Quality House, Quality Court, Chancery Lane, London WC2A
      1HP; 2b) 01-242 1198
3)   G R C Davis (Secretary to the Commission)

(continued)

72   ROYAL COMMISSION ON HISTORICAL MSS (continued)
4a)   The commission was established in 1869 to collect and disseminate
      information about the nature and location of historical manu-
      scripts outside the Public Records; 4b) As one of its activities, the
      commission maintains the National Register of Archives, which
      was established in 1945 as a central collecting point for information
      acquired by the commission
5a)   Papers and records of individuals of note, families and estates,
      local authorities, religious institutions and bodies, business and
      industrial undertakings
6a)   Over 21,000 unpublished reports on manuscript collections to
      date
7a)   Open-access in the commission's search room. Numerical classi-
      fication
8a)   No reader's ticket required; 8b) M-F 0930-1700; 8c) Various
      finding aids to the unpublished reports available including short-
      title, personal and subject indexes. No borrowing or photocopying
9)   HMSO Government Publications Sectional List 17
10)   Four articles about the Royal Commission on Historical Manu-
      scripts appeared in *Journal of the Society of Archivists*, April 1969

73   ROYAL COMMONWEALTH SOCIETY LIBRARY
1b)   The Royal Commonwealth Society
2a)   Northumberland Avenue, London WC2N 5BJ; 2b) 01-930-6733;
      2c) RECITAL RAND
3)   D H Simpson MA FLA FRGS
4a)   Established in 1868 and located on its present site since 1885;
      4b) A major reference and research collection relating to the
      commonwealth as a whole and its members past and present
5a)   The Commonwealth past and present; 5b) The collections are
      particularly strong in voyages, travels and publications of a wide
      range of societies and in official publications. Collects Nigeria,
      St Helena, Ascension, Tristan da Cunha under the SCOLMA
      area-specialisation scheme. Overall the collection is strong in
      the social sciences, literature and humanities, and bibliography
6a)   Bookstock: c400,000 items. Current serials received: c600.
      Serials retained: c2500 titles. Photographs: c30,000. Maps:
      5500 items. Portraits of members 1880-1925: c3000; 6b)
      Cobham Bequest (Cyprus pamphlets); material on countries
      formerly under British rule (eg Ionian Islands, Egypt, Heligoland,
      Burma, Sudan, South Africa); material on countries bordering
      British and Commonwealth territories where influence was sig-
      nificant (eg Middle Eastern countries, Chinese treaty ports);
      voyages and travels by land and sea since the sixteenth century;
      Library of the Kipling Society (on deposit); society archives;
      British Association of Malaysia historical collection; collection
      of material for the East African Dictionary of Biography; Com-
      monwealth Producer's Board archives; Joint African Board
                                    84

73   ROYAL COMMONWEALTH SOCIETY LIBRARY (continued)
      archives. Receives a special grant from the Canadian government
      for the purchase of Canadian publications
7a)   Own classification scheme; substantial amount of collections on
      open-access; 7b) Classified catalogue; author and societies catalogue
8a)   Admission to members of the Royal Commonwealth Society. Non-
      members may apply for readers' tickets from the librarian; 8b)
      M, F, Sat 1000-1730, Tue-Th 1000-1900; 8c) Information bureau
      with collection of current reference material is an integral part of
      the library; deals with postal, telephone and personal inquiries.
      Library exhibitions; photocopying and photographic facilities
9)   Library notes with list of accessions (monthly); series entitled
      'Notes on conditions' (relating to 26 Commonwealth countries)
      available on subscription. *Subject catalogue of the Library of
      the Royal Empire Society* 4v 1930-37 (reprinted Dawson 1967);
      *Biography catalogue of the Library of the Royal Commonwealth
      Society*. RCS, 1961; *Subject catalogue of the Royal Common-
      wealth Society* Boston (Mass) G K Hall 7v 1971, and supplement
      2v 1977; *Manuscript catalogue of the Library of the Royal Com-
      monwealth Society* Mansell, 1975; All these are in print and none
      are superseded. The first printed catalogue of the Society appeared
      in 1880. Leaflet 'The library of the Royal Commonwealth Society'
      available free of charge.
10)   References to the library appear in most specialised library direc-
      tories in the field of studies covered by the library. Among
      articles by the present librarian are: 'A century of the library'
      Library notes 1968; 'An internationally famous library' *Royal
      Commonwealth Society Centenary journal*, 1968, 55-9; 'Educational
      material in the library of the Royal Empire Society' *Education
      libraries bulletin* no 1, 1958, pp12-15; 'The St Helena exhibition
      in the library of the Royal Commonwealth Society' *St Helena
      wirebird* no 50, 1959, pp402-4; 'The library of the Royal Common-
      wealth Society and its Indian material' *Indian archives* vol 15,
      1963-64, pp25-27; 'The Royal Commonwealth Society and African
      studies' *African research and documentation* nos 8-9, 1975, pp66-68.

74   ROYAL GEOGRAPHICAL SOCIETY LIBRARY
1b)   Royal Geographical Society
2a)   Kensington Gore, London SW7 2AR; 2b) 01-589-5466; 2c)
      OBTERRAS LONDON SW7 2AR
3)   G S Dugdale MA FLA
4a)   Library and society established 1830
5a)   Geography in all its aspects; travel and exploration; cartography
      and survey; 5b) The society's map room is operated separately from
      the library under the supervision of the Keeper. The map room
      contains some 600,000 sheets available for public consultation
      together with atlases and gazetteers. A collection of slides and
      photographs is available for public consultation.

74   ROYAL GEOGRAPHICAL SOCIETY LIBRARY (continued)
6a)   Bookstock: c100,000 volumes. Current serials received: c750
       titles. Serials retained: c1550 titles. Pamphlets and offprints:
       c25,000 items; 6b) African dictionaries, grammars and phrase-
       books (late nineteenth/early twentieth centuries); Brown collec-
       tion (Morocco); Feilden collection (Polar); Fordham collection
       (Roadbooks); Gunther collection (Southern Italy); society's
       archives and MS, travel diaries and field books
7a)   Own classification scheme, based on region and subject; 7b)
       Author and subject card catalogues, including separate author
       catalogue for periodical articles.
8a)   Library available only to members of the society, including those
       duly sponsored by organisations in corporate or educational
       corporate membership; 8b) M-F 0930-1730. Closed each year
       for three weeks in May for cleaning and stocktaking; 8c) The
       library provides a reference and loan service to members of the
       society. Inquiries from the general public can be answered
       by letter or telephone.
9)   *New geographical literature and maps*, issued twice yearly.
10)   Crone, G R 'The library of the Royal Geographical Society'
       Library Association record Jan 1931; 'The library of the Royal
       Geographical Society' *Geographical journal* vol 121, pt 1, March
       1955; Mill, H R *The record of the Royal Geographical Society*,
       1930; Kelly, Christine 'The RGS archives: a handlist, in five
       parts' *Geographical journal* vol 141 pt 1, March 1975; 142 pt 1,
       March 1976; pt 2 July 1976; 143 pt 1, March 1977; pt 2, July 1977.

75   ROYAL INSTITUTE OF INTERNATIONAL AFFAIRS
       LIBRARY and CHATHAM HOUSE PRESS LIBRARY
1b)   Royal Institute of International Affairs
2a)   Chatham House, 10 St James Square, London SW1Y 4LE;
       2b) 01-930-2233
3)   Miss D Hamerton (Librarian); Miss S J Boyde (Press Librarian)
4a)   Library established 1920 and Press Library in 1924; 4b) Working
       research libraries serving the institute and its members
5a)   Library: international affairs since 1918, but concentrating on the
       period since 1945. Press Library: international affairs and domestic
       affairs of foreign countries as reflected in the world's daily news-
       papers since 1924; 5b) Related social science material
6a)   Library bookstock: c150,000 items. Current serials received:
       600 titles. Press Library: 20,000 boxes of press cuttings;
       6b) Library: Documents of the principal international organi-
       sations. Press Library: Majority of material in West European
       languages. Pre-1940 material temporarily unavailable
7a)   Library: own classification; recent material on open access.
       Press Library: own classification, detailed classification and
       cross-referencing. Closed access; 7b) Library: author and
       classified catalogue. Selective index to c200 periodicals.

75   ROYAL INSTITUTE OF INTERNATIONAL AFFAIRS (cont'd)
Press Library: handlist of headings; selective 'Author index' of
speeches

8a)   Available to members and research staff of the institute. Research
workers at postgraduate level may be granted reader's tickets; 8b)
M-F 1000-1800. Usually closed all or part of August; 8c) Information given by post and phone to members only; photocopying
facilities

9)   *Index to periodical articles 1950-1964* 2 vols, Boston (Mass), G K
Hall, 1965, and *Supplement 1965-1972*, 1973.

76   ROYAL INSTITUTION OF CHARTERED SURVEYORS
LIBRARY

1b)   Royal Institution of Chartered Surveyors
2a)   12 Great George Street, Parliament Square, London SW1P 3AD;
2b) 01-839-5600 ext 32
3)   Miss P J Lane
4b)   This is the major library collection in the field of land and land
surveying in the country
5a)   Land and related subjects; 5b) Agriculture, estate management,
land agency, land surveying, law, photogrammetry, statistics
6a)   c30,000 volumes. Current serials received: c300 titles; 6b) Historical
collections on land surveying, building economics and fine arts;
Board of Agriculture Reports; Royal Commission reports on land
use (from 19th century); topography collections, Victoria County
History; Collection of legal serials; Land Tribunal decisions
7a)   Dewey Decimal Classification; 7b) Dictionary catalogue
8a)   Open to the general public for reference, but preferably with an
introduction from a member; 8b) M-F 0930-1730; 8c) Borrowing
permitted for members only
9)   Library information service; *Abstracts and reviews* (subscription
service); *Lands tribunal index 1965-1972*

77   ROYAL PHOTOGRAPHIC SOCIETY LIBRARY
1b)   Royal Photographic Society
2a)   14 South Audley Street, London W1Y 5DP; 2b) 01-493-3967
ext 42
4a)   1853
5a)   Photography and photographic science
6a)   c8000 volumes; 6b) DuMont collection (illustrated books); collection of c8000 photographs by 19th and 20th century photographers
7a)   Own classification; 7b) Classified catalogue
8a)   For reference only on application; 8c) Information given by phone
and post to members only
9)   Author catalogue (3 vols); subject catalogue (2 vols); periodicals
catalogue; accessions list published irregularly in *Photographic
journal*

78   ROYAL SOCIETY OF MEDICINE LIBRARY
1b)   Royal Society of Medicine
2a)   1 Wimpole Street, London W1M 8AE; 2b) 01-580-2070
3)   D W C Stewart BA ALA
4a)   Established 1805 as the Medical and Chirurgical Society of
      London. Collection development has continued since then; 4b)
      To provide a broadly based postgraduate research collection in
      medicine and related subjects with supporting reference and in-
      formation services.
5a)   Medicine
6a)   c450,000 volumes. Current serials: 2200. Serials retained:
      c8500. Portrait collection; 6b) Chalmers collection of rare books.
      Some manuscript material including Jenner and Withering letters.
7a)   UDC Classification. Ninety per cent of collection open-access;
      7b) Dictionary catalogue
8a)   Available to fellows of the Royal Society of Medicine. Non-
      members may be introduced by fellows to use the library for
      reference purposes only. Corporate membership available through
      the Library Section of the society; 8b) M-F 0930-2130, Sat to
      1730; 8c) Postal loans to British Isles; worldwide photocopy service
      (also available to non-members); literature searches (manual and
      computer-based); linguistic assistance; reference paging. Inter-
      library borrowing.
9)   Pamphlet guide to library (current); List of the periodicals in the
      library, 1938; *Royal Medical and Chirurgical Society of London:
      Catalogue of the library* London, 1879. *Supplements* 1880-1901.
10)   Wade, P 'The history and development of the library of the Royal
      Society of Medicine' *Proceedings of the Royal Society of Medicine*
      55, 1962, pp627-636.   Evans, G T 'Development of an automated
      periodical system at the Royal Society of Medicine Library' *PRSM*
      62, 1969, 757-763.   Wade, P and Stewart, D W C 'The automated
      periodical system at the RSM' *Library Association (Medical Section*
      bulletin 87, 1971, pp5-9. Stewart, D W C 'RSM and BLLD: The
      Role of a back-up library' *LA(MS) bulletin* 107, 1976, pp1-4.
      Wade, P (1976) 'After forty years: the library of the RSM in retro-
      spect and prospect' *PRSM* 69, 1976, pp751-754.

79   RUTHERFORD LABORATORY LIBRARY
1b)   Science Research Council
2a)   Chilton, Didcot, Oxfordshire OX11 0QX; 2b) 0235-21900; 2c)
      83159
3)   Mrs E Marsh ALA
4a)   1961; 4b) The library serves permanent staff and university visitors
5a)   Physics, computing; 5b) Superconductors, cryogenics
6a)   25,000 items. Current serials received: 400 titles. Reports: 50,000
      6b) Preprint and report material in high energy physics and elemen-
      tary particles
7a)   UDC, open-access; 7b) Subject catalogue

79   RUTHERFORD LABORATORY LIBRARY (continued)
8a)   Generally available for reference by accredited persons; 8b) Open
      every day, 24 hours a day; 8c) Information service in cryogenics;
      computer-based information retrieval
9)   Accessions list (weekly); 'Rutherford Laboratory new publications'
      (bi-weekly); *References in cryogenics and superconductivity; References in lasers; References in energy*

80   ST BRIDE PRINTING LIBRARY
1b)   Corporation of London
2a)   St Bride Institute, Bride Lane, Fleet Street, London EC4; 2b)
      01-353-4660
4a)   The collection originated with the purchase in 1891 of the library
      of William Blades (1814-1890), the biographer and bibliographer
      of William Caxton, who had assembled one of the most comprehensive collections of books on practical printing then in existence.
      The library formed the nucleus of the collection of the Technical
      Library of the Printing School (1894-1921). The governors of
      the St Bride's Institute maintained the library as reference library
      for the trade until 1966 when it was incorporated in the City of
      London Library Service; 4b) A reference library of books and
      periodicals on the technique, design and history of printing and
      related subjects
5a)   Books and printing
6a)   Monographs: 30,000 items. Serials retained: c700 titles; 6b)
      Printing trade directories and dictionaries; technical manuals of
      printing; typefounders specimens; documents relating to early
      printing unions; photographic slide collections (typography,
      portraits of printers etc)
7b)   Catalogue of slide collection
8a)   Generally available for reference; 8b) M-F 0930-1730; 8c) Photographic service

81   SCIENCE MUSEUM LIBRARY
1b)   Science Museum
2a)   South Kensington, London SW7 5NH; 2b) 01-589-3456; 2c) 21200
3)   LR Day MSc (Keeper)
4a)   1883; 4b) A national reference library of pure and applied science
      specialising in the history of science and technology, serving the
      public, the South Kensington museums and Imperial College of
      Science and Technology
5a)   Pure and applied sciences; 5b) History of science and technology
6a)   458,000 volumes. Current serials received: 6000 titles. Serials
      retained: 12,000 titles. Microforms: extensive collection, especially of atomic energy reports; 6b) Rich collection of source
      material for the historian of science with almost complete coverage
      of secondary material; pictorial collection of prints, drawings and

(continued)

81　SCIENCE MUSEUM LIBRARY (continued)
　　　other media relating to science and technology; British patent
　　　specifications
7a)　UDC Classification; post-1945 material on open-access; earlier
　　　material on closed-access but quickly available; 7b) Alphabetical
　　　and classified catalogues
8a)　Open daily to the public for reference purposes; ticket required
　　　to consult rare material; 8b) Open daily except Sunday and bank
　　　holiday weekends 1000-1730; 8c) Enquiry and bibliographical
　　　information service to readers (and by post, telephone or telex).
　　　Reading lists prepared
9)　　Books on the chemical and allied industries; Books on engineering;
　　　Current periodicals in the Science Museum Library: a hand list;
　　　List of accessions to the Science Museum Library; Science Library
　　　bibliographical series; Short guide to the library (leaflet)

82　SCOTTISH RECORD OFFICE LIBRARY
1b)　Scottish Record Office
2a)　HM General Register House, Edinburgh EH1 3YY; 2b) 031-556-
　　　6585
3)　　F Burton MA PhD (Keeper of the Records of Scotland)
4a)　Established c1806; 4b) The library collection is for use in connec-
　　　tion with the national archives, and is available to the public in
　　　connection with use of the records
5a)　Scottish history and topography
6a)　c12,000 volumes
7a)　Own classification scheme; 7b) Classified catalogue; author
　　　catalogue
8a)　Available to members of the public using the records; 8c) M-F
　　　0900-1645, Sat to 1230

83　SHEFFIELD CITY LIBRARIES Central Library
1b)　Sheffield City Libraries
2a)　Surrey Street, Sheffield S1 1XZ; 2b) General: 0742-734711;
　　　Business library 734735/9; Arts and humanities 734747/50; Scienc
　　　and technology 734742/5; Local studies 734753; Archives 734756
　　　2c) 54243
3)　　R F Atkins FLA (Director of Libraries)
4a)　Established 1856, under the Public Libraries Act. Present
　　　central library building dates from 1934; 4b) The central library
　　　provides a major public reference and research collection covering
　　　a full range of subject fields, but with special emphasis on science
　　　and technology, and business and law. The reference divisions
　　　provide a comprehensive information service.
5a)　Collections for all subjects in both the arts and the sciences;
　　　5b) Metals, especially steel; HQ of SINTO. Research services in
　　　three divisions: Arts & humanities, including local studies section;
　　　Commerce & technology, including Science & Technology Section
　　　and Business Section; Archives

83   SHEFFIELD CITY LIBRARIES (continued)
6a)   Periodicals holdings approximately 1500 titles; bookstock 265,000;
      non-book material–slides 7500, microforms 8500, maps and
      plans 6500; 6b) Named collections include the Edward Carpenter
      collection; Wentworth Woodhouse Muniments (including Edmund
      Burke papers); Arundel and Spencer Stanhope MSS; Fairbank
      collection (draft plans, surveying books etc). Other collections
      include British and US patents; British national and International
      Standards and Specifications; world metal index; maps; trade direc-
      tories; current information files for businessman/exporter; private
      press books; glass and silverware; metallurgy; material on South
      Yorkshire and North Derbyshire; books printed in England 1765-
      1779.
7a)   Up to ten per cent of stock is on open-access in the reference li-
      braries. Classification used for monographs is Dewey Decimal
      16th edition; 7b) At present author and classified catalogues are
      publicly available in Arts and humanities, Science and technology,
      Commerce & law libraries; Alphabetico/classified catalogue in the
      Local studies section, and numerous special index catalogues give
      access to local non-book material and to the archive and MSS col-
      lections. Computerisation of the catalogue is being undertaken.
8a)   Generally available for the use of the public for research and ref-
      erence; 8b) Arts & humanities/Science & technology: M-F 0900-
      2100, Sat to 1630. Business Library and Local studies and archives:
      M-F 0900-1730, Sat to 1630; 8c) Professionally qualified staff
      offering a comprehensive information service to users via telephone,
      telex, letter and to individual enquirers; major collection of abstracts
      and indexes to compliment the extensive stock of monographs and
      periodicals. Compilation and coordination of South Yorkshire
      region periodicals holdings; locations of standards/specifications
      held by both libraries and industrial concerns in Sheffield area.
9)   Catalogue of the Arundel Castle manuscripts (1965); Catalogue of
      business and industrial records (1977); Guide to the manuscript
      collections in the Sheffield City Libraries (1956) and Supplement
      1956-1976 (1977); various local studies publications; 'Scoclis
      news' (Standing Conference of Cooperative Library and Information
      Services) (3 pa); 'Sinto news' (4 pa).
10)   'World metal index', *Aslib proceedings* January 1975; 'Archive
      collection' *Northern history* vol IX, 1974.

84   STATISTICS AND MARKET INTELLIGENCE LIBRARY
1b)   Department of Trade
2a)   Export House, 50 Ludgate Hill, London EC4M 7HU; 2b)
      01-248-5757 ext 368/369; 2c) 886143 (DTI Export LDN)
3)   Miss M H Wilson
4a)   Established in its present form in 1962
5a)   The collection of material is intended to facilitate preliminary
      desk research on overseas markets; 5b) General statistical

84 STATISTICS AND MARKET INTELLIGENCE LIB (continued)
    compilations and statistics of trade, production, distribution,
    population and other economic topics for all countries of the
    world (retained for 15 years); UK and international compilations
    of statistics (retained from 1946); trade and telephone directories
    for all countries (current editions only); market surveys; develop-
    ment plans; overseas mail order catalogues. The library also acts as
    a national reference library for public use of UK statistics, and as
    a referral centre to officially produced sources of information
    in the Government Statistical Service.
6a) 7000 statistical serials. 4000 directories. 300 foot run of other
    periodicals
7a) Partly closed access; own classification; 7b) Dictionary catalogue
8a) Open to the public for reference purposes; 8b) M-F 0900-1730;
    8c) Statistical material and directories are available for reference
    only but photocopying facilities are available. Catalogues and
    development plans are available for loan. Microfiche readers are
    provided as are print-out facilities
9) *Sources of statistics and market information* (a series of biblio-
    graphies published irregularly); *National statistical offices for
    overseas countries* (annual); *Statistics and Market Intelligence
    Library; the exporter's reference library*; *Statistics, directories
    information* (quarterly).
10) Burkett, J *Government and related libraries in the UK* LA 3rd ed
    rev, 1974. Campbell, M J *Business information services: some
    aspects of structure, organisation and problems* Bingley; Hamden
    (Conn), Linnet, 1974. Department of Industry *Permanent direc-
    tory of energy information sources*; Institute of Latin American
    Studies *Directory of libraries of special collections on Latin America
    and the West Indies*. 'DTI's Statistics and Market Intelligence
    Library: how it can help you export' *Trade and industry* 28th
    October 1971, pages 186, 188; 'Library for exporters' 15th April
    1977, pages 63, 64; 'Middle East desk research sources' 27th
    January 1978, pages 155-6.

    Details of this library are also given in a very wide range of
    publications from general details in commercially produced
    diaries to papers at conferences which refer to the library and its
    services.

85 TAVISTOCK JOINT LIBRARY
1b) Tavistock Institute of Human Relations and Tavistock Clinic
2a) Tavistock Centre, Belsize Lane, London NW3 5BA; 2b) 01-435-711
3) Mrs M Walker ALA
4a) Established 1946; 4b) To provide a practical research and teaching
    library to serve the working needs of the institute and clinic
5a) Psychology, psychiatry, psychoanalysis, social work, sociology,
    management; 5b) Medicine and statistics

(continued)

TAVISTOCK JOINT LIBRARY (continued)
6a) c15,000 items. Current serials received: 210 titles. Serials retained: 335 titles
7a) Bliss Classification; 7b) Author and classified catalogues
8a) Normally available only to those people having some formal connection with the Tavistock Centre. One-day reference tickets issued to researchers if required material is not easily available elsewhere. Tickets for a longer period only given in special circumstances; written application required; 8b) M-F 0930-1730; 8c) Brief inquiries from non-members as staff time permits
9) Accessions list; List of periodicals (both available on request); Annotated list of publications 1946-1975; *Catalogue of the Tavistock Joint Library* 2 vols, Boston (Mass), G K Hall, 1975

86 TROPICAL PRODUCTS INSTITUTE LIBRARY
1b) Ministry of Overseas Development
2a) 56-62 Grays Inn Road, London WC1X 8LU; 2b) 01-242-5412
3) J A Wright
4a) Established c1895 as part of the Library of the Imperial Institute. Underwent a series of name changes until in 1957 it became the Tropical Products Institute, a scientific unit of the Ministry of Overseas Development; 4b) To provide an information and documentation service to the staff of the institute and to organisations in developing countries
5a) Agriculture in the tropics and sub-tropics; 5b) Emphasis on post-harvest aspects including processing, preservation, transportation, quality control, marketing and the utilisation of renewable natural resources
6a) Total over 100,000 volumes: c15,000 monographs. c1200 current journal titles. c3000 journal titles bound and retained. c1000 annual reports currently taken and many other technical reports; 6b) A technical index is housed at the institute which consists of some 750,000 card entries relating to the literature since 1898. Includes material on essential oils, drugs, food, fibres, fish, fruit, oilseeds and spices. The index is arranged in alphabetico-classed sequence.
7a) UDC for library monograph stock—open-access; 7b) Classified catalogue and technical report series catalogue.
8a) Available to researchers for reference without formality; 8b) M-F 0900-1730, closed on bank holidays; 8c) Reference service and bibliographic enquiries by phone and post. Limited xerox copying service. Loan service to other libraries.
9) Accessions list; List of current periodicals (annual); Bibliography of insecticide materials of vegetable origin (2 pa).
10) Datta, V K 'The technical index of the Tropical Products Institute' *Tropical science*, 1974, 16(4), pages 237-246. Piper, K G 'The information services of the Tropical Products Institute' *African research and documentation*, 1974, (5-6), pages 12-15.

87   UNITED NATIONS London Information Centre
1b)   United Nations Organisation
2a)   14-15 Stratford Place. London W1N 9AF; 2b) 01-629-3816
3)   Mrs A-M Paterson
4a)   1947; 4b) Official information service of the United Nations
       Organisation and agencies
5a)   Official publications of the UN and its international agencies
6b)   Visual material and pamphlets published by the UN Office of
       Public Information. Catalogues of films and filmstrips
7a)   Open-access; classified by UN sales publication number/category;
       7b) UNDEX and printed publications catalogues
8a)   Generally available to the public for reference purposes; 8b) M,
       W and Th 1000-1300 and 1400-1700. Closed Tu and Fri; 8c)
       Maintains the network of depository libraries for UN publications
       established at various libraries in the UK
9)   Do-it-yourself photocopying facilities available.

88   VICTORIA AND ALBERT MUSEUM LIBRARY National Art
       Library
1b)   Victoria and Albert Museum
2a)   Cromwell Road, London, SW7 2RL; 2b) 01-589-6371
3)   R W Lightbown (Keeper)
4a)   1837; 4b) The national reference collection for the fine and
       applied arts and crafts. The main reference source for all museum
       departments, as well as serving the general public, students and
       scholars.
5a)   Fine and applied arts; 5b) Social history, religions, natural history,
       ethnology, topography, archaeology, the art of the book
6a)   650,000 items. Current serials received: 1500 titles. Retained
       serials: 2500 titles. Slides and photograph collections are housed
       in separate departments of the museum; 6b) Bookbindings (histor-
       ical styles); Clements collection (armorial bookbindings); Dyce
       and Forster collections (nineteenth century literary and historical
       material, including Dickensiana); Guy Little and Renier collections
       (children's books); Hutton Bequest (fencing and allied subjects);
       Harrod collection (Victorian illustrated books); Piot collection
       (seventeenth and eighteenth century books on ceremonial and
       pageantry). Extensive manuscript collections; illuminated manu-
       scripts of artistic, calligraphic and liturgical interest; miscellaneous
       material eg artists' letters, diaries, bills, accounts, day books and
       inventories. Postcards and some photographic material (in addition
       to that available in other departments); auction and sale catalogues
7a)   Own classification scheme (pressmarks); majority of collection is on
       closed-access with books brought to reading room. Open-access
       reference collection in reading room; 7b) General author and subject
       catalogues. Large number of special catalogues eg auction sales,
       children's books, fine bindings, illuminated manuscripts, loan exhi-
       bitions

38 VICTORIA AND ALBERT MUSEUM LIBRARY (continued)
3a) Collection available to museum staff and to accredited enquirers
    and others for reference. Reader's ticket required for full use of
    the library. Endorsement required for use of reserve collections;
    8b) M-Th 1000-1745, Sat to 1300 and 1400-1745, closed Fri and
    Sunday; 8c) Information given by telephone and post, and to
    personal visitors
9) Library rules; *National Art Library catalogue* 10 vols, Boston
    (Mass), G K Hall, 1972; Catalogue of exhibition catalogues
10) Wheen, A W (in:) Irwin, R and Staveley, R *The libraries of London*
    LA, 1964, pp54-59; Whalley, I 'The V & A Library' *ARLIS news-
    letter* April 1971.

59 WELLCOME INSTITUTE FOR THE HISTORY OF MEDICINE
    LIBRARY
b) Wellcome Trust
a) Wellcome Building, 183 Euston Road, London NW1 2BP; 2b)
    01-387-4477; 2c) 22280
) E J Freeman BA ALA
a) Established c 1890 as the private collection of Sir Henry Wellcome
    (1853-1936). Opened to the public in 1949; 4b) To provide com-
    prehensive reference coverage in all languages in the history of medi-
    cine, and to collect primary and secondary sources in that field
a) History of medicine and the allied sciences; 5b) Ethnology, travel
a) Bookstock: 400,000 items. Pamphlets and broadsides: c50,000
    items. Current serials received: 109 titles. Serials retained: 2669
    titles. Manuscripts: 5000 western; 5000 oriental. Autograph
    letters: c100,000. Prints, drawings and paintings: c100,000.
    Photographs: 38,000 items; 6b) Spanish-American collection;
    Florence Nightingale
a) Barnard classification (heavily modified, for modern reference
    books only). Substantial proportion of collection on closed-access;
    7b) Author catalogue; chronological and alphabetical subject cata-
    logue
a) Open to bona fide researchers at the librarian's discretion; 8b) M-F
    0915-1715, closed public holidays; 8c) Reference library only; photo-
    copying and photographic facilities
) List of publications

UNIVERSITY LIBRARIES

90 ABERDEEN UNIVERSITY LIBRARY
1b) University of Aberdeen
2a) King's College, Aberdeen AB9 2UB; 2b) 0224-40241;
2c) 73458 UNIABN
3)   J M Smethurst BA ALA
4a) University founded in 1494. Six library buildings, including
King's College Library (built 1870), the Science Library (1965),
and the Medical Library (1972). There is a library at Marischal
College, which was an independent institution from 1592 to
1860, when it was united with King's College to form the university. The library received material by copyright deposit from
1709 to 1836; 4b) To provide access to research and teaching materials within the scope of studies in the university
5a) General; 5b) The majority of older books, and all the books in arts
and humanities, are at King's College. The Taylor Building contains the Law Library. Marischal College Library contains material
for the science subjects taught there, and pre-clinical medicine.
The remaining collections in sciences, together with mathematics,
psychology and education, are in the Science Library. There are
separate libraries for agriculture and clinical medicine. The Library
participates in national and regional interlending schemes, and in
local cooperative information services. (See entry 246.)
6a) 750,000 volumes. 6000 current periodicals; 6b) McBean Collection (Jacobite); local collection; O'Dell Collection (railways);
King, Thomson, and Herald Collections of pamphlets; Gregory
Collection (history of science and medicine); Meldrum House Collection; Taylor Collection (psalmody); Melvin Collection (Classical history); G W Wilson Collection (photographic negatives);
European Documentation Centre; OECD Publications Collection;
Rich collections of early printed and mss material from the original
libraries of the university. University and family papers and archives.
7a) Mostly open-access. Dewey Decimal Classification (modified);
7b) Each branch has its own catalogues. King's College Library
has a union name catalogue. There are union name catalogues of
the science branches in the Science and Marischal College Libraries.
Name catalogue (slips; entries for books and periodicals); Classified subject catalogue (slips; entries for books); Alphabetical subject index; Current periodicals list. The catalogues are now being
prepared by an automated process, with recent acquisitions recorded in a microfiche catalogue. A programme of retrospective
conversion of the existing catalogues is in progress.
8a) Members of the university; others on application and payment of
a deposit; 8b) Open on Sundays in term; 8c) For general biblio
graphical and reference enquiries, and enquiries relating to
special collections there is an enquiry desk in King's College Library. Elsewhere enquiries to the issue desk.
9)   Guide to the library; Library notes; pocket guides; guides to
sources of information; annual reports

91   UNIVERSITY COLLEGE OF WALES, ABERYSTWYTH, THE
      LIBRARY
1b)   The University College of Wales, Aberystwyth, Dyfed
2a)   Hugh Owen Library, Hugh Owen Building, Penglais, Aberystwyth,
      SY23 3DZ; Biology Library, Biology Building, Penglais, Aber-
      ystwyth, SY23 3DA; Chemistry Library, Edward Davies Chem-
      ical Laboratories, Buarth Road, Aberystwyth, SY23 1NE;
      Education Library, Department of Education, Alexandra Road,
      Aberystwyth, SY23 1LN; Physical Sciences Library, Physical
      Sciences Building, Penglais, Aberystwyth, SY23 3BZ; School of
      Agricultural Sciences Library, School of Agricultural Sciences,
      Penglais, Aberystwyth, SY23 3DD; Undergraduate Reading Room,
      Old College, King Street, Aberystwyth, SY23 2AX
2b)   0970-3111; Chemistry Library 0970-617645; Education Library
      and Undergraduate Reading Room 0970-3177; 2c) 35181
      ABYUCW G
3)   W W Dieneman MA DipLib ALA
4a)   The library of the University College of Wales, Aberystwyth, the
      oldest constituent institution of the University of Wales, was
      founded in 1872. The Hugh Owen Library was opened in Sept-
      ember 1976. For further details see *The college library 1872-1976*
      T G Lloyd (1977); 4b) Primarily to support the teaching (largely
      undergraduate) and research work in the college. Facilities usually
      found in an academic library, eg microtexts, photographic depart-
      ment, study carrels, inter-library loans, exhibition area, audio-
      visual equipment, reference service, library instruction, provision
      for handicapped readers, seminar rooms
5a)   General, excluding medicine and engineering, (not studied here);
      5b) The Hugh Owen Library houses administration, technical
      services, the photographic department and stock on the arts, social
      studies, geography, geology (and law in the adjoining Law Library).
      There are a number of sectional libraries (see 2a above) covering
      the agricultural, biological and physical sciences, chemistry and
      education. There is a separate Undergraduate Reading Room for
      'arts' departments still in Old College in the town. The library is
      a member of the Wales Regional Library Scheme and the Aber-
      ystwyth Local Library Cooperation Group. It maintains a union
      list of current serials in the Aberystwyth area
6a)   Books and serials: c400,000 volumes. Current periodicals: 3000;
      Small collection of scores, microfilms, microfiches, records,
      cassettes and mss; 6b) George Powell Collection: literary and mu-
      sical mss, French and English literature, music; Private Press Books:
      modern British private presses including a complete set of Gregynog
      Press books; Early Printed Books: books printed before 1701;
      John Camden Hotten Collection: JCH publications 1856-73; Duff
      Collection (of pamphlets); classics; Rudler Collection (of pam-
      phlets): geology; 1857-59 collection; JSCLS background materials
      scheme; Richard Ellis MSS: mainly on Edward Lhuyd with some
      original literary compositions, short stories, poems, etc; David

100

UNIV COLLEGE OF WALES, THE LIBRARY (continued)
de Lloyd mss: de Lloyd's musical compositions and work on
Welsh music; T F Roberts mss: relating to the University of
Wales, and this college in particular, 1891-1919

Subject areas of 'strength': statistics; official publications (including diplomatic documents and League of Nations); law;
United States studies; agriculture; purchase of all new Welsh books
and books in English of Welsh interest (except some fugitive and
juvenile material); classics (including medieval Latin); French
Revolution; Celtic studies; Labour history

7a) Open-access. Library of Congress Classification (Dewey in Education Library); Little-used, valuable and rare material in store,
including one off-site store for least-used material;

7b) In the Hugh Owen Library: union catalogue of names and shelf-list/classified catalogue and subject index for Hugh Owen Library
stock. In sectional libraries: name catalogue and shelf-list

8a) Members of the University College of Wales and certain other approved categories (eg members of the College of Librarianship
Wales, Welsh College of Agriculture, etc). Others for reference
only, on written application; 8b) Term: M-F 0900-2200, Sat to
1300. Vacation: M-F 0900-1300 and 1400-1730, Sat varies. All
libraries closed for a week at Christmas and some also closed for
a week at Easter. Slight variations in opening hours of sectional
libraries are indicated in the individual guides; 8c) Readers'
advisers in the social studies, law, education and humanities; information desks in the Hugh Owen Library reading rooms continuously staffed; library instruction given to all new students and to
students at all levels—and to new teaching staff—on request;
special collection of bibliographies, abstracting journals and reference books.

9) Guide to the libraries (annual); lists of accessions (monthly 1959-);
broadsheets 1, 1968- (usually brief bibliographical surveys of a
subject); handlists 1, 1968- (more detailed guides to the literature
of subjects of descriptions of library facilities); library report 1967-
(previously part of UCW's Report to the Court of Governors).

Miscellaneous publications, such as Union Kwic Index of Abstracting and Indexing Journals taken in the Library (1970); Books
printed before 1701 in the Library of the University College of
Wales, Aberystwyth (1972); Union List of Current Periodicals in
the Aberystwyth area, 2nd ed (1973).

Exhibition catalogues, such as Five centuries of French printing:
catalogue of an exhibition prepared by the College Library (1970);
George Powell of Nanteos: an early benefactor of the College
Library: catalogue of an exhibition ... (1971); 1272 and all that:
an exhibition relating to people commemorated in 1972 (1972)
The University College of Wales 1872-1972: catalogue of an exhibition to mark the centenary of the college (1972).

Tape/slide introduction to the library, rev version, 1975; The
Hugh Owen Library, 1977 (a brochure prepared by the project

91 **UNIV COLLEGE OF WALES, THE LIBRARY** (continued)
architects and the staff of the college library . . . on the occasion
of the visit of HRH Prince Charles, Chancellor of the University
of Wales, 22 July 1977); The College Library 1872-1976, by T G
Lloyd. Aberystwyth, the University College of Wales Library,
1977.

10) Roberts, B F, 'Richard Ellis, MA (Edward Lhuyd and the Cymmrodorion)' Cymmrodorion *Transactions* 1977, pp 131-172;
Brinkley, R 'George Powell of Nanteos' *Anglo-Welsh review* vol
21, no 48 (1972), pp130-134; Williams, J D 'The library, UCW'
in *The college by the sea* (ed) Ieuan Morgan. Aberystwyth,
Cambrian News Ltd, 1928 pp205-210; University College of
Wales, Aberystwyth. A catalogue of (1) Welsh books; (2) Books
relating to Wales; (3) Books written by Welshmen; (4) Books
relating to Celtic literature; (5) Autograph letters, etc. Aberystwyth, Cambrian News Office, 1897; Evans, George Eyre,
(pseud Philip Sidney) 'The Welsh library at Aberystwyth', reprinted from the *Welsh gazette* March 5 1903; Cuming, Agnes
'Sketch for a classification for law on the lines of the Library of
Congress' Repr from the *Library Association record*, 1926 (Paper
on the scheme worked out for the UCW library); Cuming, Agnes
'A copy of Shakespeare's works which formerly belonged to Dr
Johnson' Repr from the *Review of English studies* vol 3 no 10,
April 1927 (Description of 'Works' in the UCW Library); Cuming,
Agnes 'The organisation of a university library' Repr from the
Library Association record 1926 (Based on the author's experi-
ence while on the staff of the UCW library); Davies, Sir W Ll *The
National Library of Wales: a survey of its history, its contents,
and its activities* Aberystwyth, The National Library of Wales,
1937 (Brief reference to the formation of the 'Welsh Library' in
the UCW library 1899-1908, pp4-6); D J Fletcher (ed) 'Nicolas
Edme Restif de la Bretonne, *Le généographe*' (an edition and
transcription of one of the George Powell mss) *Studies on Vol-
taire and the eighteenth century* vol CLXX (1977), pp125-234;
Swinburne, A C *The letters*, ed C Y Lang. 6 vols; New Haven,
1959-62. (include transcripts and comments on the letters of
Swinburne to George Powell in the possession of the college library, and now deposited in the National Library of Wales)

92 **UNIVERSITY OF ASTON IN BIRMINGHAM, THE LIBRARY**
1b) The University of Aston in Birmingham.
2a) Gosta Green, Birmingham B4 7ET. 2b) 021-359-3611;
2c) 336997
3) C R Burman BA FLA
4a) 1895. Aston received its charter as a university in 1966. Library
building occupied 1975; 4b) to support teaching and research in
the university; Provides loan and inter-library loan services, reference and information services, literature searches, library instruction, audiovisual service.

92   UNIVERSITY OF ASTON, THE LIBRARY (continued)

5a) Science, technology, social sciences, modern languages, management; 5b) Founder member Birmingham Libraries Cooperative Mechanisation Project (BLCMP); West Midlands Regional Library Bureau; Weslink.

6a) Books: 132,564. Periodical volumes: 49,387; Films: 173; Gramophone records: 584; Tapes/slide sequences: 408; Periodicals taken 2339.

7a) All material on open access except short-loan collection. Dewey 18 and modified UDC in use; 7b) Microfilm catalogue for post 1972 additions: a) alphabetical name/title, b) classified; Card catalogue for pre-1972 additions: a) alphabetical name, b) alphabetical title, c) classified; Periodicals catalogue by title, alphabetically; Birmingham Libraries (BLCMP) Union Catalogue for post 1972 additions: a) alphabetical name, b) periodicals, alphabetical by title; Alphabetical subject index; Course books list; Short loan list

8a) All staff and students of the university; graduates of the university and others by application on payment of a deposit; 8b) M-F 0900-2300 (no service 2130-2300), Sat to 1700 (no service after 1200). Vacations: M-F 0900-1700 except Easter and Christmas— M-Th 0900-1900, F to 1700;

8c) Loan services including renewals and reservations; inter-library loans; enquiries; literature searches; library instruction; translations; library publications ('Current contents' bulletins. subject guides); Audiovisual services (tapes, records, cinefilms, film loops, tape/slide programmes, TV & radio, microforms), photocopying;

9) Library guide; guide to the catalogues; library newsletter; Current contents bulletins (economics and management, education, ophthalmic optics, psychology, safety and hygiene, sociology and politics); subject guides (10 so far in series); detailed guides to publications & information services. 'Small business bibliography'; Index to Aston theses.

10) *Program* vol 4(4), October 1970, pp150-155

93   UNIVERSITY COLLEGE OF NORTH WALES LIBRARY, BANGOR

1b) University College of North Wales

2a) Bangor, Gwynedd LL57 2DG; 2b) 0248-51151; 2c) 61100

3) L G Heywood MA

4a) 1884

5a) General; 5b) Main Library houses the arts collections and the Science Library the main science collections. In addition, there are departmental libraries for zoology, mathematics and computer science, electronic engineering and marine science

6a) 400,000 volumes; 3650 current periodicals; 6b) Welsh Library (books and periodicals) estate and private papers of North Wales families; Germanic philology; theology; Hebrew and other Semitic languages and literature; J R Firth Collection (comparative

103

93   UNIV. COL. OF NORTH WALES LIBRARY (continued)
      linguistics); Sir Frank Brangwyn collection (painting and art
      generally); Bangor Cathedral library; Talfourd-Jones Collection
      (botany and zoology); Phillips Collection (marine algology);
      Edward Greenly Collection (books and periodicals on geology);
      the library of the Forensic Science Society
8a)   Members of the college; others, for reference, on written appli-
      cation; 8b) Open on Sundays in term
9)   Readers' guide; Notes for readers in the Science Library; List of
      science periodicals

94   BATH UNIVERSITY LIBRARY
lb)   University of Bath
2a)   Claverton Down, Bath BA2 7AY; 2b) 0225-6941; 2c) 44907
3)   J H Lamble MA
4a)   Established 1856, Bath University received its charter in 1966.
      The library building was occupied in 1971; 4b) To provide a li-
      brary service to all the functions of the university
5a)   Science, technology, social sciences, management, education,
      modern languages; 5b) The library is one central organisation.
      However, the senior library staff are assigned as librarians of the
      various schools of the university and are responsible for stock
      selection etc on behalf of these schools
6a)   127,000 volumes; 1900 current periodicals; 6b) Bath and West and
      Southern Counties Society library; Pitman Collection (shorthand);
      Garden History Society library; collection of early nurserymen's
      catalogues
7a)   Open-access for most of stock, except short loan collection,
      theses and stack rooms. UDC; 7b) COM catalogues (fiche) in
      author, title, KWOC title and classified (with subject index) se-
      quences
8a)   Members of the university; others on recommendation; 8b) Open
      on Sundays in term; closed Saturdays; 8c) Seats for some 600
      readers. Loan facilities by category of book to members of uni-
      versity; Assistance with literature searches and use of on-line
      retrieval services
9)   Physics and materials science (Jean MacGregor); Early horti-
      cultural catalogues: a checklist (John Harvey); Pounds or pin-
      folds and lock-ups (B M W Dobbie)
10)   Lamble, J H 'Die Bibliothek der Universität von Bath, England'
      DFW Dokumentation Information 23, 1975.

95   QUEEN'S UNIVERSITY LIBRARY, BELFAST
lb)   Queen's University of Belfast
2a)   Main Library, Belfast BT7 1NN (tel: 0232-45133). Science Li-
      brary, Chlorine Gardens, Belfast BT9 5EQ (tel: 0232-66111);
      Medical Library, Belfast BT12 6BJ (tel: 0232-22043/21487);
      Agriculture Library, Belfast BT9 5BX (tel: 0232-661166);

95   QUEEN'S UNIVERSITY LIBRARY (continued)
2c) Science Library: 747691 QUBSCI G: Medical Library:
747578 QUBMED G

3)   A Blamire MA DipLib ALA

4a)   Queen's College, Belfast opened in 1849, becoming Queen's University in 1908. Library opened 1850; 4b) Serves staff and students in the nine faculties of the university. Medical Library also offers a regional service under the auspices of the Department of Health and Social Services

5a)   General; 5b) The university library comprises the Main Library (humanities, law, social sciences), the Medical Library, the Science Library, and the Agriculture Library

6a)   700,000 volumes; 8000 current periodicals; 6b) Thomas Percy Collection; Somerville and Ross Collection (manuscripts); McDouall Collection (Comparative Philology); Hamilton Harty Collection (music); Hibernica Collection; Edward Bunting Collection (Irish music manuscripts); Sir Robert Hart papers (Chinese Customs Service); Simms Collection (History of Medicine)

7a)   Open-access; Library of Congress Classification; 7b) Name catalogue; classified subject catalogue (which contain entries for the university library system, and the departmental and class libraries)

8a)   Members of the university; external readers, on payment of a deposit; others, for reference, on application; 8b) Term: 0900-2300, Vacation to 1730; 8c) Blaise and Dialog information retrieval services

9)   Reader guides to the four libraries in the system; *Architecture and planning information service bulletin; List of books required for the Library of the Queen's College, Belfast* (1849); *Catalogue of books in the department of logic and metaphysics, and on kindred subjects* (February 1856); *Catalogue of books in the department of medicine* (November 1856); *Catalogue of books in the departments of mathematics and natural philosophy* (1856); *Catalogue of books in the department of chemistry* (1858); *Catalogue of books in the Library of Queen's College, Belfast* (1859) and *supplements I-IV* (1860-1878); *Catalogue of books in the Antrim Library, now deposited in Queen's College, Belfast* (1874); *Catalogue of classical books and works relating to Patristic literature in the Library of Queen's College, Belfast* (1887); *Catalogue of books in the library of Queen's College, Belfast* (1897)

10)   Jessie B Webster 'Queen's University Medical Library; a province-wide service' *Hospital news* 6(4) 1964, pp3-9; W D Linton 'Queen's University Science Library, Belfast' *Northern Ireland libraries* 8(2) 1969, pp47-53; P Havard-Williams 'The new Science Library at Queen's University, Belfast' *Library world* 71 1970, pp263-266; J R Watson 'Photography at the Queen's University of Belfast' *Industrial and commercial photographer* 9(10), 1969, pp38-44; H J Heaney 'Special collections in the University Library' *Queen's University Association, annual record* 1973, pp71-78.

96   UNIVERSITY OF BIRMINGHAM LIBRARY

1b)   University of Birmingham

2a)   PO Box 363, Edgbaston, Birmingham B15 2TT; 2b) 021-472-1301;
       2c) 338160 ULBHAM G

3)   M A Pegg BA PhD

4a)   Founded 1875, became a university in 1900. Main Library opened
       1960, extended in 1971.

5a)   General; 5b) Main library houses the general science, social science,
       languages and literatures, and history collections. Separate build-
       ings house the Barnes Medical Library, the Barber Music Library,
       the Dental Library, and the Harding Law Library.

6a)   About 1 million volumes; 7700 current periodicals; 6b) The li-
       brary houses the National Documentation Centre for Sport,
       Physical Education and Recreation; and the National Centre for
       Athletics Literature. Papers of Joseph, Austen and Neville Cham-
       berlain, and Anthony Eden, 1st Earl of Avon (political archives);
       papers of John Galsworthy and Francis Brett Young (literary ar-
       chives); Sceptre Press Collection (modern English poetry); Sel-
       bourne Library (early books on science and medicine, early
       English drama, modern English literature, fine bindings); Birming-
       ham Medical Institute Collection; Midland Institute of Otology
       Collection; Wedgwood Library (philology), parish libraries of St
       Mary's Warwick, St John's Bewdley (Wigan Collection), and St
       Peter's Bengeworth (17th to 19th century theology and history);
       Baskerville Collection; Modern Poetry Collection; European Docu-
       mentation Centre

7a)   Mainly open-access. Library of Congress Classification; 7b) Name
       and classified catalogues (microfiche); periodicals title catalogue
       (card)

8a)   Members of the university; graduates of the university, with the
       permission of the librarian; external borrowers, with the permission
       of the library committee (registration fee payable). The Barnes
       Medical Library is also open to members of the West Midlands
       Area Health Authority; 8b) The General Reading Room is open
       on Sunday afternoons in term; 8c) enquiries in the Main Library
       to a general enquiry desk and enquiry desks in the Official Publi-
       cations Department, the Current Periodicals Room, and the
       Special Collections Department. Specialised enquiries are also
       dealt with in the subject reading rooms. On-line biomedical in-
       formation retrieval services in the Barnes Medical Library.

9)   Guide to the library; a series of 'Quick lists' (student guides to
       subject areas); a series of 'Special guides' (going into greater
       detail on various topics or for specific groups); University of Bir-
       mingham Music Library. *Catalogue of the printed music and mu-*
       sic manuscripts before 1801 by Iain Fenton London, Mansell,
       1976

10)   Buckle, D G R 'The Birmingham Libraries' Cooperative Mechanis-
       ation Project' *LIBER Bulletin* 5/6, 1975, pp74-95; Humphreys, K W

96   UNIVERSITY OF BIRMINGHAM LIBRARY (continued)
      'Birmingham University Library' in *Encyclopedia of Library and
      Information Science*; Smith, B R 'The Library Film Information
      Service at the University of Birmingham' *University vision* 13,
      1975, pp35-43; 'Main library' *Library Association record*, 63,
      1961, pp40-1.

97   UNIVERSITY OF BRADFORD LIBRARY
lb)   University of Bradford
2a)   J B Priestley Library, University of Bradford, Bradford BD7 1DP;
      Social Sciences and Modern Languages Library, University of
      Bradford, Wardley House, Little Horton Lane, Bradford BD5 OAJ;
      Yvette Jacobson Library, Management Centre, University of Brad-
      ford, Emm Lane, Bradford BD9 4JL; 2b) 0274-33466; Yvette
      Jacobson Library: 0274-42299; 2c) 51309
3)   F Earnshaw BA ALA
4a)   Founded 1957, became a university in 1966; The Yvette Jacob-
      son Library opened in 1974, and the J B Priestley Library in 1975;
      4b) To support the teaching and research programmes of the uni-
      versity;
5a)   Science, engineering, social sciences, management, modern lan-
      guages, human studies; 5b) The university library is housed in
      three separate building: the J B Priestley Library (mainly science
      and technology); the Social Sciences and Modern Languages Li-
      brary; the Yvette Jacobson Library (business and management
      studies);
6a)   280,000 volumes; 2800 current serials; 6b) Commonweal Collec-
      tion (peace studies), European Documentation Centre;
7a)   Open-access. Universal Decimal Classification (science and engin-
      eering) and Dewey Decimal Classification (other subjects);
      7b) Author and title catalogue (title entries for all recently-
      catalogued books); classified subject catalogue; alphabetical sub-
      ject index (computer printout); Central union catalogue on cards
      in J B Priestley Library; other libraries have microfilm catalogues.
8a)   Members of the university; staff and postgraduate research students
      of Leeds, Sheffield, Hull and York universities; others, for refer-
      ence, on written application; 8b) J B Priestley Library open on
      Sunday afternoons in term; Social Sciences and Modern Languages
      Library open on Sunday afternoons in summer term; 8c) Senior
      library staff organised on subject specialisation basis, with empha-
      sis on bibliographical and information services.
9)   Know your library; Periodicals and serials in the university library;
      Annual report of the librarian; Library bulletin; Library notes
      (9 titles).

98   UNIVERSITY OF BRISTOL LIBRARY
lb)   University of Bristol
2a)   Tyndall Avenue, Bristol BS8 1TJ; 2b) 0272-24161; 2c) 449174 BRIS

98   UNIVERSITY OF BRISTOL LIBRARY (continued)
3)   N Higham MA ALA
4a)   Established 1876, university received its charter in 1909. The
      library's main building was opened in 1976
5a)   General; 5b) The Tyndall Avenue building houses the Arts and
      Social Sciences Library. Other libraries are the Medical Library;
      Queen's Library (engineering, geology, and mathematics); School
      of Education Library; Worsley Chemical Library; Maria Mercer
      Library (physics); Law Library; Biological Sciences Library; Geo-
      graphy Library; those for architecture, dental surgery, veterinary
      science, horticultural science, and community health libraries;
      the library of the computer centre
6a)   620,000 volumes (excluding manuscripts). 140,000 pamphlets;
      10,900 periodicals, of which 5500 are current; 6b) British philos-
      ophers; early English novels. Allen Lane Collection (autographed
      Penguin books); published business histories; early medical books;
      mineral waters and spas; British local history; courtesy books;
      history of education; early English dictionaries; cartography; land-
      scape gardening; Exley Library (early mathematical books);
      Worsley Library (early works on chemistry and alchemy); Wigles-
      worth Collection (ornithology); Gladstone memorial collection of
      election addresses and of political pamphlets.
          Manuscripts: I K Brunel collection of sketch books, notebooks
      and correspondence; papers of the Pinney family (17th to 19th
      centuries); Somerset Miners' Federation archives (20th century);
      National Liberal Club archives
7a)   Mainly open-access. Library of Congress Classification (arts,
      social science and education); INSPEC classification (Maria Mercer
      Library); Moys (Law Library); Cunningham (Medical Library);
      locally-created schemes in other branches; 7b) Main catalogue
      includes entries for all books in the university library system (in-
      cluding departmental libraries), except the Medical Library. Com-
      prises name catalogue and shelf catalogue (classified catalogue).
      Separate catalogues for periodicals, parliamentary papers, music
      scores and theses
8a)   Academic staff of the university and fee-paying students; full
      facilities; others, at the discretion of the librarian: limited fa-
      cilities; 8b) Most branches open some or all evenings and Sat morn-
      ings. Undergraduate reading room opens in addition Sat and Sun
      pm and weekday evenings until 2300 during term; 8c) Readers'
      assistance provided by head of reader services, and divisional li-
      brarians (Main Library), and senior librarians in branch libraries
9)   Readers' guides to main and branch libraries; Annual report of
      the librarian

99   BRUNEL UNIVERSITY LIBRARY
1b)   Brunel University
2a)   Kingston Lane, Uxbridge, Middlesex UB8 3PH; 2b) 0895-37188;
      2c) 261173

(continued)

99   BRUNEL UNIVERSITY LIBRARY (continued)
3)   C E N Childs BA
4a)   Established as a regional college of technology in 1957, received
      its charter as a university in 1966; 4b) All the usual facilities
      and services
5a)   Science; technology; social sciences; well-developed audiovisual
      section; 5b) CICRIS member
6a)   140,000 volumes; 2000 current periodicals
7a)   Open-access. Library of Congress Classification: 7b) Author/title
      and subject catalogues (cards); serials list and catalogue of Reserve
      Book Collection (computer-based)
8a)   Members of the university; others, for reference, on written appli-
      cation; 8b) Open Sun pm in term; 8c) On-line information retrieval
      service
9)   Library guide; subject guides; guide to A/V services; guide to gov-
      ernment publications; list of dictionaries; subject lists of Reserve
      Book Collection holdings. serials list; source literature

100   UNIVERSITY COLLEGE AT BUCKINGHAM LIBRARY
1b)   University College at Buckingham
2a)   Hunter Street, Buckingham MK18 1EG; 2b) 02802-4161
3)   J E Pemberton MA FLA FRSA
4a)   The college was established in 1973 and opened in 1976; 4b) To
      provide a comprehensive library service to support undergraduate
      teaching in subject courses offered by the college
5a)   Law; economics; politics; history; accountancy; English literature;
      mathematics; life sciences; 5b) Separate Denning Law Library;
      Language Library; James Meade Library of Economics
6a)   30,000 volumes; 175 current periodicals
7a)   Open-access; Dewey Decimal Classification (18th edition); special
      coding scheme for primary materials in the social sciences;
      7b) Author catalogue; title catalogue; classified catalogue and sub-
      ject index
8a)   Members of the college; others, for reference, on written appli-
      cation; 8b) Open Sun; open until 12pm on weekdays in term;
      8c) Reader services (including instruction); on-line access to book-
      seller's database via VDU
9)   Subject guides

CAMBRIDGE
The entries for the University of Cambridge comprise the University Library, a selection of departmental libraries (mainly those
with larger or more important collections which permit a reasonable degree of access), and the Fitzwilliam Museum Library.
    A full list of departmental libraries is given, and intending users
are advised to make adequate individual contact with librarians
before attempting to use the collections. A good account of departmental collections in Cambridge is given in the 'First report of
the General Board's Committee on Libraries', *Cambridge University reporter* 99 (29), Friday March 28 1969;

CAMBRIDGE (continued)

The constituent colleges of the university each possess libraries which range from undergraduate working collections to unique historical and research collections. Intending readers should make contact with librarians before attempting to use these collections. A good description of college libraries is given in Munby, A N L *Cambridge college libraries: aids for research students* 2nd ed rev Cambridge, Heffer, 1962;

A compendium of current information on opening hours and staff of other libraries in the university (excluding college libraries) is given in the *Libraries directory*, published as a supplement to the *Libraries information bulletin* (12 pa).

Departmental libraries:
AFRICAN STUDIES CENTRE LIBRARY
Sidgwick Avenue, Cambridge CB3 9DA (Phone: 0223-58944)
ANATOMY
Department Library, Downing Site, Cambridge (Phone: 0223-58761)
APPLIED BIOLOGY
Department Library, Downing Site, Cambridge (Phone: 0223-58381)
APPLIED ECONOMICS
Department Library, Sidgwick Avenue, Cambridge (Phone: 0223-58944)
APPLIED MATHEMATICS AND THEORETICAL PHYSICS
Departmental Library, Silver Street, Cambridge (Phone: 0223-51645)
ARCHAEOLOGY AND ANTHROPOLOGY FACULTY
Haddon Library, Downing Street, Cambridge CB2 3BZ (Phone: 0223-59714/6)
BIOCHEMISTRY DEPARTMENT COLMAN LIBRARY
Tennis Court Road, Cambridge CB2 1QW (Phone: 0223-51781)
BIOPHYSICAL CHEMISTRY AND COLLOID SCIENCE
Colloid Science Laboratory, Free School Lane, Cambridge (Phone: 0223-58381)
BOTANIC GARDEN
Library, 1 Brookside, Cambridge (Phone: 0223-50101)
BOTANY SCHOOL LIBRARY
Downing Street, Cambridge CB2 3AE (Phone: 0223-61414)
CHEMICAL ENGINEERING DEPARTMENT LIBRARY
Pembroke Street, Cambridge CB2 3RA (Phone: 0223-58231)
CLASSICAL ARCHAEOLOGY, MUSEUM OF
Little St Mary's Lane, Cambridge CB2 1RR (Phone: 0223-65621)
CLASSICS
Classical Faculty Library, Mill Lane Lecture Rooms, Mill Lane, Cambridge CB2 1RR (Phone: 0223-65621)
CRIMINOLOGY
Radzinowicz Library, West Road, Cambridge, CB3 9DT (Phone: 0223-68511)

CAMBRIDGE *Departmental libraries* (continued)
DIVINITY
Divinity Faculty Library, St John's Street, Cambridge CB2 1TW
(Phone: 0223-58933)
ECONOMICS FACULTY
Marshall Library, Sidgwick Avenue, Cambridge CB3 9DB (Phone:
0223-58944)
EDUCATION
Education Department Library, 17 Brookside, Cambridge CB2 1JG
(Phone: 0223-5527)
ENGLISH FACULTY
Faculty Library, Sidgwick Avenue, Cambridge (Phone: 0223-56411)
ENGINEERING FACULTY
Engineering Faculty Library, Trumpington Street, Cambridge CB2
1PZ (Phone: 0223-66466)
EXPERIMENTAL PSYCHOLOGY
Departmental Library, Downing Street, Cambridge (Phone: 0223-
51386)
FINE ARTS
Architecture and History of Art Faculty Library, 1-3 Scroope
Terrace, Cambridge (Phone: 0223-54265)
GENETICS
Department Library, Milton Road, Cambridge CB4 1XH (Phone:
0223-58694)
GEOGRAPHY
Department Library, Downing Place, Cambridge (Phone: 0223-
64416)
GEOLOGY
Sedgwick Geology Library, Downing Street, Cambridge CB2 3EQ
(Phone: 0223-51585)
HISTORY FACULTY
Seeley Historical Library, West Road, Cambridge CB3 9DF (Phone:
0223-61661)
HISTORY AND PHILOSOPHY OF SCIENCE
Whipple Library, Free School Lane, Cambridge CB2 3RH (Phone:
0223-58381)
INSTITUTE OF ASTRONOMY
Library, The Observatories, Madingley Road, Cambridge CB3 0HA
(Phone: 0223-62204)
INVESTIGATIVE MEDICINE
Department of Investigative Medicine, Addenbrooke's Hospital,
Hills Road, Cambridge (Phone: 0223-44014)
LAND ECONOMY
Department Library, Laundress Lane, Cambridge CB2 1SD (Phone:
0223-55262)
LATIN AMERICAN STUDIES
Centre of Latin American Studies Library, West Road, Cambridge
(Phone: 0223-61661)

CAMBRIDGE *Departmental libraries* (continued)
LAW FACULTY
Squire Library, Old Schools, Cambridge CB2 1TU (Phone: 0223-58933)
MATHEMATICAL STATISTICS
Wishart Library, 16 Mill Lane, Cambridge CB2 1SB (Phone: 0223-65621)
MEDICAL SCHOOL
University Medical Library, Addenbrooke's Hospital, Hills Road, Cambridge CB2 2QQ (Phone: 0223-44014)
METALLURGY AND MATERIALS SCIENCE DEPARTMENT
Department Library, Pembroke Street, Cambridge CB2 3QZ (Phone: 0223-65151)
METEOROLOGY
Napier Shaw Library, Cavendish Road, Madingley Road, Cambridge (Phone: 0223-66477)
MINERALOGY AND PETROLOGY DEPARTMENT
Department Library, Downing Place, Cambridge, CB2 3EW (Phone: 0223-64131)
MODERN LANGUAGES
Modern and Medieval Languages Library, Sidgwick Avenue, Cambridge CB3 9DA (Phone: 0223-56411)
MUSIC FACULTY
Pendlebury Library, Downing Place, Cambridge CB2 3EL (Phone: 0223-63322)
OBSERVATORIES
Astronomy Library, The Observatories, Madingley Road, Cambridge CB3 OHA(Phone: 0223-62204)
ORIENTAL STUDIES FACULTY
Faculty Library, Sidgwick Avenue, Cambridge CB3 9DA (Phone: 0223-62253)
PARASITOLOGY
Nuttall Library, Molteno Institute, Downing Street, Cambridge (Phone: 0223-50577)
PATHOLOGY DEPARTMENT
Kanthak Library, Tennis Court Road, Cambridge CB2 1QP (Phone: 0223-58251)
PHARMACOLOGY DEPARTMENT
Department Library, Medical School, Hills Road, Cambridge CB2 3QD (Phone: 0223-45171)
PHILOSOPHY
Faculty of Philosophy Library, Sidgwick Avenue, Cambridge (Phone: 0223-56411)
PHYSICS DEPARTMENT
Rayleigh Library, Cavendish Laboratory, Madingley Road, Cambridge CB3 OHE (Phone: 0223-66477)
PHYSIOLOGY
Physiological Laboratory Library, Downing Street, Cambridge CB2 3EG (Phone: 0223-64131)

CAMBRIDGE *Departmental libraries* (continued)
POLAR RESEARCH
Scott Polar Research Institute Library, Lensfield Road, Cambridge
CB2 1ER (Phone: 0223-66499)
PURE MATHEMATICS
Pure Mathematics Library, 16 Mill Lane, Cambridge CB2 1SB
(Phone: 0223-65621)
RADIOTHERAPEUTICS
Department of Radiotherapeutics, Hills Road, Cambridge (Phone:
0223-45171)
SCIENTIFIC PERIODICALS LIBRARY
Bene't Street, Cambridge CB2 3PY (Phone: 0223-54724)
SLAVONIC STUDIES
Department Library, Sidgwick Avenue, Cambridge (Phone: 0223-
56411)
SOUTH ASIAN STUDIES (CENTRE OF SOUTH ASIAN STUDIES)
Faculty Rooms, Laundress Lane, Cambridge CB2 1SD (Phone:
0223-65621)
SURGERY
Department Library, Addenbrooke's Hospital, Hills Road, Cam-
bridge (Phone: 0223-61467)
VETERINARY ANATOMY
Department Library, Downing Site, Cambridge (Phone: 0223-
58761)
VETERINARY MEDICINE
Department Library, Madingley Road, Cambridge (Phone: 0223-
55641)
ZOOLOGY DEPARTMENT
Balfour and Newton Library, Downing Street, Cambridge CB2 3EJ
(Phone: 0223-58717)

College libraries:
CHRIST'S COLLEGE
Cambridge CB2 3BU (Phone: 0223-67641)
CHURCHILL COLLEGE
Cambridge CB3 ODS (Phone: 0223-61200)
CLARE COLLEGE
Cambridge CB2 1TL (Phone: 0223-58681)
CLARE HALL
Cambridge CB3 9AL (Phone: 0223-63330)
CORPUS CHRISTI COLLEGE
Cambridge CB2 1RH (Phone: 0223-59418)
DARWIN COLLEGE
Cambridge CB3 9EU (Phone: 0223-51761)
DOWNING COLLEGE
Cambridge CB2 1DQ (Phone: 0223-59491)
EMMANUEL COLLEGE
Cambridge CB2 3AP (Phone: 0223-65411)

(continued)

CAMBRIDGE *College libraries* (continued)
FITZWILLIAM COLLEGE
Cambridge CB3 ODG (Phone: 0223-58657)
GIRTON COLLEGE
Cambridge CB3 OJG (Phone 0223-76219)
GONVILLE AND CAIUS COLLEGE
Cambridge CB2 1TA (Phone: 0223-53275)
HUGHES HALL
Cambridge CB1 2EW (Phone: 0223-52866)
JESUS COLLEGE
Cambridge CB5 8BL (Phone: 0223-68611)
KING'S COLLEGE
Cambridge CB2 1ST (Phone: 0223-50411)
LUCY CAVENDISH COLLEGIATE SOCIETY
Cambridge CB3 OBU (Phone 0223-63409)
MAGDALENE COLLEGE
Cambridge CB3 OAG (Phone: 0223-61543)
NEW HALL
Cambridge CB3 ODF (Phone: 0223-51721)
NEWHAM COLLEGE
Cambridge CB3 9DF (Phone: 0223-62273)
PEMBROKE COLLEGE
Cambridge CB2 1RF (Phone: 0223-52241)
PETERHOUSE
Cambridge CB2 1RD (Phone: 0223-50256)
QUEEN'S COLLEGE
Cambridge CB3 9ET (Phone: 0223-65511)
ST CATHARINE'S COLLEGE
Cambridge CB2 1RL (Phone: 0223-59445)
ST EDMUND'S HOUSE
Cambridge CB3 OBN (Phone: 0223-50398)
ST JOHN'S COLLEGE
Cambridge CB2 1TP (Phone: 0223-61621)
SELWYN COLLEGE
Cambridge CB3 9DQ (Phone: 0223-62381)
SIDNEY SUSSEX COLLEGE
Cambridge CB2 3HU (Phone: 0223-61501)
TRINITY COLLEGE
Cambridge CB2 1TQ (Phone: 0223-58201)
TRINITY HALL
Cambridge CB2 1TJ (Phone: 0223-51401)
WOLFSON COLLEGE
Cambridge CB3 9BB (Phone: 0223-64811)

101   CAMBRIDGE UNIVERSITY LIBRARY
1b)   University of Cambridge
2a)   West Road, Cambridge CB3 9DR; 2b) 0223-61441; 2c) 81395
3)   E B Ceadel MA

01

CAMBRIDGE UNIVERSITY LIBRARY (continued)

4a) The university library has had a continuous existence since the early fifteenth century. The present building has been occupied since 1934; 4b) Research library serving the needs of the university and visiting scholars. Depository library for the publications of the United Nations and various international agencies. It is a collection of both major national and international importance.

5a) Comprehensive subject coverage, except that most current British law books and periodicals are deposited in the Squire Law Library. Nearly all British publications are received under the Copyright Act. Foreign publications are obtained by purchase and exchange; 5b) The collections are particularly strong in the humanities and social sciences. The stock comprises printed books as well as Western and Oriental manuscripts. Specialist departments for maps, music, manuscripts and official publications

6a) Bookstock: nearly 2,750,000 items (monographs and bound serials). Maps: c600,000 items. Music scores: 250,000; Manuscripts: over 15,000 volumes, together with many other collections of papers; 6b) Acton Library (historical: 60,000 volumes); Royal (Bishop Moore's) Library (30,000 volumes); Bradshaw (Irish books); Wade and Aston (Chinese and Japanese books); Cambridge Collection; Chapbook Collection: War Collection 1914-1919; adversaria (printed books with ms notes); incunabula (4300 works); Darwin Library (Charles Darwin, on deposit);

Manuscripts include: Baldwin papers; Crewe papers; Darwin papers; Hardinge papers; Jardine Matheson archives; Taylor-Schechter (Genizah) fragments; Templewood papers; Cholmondeley (Houghton) mss (on deposit); Ely Diocesan Records (on deposit); mss deposited by Cambridge colleges (Pembroke, Peterhouse, Sidney Sussex)

7a) No unified scheme of classification was applied to the earlier collections and many older schemes survive. A new classification introduced in 1900 now covers most of the modern books and periodicals. A very large proportion of the book stock is on open access; fetching service to the reading room or to specialist departments for the remainder.

7b) Author catalogue (cards and guardbook); subject catalogue for official publications. The author catalogue is divided into two sequences. Main catalogue for the majority of books and periodicals required for academic study. Supplementary catalogue (in two parts 1800-1905 and 1906-) contains books not in the main catalogue considered to be of secondary importance. Separate catalogues for periodicals, official publications, maps, music, manuscripts, Far Eastern books.

A number of printed catalogues are available including: Catalogue of a collection of books on logic presented by J Venn (1889); Catalogue of the Wade Collection of Chinese and Manchu books, by H A Giles (2 vols, 1898-1915); Early English printed

101 CAMBRIDGE UNIVERSITY LIBRARY (continued)
books in the University Library, Cambridge (1475-1640), by C E
Sayle (4 vols, 1900-1907); Catalogue of the Maccoll Collection
and other Spanish books (1910); Catalogue of the Bradshaw Collection of Irish books, by C E Sayle (3vols, 1916); Catalogue of
the fifteenth century printed books, compiled by J C T Oates
(1954); Classified catalogue of modern Japanese books, by E B
Ceadel (1961).
There are a number of catalogues and lists of Western and
Oriental manuscripts including: Catalogue of the manuscripts
(5 vols plus index, 1856-1867); Handlist of Darwin papers (1960);
Summary guide to accessions of Western manuscripts (other than
medieval) since 1867, by A E B Owen (1966). There are also
specialist catalogues of Hebrew manuscripts, Buddhist Sanskrit
manuscripts, Persian manuscripts, Muhammadan manuscripts,
Syriac manuscripts, Georgian manuscripts, Indonesian manuscripts, Mongol manuscripts, and Ethiopian manuscripts.

8a)   Members of the university; others in accordance with the ordi-
nances and rules made by the Library Syndicate; 8c) Microcard,
microfilm and microfiche readers; full photographic and photocopying services

9)   Information for new readers; Readers handbook; Current serials;
Classified list of current periodicals; Checklist of the British
Parliamentary Papers 1801-1950, by K A C Parsons; Guide to
official publications in the University Library; Summary guide to
accessions of Western manuscripts (other than medieval) since
1867; Guide to faculty and departmental libraries in the University of Cambridge; Subject guide to class REF; weekly list of
accessions

10)   Oates, J C T 'Cambridge University Library' in Kent, A (ed)
Encyclopedia of library and information science vol 4. New York,
Dekker, 1970

102 AFRICAN STUDIES CENTRE LIBRARY
1b)   University of Cambridge, African Studies Centre
2a)   Free School Lane, Cambridge CB2 3RQ; 2b) 0223-58381 ext 314;
3)   A F Robertson (Director), Ms J A Ahola (Librarian)
4a)   1960; 4b) The centre's main function is to provide an interdisci-
plinary library for research in modern African studies covering
subjects in the social sciences.
5a)   Africa; 5b) Political, economic and social aspects of modern
African life plus material on law, ethnography, geography and
agriculture.
6a)   Books, serials, and microfiche; 6b) African contemporary documents—government publications, statistics and legal documents
as available.
7a)   Modified UDC; 7b) Author, regional and subject catalogues
116

02

AFRICAN STUDIES CENTRE LIBRARY (continued)

a) Members of the university. Other researchers on application to
the director of the centre or the librarian; 8b) M-F 0900-1730;
8c) The author catalogue is maintained as a bibliography to
which are added CARDAN cards as obtained and references from
accessions lists of other university libraries in Cambridge.

) 'African Women: a select bibliography' by L Kratochvil and
S Shaw, 1975; publications list

03 ARCHAEOLOGY AND ANTHROPOLOGY FACULTY–Haddon
Library

b) University of Cambridge

a) Downing Street, Cambridge CB2 3BZ; 2b) 0223-59714/6

) Lynda Oates BSc ALA

4a) The nucleus of the library originated in the collection assembled
by the Cambridge Antiquarian Society from 1840, which was
presented to the university in 1883; 4b) Mainly an undergraduate
library but contains some research material

5a) Archaeology; social anthropology and physical anthropology

6a) Monograph holdings: 18,000. Current serials: 448. Total serial
titles: 780. Some microfilms/maps; 6b) Cambridge Antiquarian
Society Collection. Volumes from libraries of Dr A C Haddon
(including the Haddon photographic collection), W K Foster,
James Hornell, M C Burkitt, and Sir James Frazer. Books printed
before 1850 are housed separately (possibly soon to be transferred
to University Library).

7a) Own classification scheme with a geographical basis–(soon to be
reclassified: probably Bliss, rev ed); 7b) Main author catalogue and
subsidiary catalogues (1956–) arranged by subject, country and
period: To be replaced by classified catalogue on reclassification

8a) Members of the university. Other researchers admitted by prior
arrangement; 8b) Term: M-F 0900-1730, Sat 0930-1230.
Vacation: 0915-1700, closed Sat;

104 BOTANY SCHOOL LIBRARY

1b) University of Cambridge

2a) Downing Street, Cambridge CB2 3AE; 2b) 0223-61414

3) K R Sporne MA PhD

4a) Original collection dates back to 1785 but the main growth
commenced towards the end of the 19th century; 4b) A collection
for undergraduates and researchers

5a) All aspects of botany except agriculture and forestry

6a) Bookstock: c20,000 volumes (monographs and bound serials);
6b) Blackman Collection (physiology), Martyn and Babington Collection (herbals and early botanical works). Various collections
of offprints donated by botanical researchers. The major portion
of the Ethel Sargant Collection (anatomy, morphology and

104   BOTANY SCHOOL LIBRARY (continued)
       taxonomy) from Girton College was received on permanent loan
       in 1957. The large Darwin Collection of books formerly lodged
       in the library is now divided between Down House (Kent) and the
       University Library
7a)   Own classification scheme modified from Bliss; 7b) Author cata-
       logue. Separate indexes for offprints and periodicals
8a)   Members of the university. Other researchers may use the library
       at the discretion of the Professor of Botany

105   DEPARTMENT OF ZOOLOGY Balfour and Newton Libraries
1b)   University of Cambridge
2a)   Downing Street, Cambridge CB2 3EJ; 2b) 0223-58717
3)   R Hughes
4a)   Nucleus of the collection was established in 1883 by the bequest
       of the library of Francis Maitland Balfour, Professor of Animal
       Morphology. The library of Alfred Newton the first Professor of
       Zoology was bequeathed in 1907; 4b) Provides material for under
       graduate and advanced research use
5a)   Zoology and allied subjects
6a)   Bookstock: c33,000 items. Current serials received: c400 titles;
       6b) Newton Collection (outstanding collection of works in orni-
       thology), Strickland Collection (ornithology), Mac Andrew Col-
       lection (conchology), Buckley Collection (fauna of Africa), Nor-
       man Collection, Watson Collection (malacology), Doncaster Col-
       lection (cytology), Hogg Collection (spiders). Also a collection
       of old books from the 16th century onwards
7a)   Modified Bliss Classification; 7b) Separate author catalogues to
       the main collection, the offprint collection and the Newton Col-
       lection
8a)   Members of the university. Other researchers on application to
       the librarian

106   DEPARTMENT OF GEOGRAPHY LIBRARY
1b)   University of Cambridge
2a)   Downing Place, Cambridge; 2b) 0223-64416
3)   Mrs J E Powell
4a)   Established in the years following 1903; 4b) Essentially a teaching
       library covering the field of the geographical tripos
5a)   Geographical literature, maps and atlases; 5b) Some material on
       topographical and geodetic surveying formerly kept in the survey
       laboratory is now held in the Department of Geography
6a)   Bookstock: c15,000 columes (monographs and bound serials).
       Current serials received: 135 titles. Pamphlets and offprints:
       8000 items. Maps: 50,000 items; 6b) Clark Collection (travel
       books)
7a)   Own classification scheme. Open and closed access; 7b) Author
       catalogue
8a)   Members of the university and other researchers by arrangement
       with the librarian

107 FITZWILLIAM MUSEUM LIBRARY
1b) University of Cambridge; Fitzwilliam Museum
2a) Trumpington Street, Cambridge CB2 1RB; 2b) 0223-69501
3) P Woudhuysen
4a) The museum collection was bequeathed to the university by
Richard, Viscount Fitzwilliam, of Trinity Hall (d1816). The
museum was completed in 1875. The viscount's library of c10,000
volumes formed the nucleus of the collection; 4b) The library provides a reference collection serving the needs of the museum, the
faculty of fine arts and students of art in general
5a) Fine and applied arts; 5b) Music, numismatics, eighteenth century
works on history, topography and natural history, ceramics, antiquities, prints, drawings, manuscript illumination
6a) Bookstock: c60,000 items. Pamphlets: c5000 items; 6b) The library contains important collections of early printed books and
manuscripts, music (printed and manuscript), literary autographs
and autograph letters, fine illustrated books, private press books,
fine bindings
7a) Library of Congress Classification for fine arts material. University Library 'Select books' classification for other subjects;
7b) Author and classified catalogues (slip form)
8a) Available to museum staff, members of the university and others
for special inquiry and reference
9) List of main additions to the library (annual)

108 GENETICS DEPARTMENT LIBRARY
1b) University of Cambridge
2a) Downing Street, Cambridge CB2 3EH; 2b) 0223-69551
3) K J R Edwards MA PhD
4a) 1914; 4b) The library functions as an undergraduate and research
collection. Probably the most comprehensive collection of genetics literature in the UK, owing to its strong offprint collection
5a) Genetics (plant, animal, microbial, and human) and related subjects
6a) Bookstock: 6800 volumes (monographs and bound serials);
Serials retained: 204 titles; 6b) Important collections of offprints
gathered together by former members of the department (Professor R C Punnett, Professor Sir Ronald Fisher, Mr Michael Pease,
Professor J M Thoday); Coverage of papers is particularly strong
between 1900 and 1950; Bateson's, Punnett's and Fisher's ms
record books of experimental work on poultry, rats and mice
7a) Bliss Classification; 7b) Author catalogues of books and offprints.
Index to periodicals
8a) Members of the department, but other researchers permitted
access on application

109 INSTITUTE OF ASTRONOMY LIBRARY
1b) University of Cambridge
2a) The Observatories, Madingley Road, Cambridge; 2b) 0223-62204
3) D W Dewhirst MA PhD

109   INSTITUTE OF ASTRONOMY LIBRARY (continued)
4a)   About 1824; 4b) The library has one of the major collections of
       works on observational astronomy in the UK. Theoretical
       astronomy is covered by the collection at the Institute of Theor-
       etical Astronomy.
5a)   Astronomy and observational techniques in particular; 5b) Astro-
       physics, radio astronomy, space research, optics, electronics,
       general physics and mathematics
6a)   Bookstock: over 2000 volumes. Pamphlets and offprints: over
       6000 items; 6b) John Couch Adams Collection (17th and 18th
       century works on astronomy etc); archives collection
7a)   Own classification scheme; 7b) Author and subject catalogues;
       separate author catalogue of offprints and pamphlets
8a)   Members of the university. Visiting researchers and members of
       the public suitably qualified may arrange to use the collection
9)   Notes on the use of the library

110   INSTITUTE OF CRIMINOLOGY LIBRARY Radzinowicz Library
       of Criminology
1b)   University of Cambridge
2a)   7 West Road, Cambridge CB3 9DT; 2b) 0223-68511
3)   Post vacant
4a)   The Institute of Criminology was established in 1960 but the
       present collection incorporates stock from the Department of
       Criminal Science founded in 1941; 4b) The library serves both
       research and teaching needs. The library is regarded as the prin-
       cipal criminological collection in the UK and has an international
       reputation in its field
5a)   Criminology; 5b) Penology, crime prevention and treatment of
       offenders, psychology, forensic psychiatry, sociology of deviance,
       criminal law
6a)   Bookstock: c20,000 volumes (monographs and bound serials);
       pamphlets and offprints: c10,000 items; Current serials received:
       c200 titles; 6b) Important collection of historical material; UK
       official publications on criminology and related fields
7a)   Bliss Classification, with modifications. Historical and confiden-
       tial material on closed access; 7b) Author and classified catalogues,
       alphabetical subject index. Catalogue to be published by G K Hall
       during 1977/8
8a)   Available to anyone with a serious interest in criminology; prior
       application should be made to the librarian
9)   Guide and regulations (annual); List of additions (3 pa, rates on
       application); Bibliographic series (titles for sale)
10)   Perry, R 'The Radzinowicz Library of Criminology' *Law librarian*
       7 (1), 1976.

111   METEOROLOGY LIBRARY Napier Shaw Library
1b)   University of Cambridge
2a)   Cavendish Laboratory, Madingley Road, Cambridge; 2b) 0223-
       66477; 2c) 81292

111 METEOROLOGY LIBRARY Napier Shaw Library (continued)
3)   Mrs R Powell
4a) Established in 1946 on the bequest of Sir William Napier Shaw;
     4b) A research and reference library which next to the libraries
     of the Meteorological Office and the Royal Meteorological Society
     is the most important collection in the country in this field
5a) Meteorology; 5b) Climatology; physics of the atmosphere
6a) Current serials received: 13 titles; Serials retained: 42 titles;
     6b) Small collection of mainly 19th century historical works
7a) Own classification scheme; 7b) Author catalogue; index to period-
     ical articles
8a) Members of the university; members of the Meteorological Society;
     others on application to the librarian

112 MUSEUM OF CLASSICAL ARCHAEOLOGY LIBRARY
1b) University of Cambridge
2a) Little St Mary's Lane, Cambridge CB2 1RR ; 2b) 0223-65621
3)   Professor A M Snodgrass (Curator)
4a) 1884; 4b) A working library for users of the museum but with
     much important research material. Of the four important libraries
     in the UK devoted to classical archaeology this is second in its
     coverage
5a) Classical archaeology; 5b) The main Cambridge collections of
     classical numismatics and Romano-British studies are located in
     the Fitzwilliam Museum and the University and Haddon Libraries
     respectively
6a) Bookstock: 13,000 volumes (monographs and bound serials).
     Current serials received: 74 titles. Serials retained: 108 titles.
     Slides: 19,000. Photographs: c9,000. Maps: c4000; 6b) Colonel
     W M Leake Collection (manuscript notebooks of travels in Asia
     Minor, Palestine, Egypt, Greece and Switzerland, 1799-1815)
7a) Own classification scheme; 7b) Author catalogue. Separate index
     by sites and museums
8a) Members of the university. Others on application to the librarian

113 SCOTT POLAR RESEARCH INSTITUTE LIBRARY
1b) University of Cambridge
2a) Lensfield Road, Cambridge, CB2 1ER; 2b) 0223-66499
3)   H G R King MA
4a) Library founded as an integral part of the institute in 1920;
     4b) The library is internationally known as a research collection
     in its field and in addition serves the needs of government, industry,
     commerce and the general public as an information source on
     polar matters.
5a) Polar research; 5b) Forms the world's most comprehensive collec-
     tion of polar literature, manuscripts and allied material in associ-
     ation with an active centre for research in the subject. Covers all
     the sciences and the arts relating to polar and sub-polar regions;
     snow and ice studies in all regions; applied glaciology in all regions;
     related subjects of whaling, sealing and typical Arctic and Antarctic life.

113 SCOTT POLAR RESEARCH INSTITUTE LIBRARY (continued)
6a) Bookstock: 14,000 volumes (monographs and bound serials).
     Current serials received: 811 titles. Serials retained: 950 titles.
     Pamphlets: 20,000 items. Maps and charts: 19,000 items.
     Pictures: 3000. Photographs: 5000; 6b) Lefroy Bequest of books
     and mss relating to Sir John and Lady Franklin; Vaino Tanner
     Library (Scandinavian subjects); Parry papers mss; Sir George
     Back Collection mss; Penny Craik gift mss; Cherry-Garrard Collec-
     tion mss; administrative papers of South Georgia; Compañía Ar-
     gentina de Pesca papers (whaling company archives 1904-1960)
7a) UDC; 7b) Main catalogues contain published material of polar
     interest held in other libraries. Author, subject and regional
     bibliography catalogues; manuscript collection catalogues; art col-
     lection catalogues
8a) Available to researchers on application to the librarian; 8b) M-F
     0900-1300 and 1415-1730; 8c) Information service available to
     the public; photocopying
9)   Guide to the SPRI library; Recent polar literature (3 pa); Library
     Catalogue of the Scott Polar Research Institute (19 volumes,
     Boston, G K Hall, 1976); Universal Decimal Classification for use
     in Polar libraries (Cambridge, the Institute, 1976. FID publication
     no 552).
10) Savours, A 'The manuscript collection of the Scott Polar Research
     Institute, Cambridge' *Archives*, 4, 1952, pp102-108; King, H G R
     'The Library of the Scott Polar Research Institute' *Geography
     and Map Division bulletin* 61 1965, pp7-12.

114 SEELEY HISTORICAL LIBRARY
1b) University of Cambridge
2a) Faculty of History, West Road, Cambridge CB3 9EF; 2b) 0223-
     61661
3)   Miss A C Cunninghame ALA
4a) Founded 1807, its nucleus being the collection of John Symonds,
     Regius Professor of Modern History from 1771-1807. On the
     death of Sir John Seeley in 1895 a memorial fund was raised to
     commemorate his services to the empire and to the university,
     and the greater part of this fund was devoted to the endowment
     of the library. As a consequence the library was renamed the
     Seeley Historical Library in 1897; 4b) Basically an undergraduate
     library; the stock therefore consists mostly of books required for
     the study of the history tripos and no attempt at an overall sub-
     ject coverage is intended. General library facilities are offered
     for senior members of the faculty, and there are some special
     facilities for graduate students.
5a) History and allied subjects.
6a) Monographs: 48,538. Bound serials: 4243 volumes. Current
     serials received: 73. Total serials in stock: 168. Non-book ma-
     terials: 4097 microfilms. 390 colour slides; 6b) Whitney

14 SEELEY HISTORICAL LIBRARY (continued)
Collection (medieval ecclesiastical history); Gray Collection
(African history); Harper Collection (Commonwealth history);
Hadley Collection (French Revolution and Napoleonic era);
Symonds Collection (tracts). Microfilms of British Cabinet
papers; Colonial Office confidential print, 1642-1925; German
naval archives; American state papers; Papal registers and other
ecclesiastical archives; Colborne papers (Canadian archives);
Kenya national archives.

a) Open access. Own classification scheme; 7b) General catalogue—
alphabetical sequence of entries for authors and for persons who
are the subjects of books (biographies, etc). Supplementary
catalogue consists of a sequence for the publications of learned
societies; a catalogue of periodical articles (ie from all the periodicals in the library's stock); catalogue of pamphlet material.
Dictionary subject catalogue (not yet complete)

a) Open to all members of the university. Non-members of the university may use the library, at the librarian's discretion, but may
not have borrowing rights; 8b) Term: M-F 0845-1915, Sat to
1200 and 1400-1800. Vacation: M-F 0900-1700; 8c) The reading
area of the library accommodates over 300 students. Books are
available for loan to all members of the university, but the loan
period is restricted during term. The research room and the microfilm room are intended to meet the needs of graduate students.
The former houses a small collection of bibliographies etc and the
students can use the room to work in privacy. The microfilm
room mostly contains research material, and there are 5 microfilm readers and 1 microcard reader available for use. 4 portable
microfilm readers are kept available for loan. Xerox copying
facilities are available in the faculty building.

General guide to the library service mainly intended for freshmen.
Visitors guide to the library and its building intended for casual
visitors; List of periodical articles, issued monthly and circulated
to the faculty teaching officers.

15 SOUTH ASIAN STUDIES CENTRE LIBRARY
o) University of Cambridge, Centre of South Asian Studies
a) Faculty Rooms, Laundress Lane, Cambridge CB2 1SD; 2b) 0223-
65621

A J N Richards (Secretary-Librarian)

a) 1964; 4b) The library aims to organise and maintain a union catalogue of all modern South Asian material held in other libraries
in Cambridge, and to build up a reference library of such material
as is not otherwise available in Cambridge. The centre is also
gathering archival material relating to these countries under a
separate project.

a) Modern studies of South Asia; 5b) Principally the countries of
India, Pakistan, Bangladesh, Afghanistan, Nepal, Burma and Sri

115 SOUTH ASIAN STUDIES CENTRE LIBRARY (continued)
Lanka. Plans to extend coverage to South-east Asian material
where relevant

6a) Bookstock: 12,000 volumes (monographs and bound serials).
Pamphlets and offprints: 3000 items. Current serials received:
176 titles. Serials retained: 308 titles. Small map collection;
6b) Cambridge South Asian Archive; collection of Indian newspapers on microfilm (1870 rolls)

7a) UDC; mostly open access; 7b) Author, subject and regional
catalogues, including union entries for relevant holdings elsewhere for South and South-east Asian material. Author index of
some periodicals

8a) Members of the university. Others by academic introduction;
8c) Reference only collection

9) Datta, R (comp) *Guide to South Asian material in the libraries of
London, Oxford and Cambridge* 1966; Datta, R (comp) *Union
catalogue of the Government of Pakistan publications held by
libraries in London, Oxford and Cambridge*, 1967.

116 UNIVERSITY COLLEGE, CARDIFF, THE LIBRARY
1b) University College, Cardiff
2a) PO Box 98, Cardiff CF1 1XQ; 2b) 0222-44211; 2c) 49635
ULIBCF
3) R J E Horrill BA
4a) 1883; 4b) To serve library needs of the college. All usual facilities provided, including inter-library loans service, photographic
and reprographic services, microform facilities, etc
5a) General; 5b) The Arts and Social Studies Library houses the administration, and the main arts and social sciences collections.
The main science collections are in the Pure Sciences and Applied
Sciences Libraries. There are also collections in the Departments
of Anatomy, Biochemistry, Music and Physiology, and the
Faculty of Education
6a) 400,000 volumes; 2500 current periodicals; 6b) Salisbury Library
(Welsh and Celtic); Mazzini and Tennyson Collections (works by
and about Mazzini and Tennyson); pre-1800 printed books
7a) Mostly open-access; Library of Congress Classification; 7b) Autho
and classified union catalogue. Catalogues in each separate library.
8a) Members of the college; staff and postgraduate students of UWIS1
and the Welsh National School of Medicine; others, for reference,
on written application; 8b) Closed on Saturdays in the Christmas
and summer vacations; 8c) Readers' adviser and some subject
specialist help. Information officer in Science Library
9) Readers' guide; Annual report; various specialised leaflets

117 CITY UNIVERSITY LIBRARY
1b) The City University
2a) Skinners' Library, St John Street, London EC1V 4PB; Business
School Library, Lionel Denny House, 23 Goswell Road, London

117 CITY UNIVERSITY LIBRARY (continued)
EC1M 7BB; 2b) 01-253-4399; 2c) 263896
3)   S J Teague BSc(Econ) FLA FRSA
4a)   Founded as Northampton Institute in 1891, The City University
       received its charter in 1966. The new library building was occu-
       pied in 1970; 4b) The university library provides books, period-
       icals and other media for the use of members of staff of the uni-
       versity, postgraduate students, and undergraduates. It also pro-
       vides an information service and instruction on the use of the li-
       brary and literature.
5a)   Engineering; applied science; social science; optics
6a)   166,000 volumes; 1500 current periodicals. 10,000 microforms;
       6b) London Society Library; Walter Fincham Collection (optics);
       Erna Auerbach Collection; the Library of Tracked Hovercraft
       Ltd
7a)   Dewey Decimal Classification; 7b) Name catalogue and classified
       catalogue (not comprehensive for pre-1970 stock); catalogue on
       microfiche (1976- stock) and cards (pre-1976 stock). Alphabeti-
       cal subject index. Periodicals catalogue
8a)   Members of the university. Others for reference on written appli-
       cation; 8b) Skinners' Library—Term: M-Th 0900-2100, Fri to
       2000, Sat 0930-1230. Vacation; M-F 1700. Business School
       Library—Term: M-Th 0900-2000, Fri 0900-1800. Vacation M-F
       0900-1700; 8c) General enquiries to reference librarian; Infor-
       mation and Research Division provides reference and user edu-
       cation services
9)   Introductory guide; Periodicals list; Finding information; Cata-
       logue of the London Collection
10)   Enright, B J 'The university library: key to education and com-
       munication' *Quest* 4 March 1968, pp6-14; Lewis, P 'Putting the
       new Skinners' Library to work' *Quest* 16 March 1971, pp6-9;
       Hancock, M M 'Media resources in the Skinners' Library' *Quest*
       27, summer 1974, pp25-27; Corney, E 'The information service
       in practice: an experiment at the City University Library' *Journal
       of librarianship* 1 (4) 1969, pp225-235.

118   CRANFIELD INSTITUTE OF TECHNOLOGY LIBRARY
1b)   Cranfield Institute of Technology
2a)   Cranfield, Bedford MK43 OAL; 2b) 0234-750111; 2c) 825072
3)   Professor C W Cleverdon
4a)   Founded as the College of Aeronautics in 1946, the institute
       received its charter in 1969
5a)   Engineering; management; 5b) The main library houses the stock
       on science and technology. There are separate School of Manage-
       ment, Centre for Transport Studies, and National College of Agri-
       cultural Engineering Libraries
6a)   100,000 volumes; 1000 current periodicals
8a)   Members of the institute. Others, for reference, on written appli-
       cation; 8b) Closed Sat

119　UNIVERSITY LIBRARY, DUNDEE

1b)　University of Dundee

2a)　Dundee DD1 4HN; Ninewells Medical Library, Ninewells Hospital
　　　and Medical School, Dundee DD1 9SY; 2b) 0382-23181; Ninewells
　　　Medical Library: 0382-60111; 2c) 76293 UNIVLIB DUNDEE

3)　J R Barker MA FLA

4a)　The university was founded in 1883. The Ninewells Medical Li-
　　　brary opened in 1974; 4b) To provide materials and services as
　　　appropriate in support of the teaching and research programmes
　　　conducted by the university. Collections very largely open-
　　　access and borrowable; ILL; photographic service; all types of
　　　microform reading facilities; AV equipment.

5a)　Arts and social sciences; engineering and applied science; environ-
　　　mental studies; law; medicine and dentistry; science; 5b) There
　　　are separate Law and Ninewells Medical Libraries, and 16 de-
　　　partmental libraries. Member of Scottish Libraries Cooperative
　　　Automation Project

6a)　350,000 volumes. 4300 current serials. c4750 serials retained.
　　　Large collections of non-book materials (mss, slides, photographs,
　　　maps, microforms etc); 6b) Brechin Diocesan Library (including
　　　incunabula, illuminated manuscripts); Thoms Collection (mineral-
　　　ogy); Valentine Collection (medical education); oil and gas law;
　　　local business archives; Leng Collection (Scottish philosophy);
　　　William Lyon MacKenzie Collection (Canadiana); Nicoll Collec-
　　　tion (fine arts); European Documentation Centre

7a)　Dewey Decimal Classification; Moys Classification (Law Library);
　　　own classification (Ninewells Medical Library); 7b) Author cata-
　　　logue; classified catalogue; subject index card to December 1977.
　　　Fiche January 1978-

8a)　Members of the university; others, for reference, on written appli-
　　　cation or with full library privileges, on payment of annual sub-
　　　scriptions; 8b) Standard hours; main library reading room open on
　　　Sunday during term 1200-1800; 8c) Reader advisory service in
　　　main library and Ninewells Medical Library. Instruction to
　　　readers in use of the library and its collections provided both
　　　formally and informally at all levels.

9)　Library guide; Annual reports; guides to particular collections

120　UNIVERSITY LIBRARY, DURHAM

1b)　University of Durham

2a)　Palace Green, Durham DH1 3RN (phone 0385-61262/3); Science
　　　Section, Science Site, University of Durham, South Road,
　　　Durham (phone 0385-64971); Oriental Section, University of
　　　Durham, Elvet Hill, Durham (phone 0385-64731).

3)　Miss A M McAulay BA, FLA

4a)　The university was founded in 1832; The main library is housed
　　　in a series of buildings, built from the 15th to 20th centuries,
　　　including an extension occupied in 1967

20 UNIVERSITY LIBRARY, DURHAM (continued)
a) General, except medicine and architecture; 5b) The library comprises the main library, science section and oriental section
a) 481,000 volumes. 3400 current serials; 6b) Oriental collections, including the Sudan Archive; Gunn Collection (Egyptology); Cant and Yetts Collection (Far Eastern); early printed books and manuscripts, including Cosin, Routh and Winterbottom Collections; local material; English Printed Background Material Scheme (1670-1689); European Documentation Centre
a) Members of the university; others, for reference, on written application; 8b) Standard hours
) Special guides; Annual reports; 10) Burnett, A D 'History of science in Durham libraries' *British journal for the history of science* 8, 1975, 94-99; Doyle, S M 'Law in Durham University Library' *Law librarian* 8, 1977, 19-21.

21 UNIVERSITY OF EAST ANGLIA LIBRARY
) University of East Anglia
) University Plain, Norwich NR4 7TJ; 2b) 0603-56161; 2c) 97154
 W L Guttsman MSc (Econ)
) The university received its charter in 1964. The library building was occupied in 1968, with an extension added in 1974; 4b) The academic needs of the university
) Humanities, social sciences, pure sciences, law and education; 5b) Senior staff act as subject specialists
) Total stock: c360,000 including c2000 periodical titles, c2300 non-book materials; 6b) Military history; Abbott Collection (English Literature); Ketton-Cremer Collection (local history)
) Open-access. Library of Congress (modified) Classification; 7b) Name, subject and periodicals catalogues. Short-title computerised catalogue.
) Members and staff of the university and affiliated institutes. Other persons admitted at the discretion of the librarian; 8b) Term: M-F 0900-2200; Sat to 1700; Sun to 1900. Vacation: 0900-1800 (M-F only); 8c) Enquiry desk; audiovisual service; restricted loan collection; photocopying; record library. Subject specialists offer bibliographic advice.
 Annual report; Library guide; Union list of periodicals in Norwich (presently being revised);

22 EDINBURGH UNIVERSITY LIBRARY
) University of Edinburgh
) George Square, Edinburgh EH8 9LJ. Central Medical Library and Medical Reading Room, School of Medicine, Teviot Place, Edinburgh EH8 9AG. Centre of European Governmental Studies Library and Law Library, Old College, South Bridge, Edinburgh EH8 9YL. New College Library, Mound Place, Edinburgh EH1 2LU. Reid Music Library, Alison House, Nicolson Square, Edinburgh EH8 9BH. Veterinary Library, Royal (Dick) School of Veterinary

122 EDINBURGH UNIVERSITY LIBRARY (continued)
Studies, Summerhall, Edinburgh EH9 1QH; 2b) 031-667-1011
3)   E R S Fifoot MC MA ALA
4a) The library was founded in 1580. The present main library build-
     ing was occupied in 1967; 4b) University library
5a) General academic subjects; 5b) The university library includes the
     following libraries: Central Medical, Centre of African Studies,
     Centre of European Governmental Studies, Law, New College
     (Theological), Reid Music, Veterinary, School of Scottish Studies.
     There are approximately 70 departmental libraries which hold
     only duplicate material, except for: dentistry, psychiatry, social
     medicine and the science departments.
6a) 700,000 volumes (main library); 2700 current periodicals (main
     library);
6b) Clement Litil Collection; Drummond of Hawthornden Collection;
     Halliwell-Phillips Collections (Shakespeare, drama). Cameron Col-
     lection (Celtic); Forbes Collection (Philippines); W B Hodgson Col
     lection (history of economics); Bruce Collection (oceanography);
     Geikie Collection (geology offprints); Murray Collection (zoology
     geography, geology); Cleghorn Collection (forestry); Thomson-
     Walker Collection (portraits of medical men); Agriculture Collec-
     tion (18th and 19th century); Appleton Collection (books and
     papers of Sir Edward Appleton); Royal Physical Society Library;
     Royal Scottish Forestry Society Library; Edinburgh Geological
     Society Library; Adam Smith's Library; Dugald Stewart Collec-
     tion; Records of Scottish firms: shipping, whaling, publishing,
     distilling, tweed manufacturing
        Manuscripts: Laing Collection (medieval, miscellaneous); Halli-
     well-Phillips Collection; Scottish Literary Renaissance Collection
     (McDiarmid, MacCaig, Cruickshank, G M Brown); John Wain Col-
     lection.
7a) Much of the collection is open-access. Main library uses Dewey
     Decimal Classification (modified); 7b) Name catalogue (typed-
     volume form, union catalogue for university library); subject
     catalogue (sheaf, entries for post-1915 books only); current
     serials catalogue; Chinese books catalogue; audio catalogue; read-
     ing room catalogue; statistical reference catalogue; government
     publications catalogue; maps and atlases catalogue. All catalogues
     except the name catalogue, for main library only. Separate cata-
     logues in other libraries.
8a) Members of the university; General Council subscribers; others,
     for reference, on written application; 8b) standard hours: vary
     from section to section; 8c) Usual university library services
9)   Guide to the library; Annual reports; Catalogue of the printed
     books in the Library of the University of Edinburgh 3 vols, 1919-
     1923; *Index to manuscripts: Edinburgh University library* 2 vols,
     Boston, G K Hall, 1964; various other catalogues and publi-
     cations

23   UNIVERSITY OF ESSEX LIBRARY
 b)   University of Essex
 a)   PO Box 24, Colchester CO4 3UA; 2b) 0206-44144; 2c) 98440
       UNILIB COLCHSTR
)   F J Friend BA AKC Dip Lib
 a)   The university received its charter in 1965. The library building
       was occupied in 1967
 a)   General range of subjects
 a)   245,000 volumes; 2800 current serials; 6b) Slavonic materials;
       Latin American materials; Society for Cultural Relations with the
       USSR Collection (journals); S L Bensuson Collection; John Hassall
       Collection; Rowhedge Ironworks archives; Bassingbourn Parish
       Library; Gaudier-Brzeska papers
 a)   Library of Congress Classification; 7b) Name catalogue (slips)
       Classified subject catalogue (slips); alphabetical subject index;
       periodicals catalogue (title and institution entries); government
       publications catalogue (British parliamentary papers only)
 a)   Members of the university; others, for reference, on written appli-
       cation; 8b) Open on Sunday afternoons in term; closed on Satur-
       days in vacation
)   Guide to the use of the library; Reference booklets; Bibliographies
       (of reference materials held by the Library)

24   EXETER UNIVERSITY LIBRARY
 b)   University of Exeter
 a)   Prince of Wales Road, Exeter EX4 4PT; 2b) 0392-77911;
       2c) 42894 EXUNIV G
)   J F Stirling JP MA
 a)   University College of the South-west of England was recognised
       as a university institution in 1922; it became the University of
       Exeter in 1955; 4b) Primarily to serve the staff and students of
       the university and then, as far as possible, the community and
       beyond
 a)   General; 5b) The Roborough Reading Room contains under-
       graduate materials. The Library also staffs and administers the
       Law Library, School of Education Library, Exeter Cathedral Li-
       brary and Archives, Library of the Devon and Exeter Institution.
 a)   500,000 volumes; 3000 current periodicals, 50,000 records, tapes
       and microforms; 6b) Crediton Parochial Library; Dodderidge
       Theological Library; Ottery St Mary Parochial Library; Totnes
       Parochial Library; Ghana Collection (part of 'area specialisation
       scheme' of SCOLMA);
 7a)   Mainly open-access. Dewey Decimal Classification; 7b) Union
       catalogue of most university holdings: name, subject, classified
       catalogue and index, conference index, periodicals, mss/autographs/
       bookplates. Card catalogues being replaced by microfiche.
 8a)   Members of the university; others, for reference, on written appli-
       cation; 8b) Standard hours. Roborough Reading Room open on

124   EXETER UNIVERSITY LIBRARY (continued)
some Sundays in term; 8c) Enquiry desk service; 'subject specialisation', bibliographical tours and seminars on request; inter-
library loan service; photographic and reprographic services (including some self-service)

9)   'Beethoven and England 1793-1855', Catalogue of a bi-centenary
exhibition at the university library, March 2nd-25th, 1970; 'A
Catalogue of Italian Books 1471-1600 in the Libraries of Exeter
University, Exeter Cathedral and the Devon & Exeter Institution'
with 184 illustrations, comp Roberto L Bruni and D Wyn Evans
(in preparation); Classified list of books catalogued (monthly, free
on special application); Devon union list: A Collection of written
material relating to Devon by Allan Brockett; Folklore, a list of
books in the university library, 3rd edn, 1972 (free); Ghana collection list of holdings, 1976 (free); Index to theses accepted for high
degrees 4th edn, 1955-1975; Information leaflets at present include the following: 2 Some guides to the literature of science and
technology, 4 The card catalogues and how to use them, 5 History
and the Decimal Classification, 7 Departmental collections, 8 A
short guide to government publications, 19 Report literature,
20 A short guide to chemistry, 21 Guide to economic history,
24 Spanish & Portuguese studies (all free); An introduction to the
law library and the law collection (free); Library guide (Annual:
free); Library information sheets (For most subjects, principally
designed for internal use; free); A list of books in the university
library of the University of Exeter in Spanish and Portuguese or
on Spanish and Portuguese topics which are not on general access
comp R Hitchcock, 1975 (free); Lloyd, L J The Library of Exeter
Cathedral . . . with a description of the archives by A M Erskine
. . . 1967, repr 1974; Manuscript collections (free); Photocopying
services and regulations (free); Self-guided tour (broadsheet, free);
A Spanish-English Vocabulary Book in Exeter: an edition of 'A
compendious manual of the Spanish Dictionarie' with an introduction by C F Scott, 1972; Special collections in the university library (free); Subject guides to the library: 2 Guide to statistical
sources in the library (free), 3 The American west: a bibliography
of books in Exeter University library by June Cooling, 1973;
Subject specialisation at Exeter University Library (free);
Union list of current publications at the University of Exeter,
1976. (first issued in 1974; supplement 1975) 1978 ed in preparation;

10)   Guthrie, D H and Scott, C F 'A progress report on the Ghana
Collection at Exeter University Library, a part of SCOLMA's
"area specialisation plan", from 1969-1973' *African research and
documentation* no 3, 1973, pp9-10; Lloyd, L J 'Exeter', in 'Four
university libraries' *The library world* vol 68 March 1967 pp239-53
Scott, C F 'Ghana' in Standing Conference on Library Materials
on Africa: *Conference on acquisition of material from Africa*, Zug,
1969; Scott, C F 'Microform provision at Exeter University Library
Microdoc vol 13, no 3, 1974, pp75-79.

25 GLASGOW UNIVERSITY LIBRARY
1b) University of Glasgow
2a) Hillhead Street, Glasgow G12 8QE (University Library—phone: 041-334-2122); Veterinary Branch Library, Veterinary Hospital, Bearsden Road, Glasgow G61 1QH (phone 041-942-2301); Soviet and East European Studies Branch Library, Institute of Soviet and East European Studies, 10 Southpark Terrace, Glasgow G12 8LQ (phone 041-339-8855); Dental Branch Library, Dental Hospital & School, 211 Renfrew Street, Glasgow G2 3JZ (phone 041-332-7020); 2c) 778421 GLASUL
3) H J Heaney MA FLA
4a) The university was founded in 1451. The library has had a continuous history for over 400 years, and during this time has attracted a large number of gifts and bequests. The most important of these is the collection of c10,000 volumes bequeathed by William Hunter in 1783. The largest single gift is that from the General Assembly of the Church of Scotland in 1974 of the library of Trinity College, Glasgow, which comprises over 75,000 volumes. The library enjoyed copyright deposit from Stationers' Hall from 1709 until 1836 when it was commuted to an annual payment from the Treasury of £707, which is still received.
4b) Serves the university community of over 12,000 students and staff, and is also extensively used by scholars, not only from the west of Scotland but also from all over the world. The majority of the collections are on open-access for consultation by all readers; most of the books are available for loan to registered readers. Other facilities available include reference and enquiry services, inter-library loans, photocopying, use of microforms and audiovisual materials
5a) Whole range of university interests for the faculties of arts, divinity, engineering, law, medicine (including dentistry), science, social sciences, and veterinary medicine; 5b) Main stock of veterinary medicine, Soviet & East European studies, dentistry, and chemistry in branch libraries. About 90 faculty, departmental and class libraries, the stock of which mainly duplicates that in the university library. An undergraduate reading room serves the needs of first and second year undergraduates with a closed-access short-loan collection. Wide subject coverage, special strengths include Glasgow and west of Scotland history, the history of science, theology, and medical and life sciences. Latin America and Soviet and East European area studies. Background material scheme of JSCLC (1690-1699).
6a) Books & bound periodicals: 1,250,000. Pamphlets: 43,000. Manuscripts: 13,000. Maps: 11,000. Microforms: 60,000. Theses: 7500. Bound parliamentary papers: 5000. Current serial titles received: 8025. Serial titles retained (current and dead) c20,000; 6b) Hunterian Collection (incunabula, manuscripts); Euing Collection (Bibles, black-letter ballads, 15th and 16th century books); Euing Music Collection (scores, early printed music, history of music); Ferguson Collection (history of chemistry,

125　GLASGOW UNIVERSITY LIBRARY (continued)
alchemy, demonology, witchcraft); Hamilton Collection (philosophy); T K Munro Collection (editions of Sir Thomas Browne);
David Murray Collection (local history; Ogilvie Collection (17th
century material, Civil War pamphlets); Simson Collection (early
mathematics works); Spencer Collection (books and manuscripts
relating to the Darien scheme); Stirling Maxwell Collection (emblem
books); Veitch Collection (medieval philosophy); Whistler Collection (papers of James McNeill Whistler); Wylie Collection (history
and antiquities of Glasgow); Eadie Collection (Biblical studies,
early printing); Mearns Collection (hymnology); Tischendorf Collection (Biblical studies, codicology; Near Eastern typography);
European Documentation Centre. Dougan Collection (D O Hill
photographs); Farmer Collection (oriental music); McEwen,
MacCunn, Stillie Collections (all music); Kelvin (papers & pamphlets; Citizens' Theatre (prompt books, photographs & other
records). Geological Society of Glasgow—foreign periodicals
formerly in their library; Institution of Engineers & Shipbuilders
in Scotland—those books and periodicals from their library not
already in the university library

7a)　Majority of material on open-access. Eclectic classification
scheme based mainly on Library of Congress. Some material still
in fixed location (press-marked) within broad subject groups;
7b) Name catalogues—Guard book to 1967; Sheaf catalogue
(AACR). All items catalogued since 1968; Supplementary catalogue for pamphlets, some donations, and works considered to
be of lesser importance acquired between 1930 and 1967; Union
catalogue of holdings in departmental libraries. Classified subject
catalogue (excludes material still press-marked); periodicals card
catalogue; short-title computer listing of periodicals; thesis catalogue; map catalogue; various special indexes of rare books and
manuscripts;

8a)　Open to staff, students and employees of the university; graduates of Scottish universities; and others by arrangement at the
librarian's discretion; 8b) Term: M-F 0900-2130, Sat to 1230
(Reading Room 1300-2130 only), Sun closed (Reading Room
1400-2000 only); Vacation: M-F 0900-1700, Sat to 1230;
Closed Christmas Day, New Year's Day and the next working
day, but open on other public holidays; 8c) Study places (975 in
university library, 510 in reading room), study rooms for research
workers, seminar rooms, enquiry and general information services
from 10 service points, loans, and short loans of material in great
demand, inter-library loans, Xerox copying, instruction in the use
of the library, Medline.

9)　Reader's guide to the university library (annual); Student's guide
to the reading room (annual); Directory of departmental libraries
3rd ed, 1975; Current scientific periodicals in Glasgow University
Library, 2nd ed, 1976 (ULP 1); British government publications

25 GLASGOW UNIVERSITY LIBRARY (continued)
in GUL 2nd ed, 1978 (ULP 2); Engineering reference sources in
GUL 2nd ed, 1977 (ULP 3); Slavonic and East European studies:
selected reference works in the University of Glasgow, 1977
(ULP 4); Brief notes on some of the more important collections
in . . . special collections, 1977 (ULP 5); Kelvin papers; index to
the manuscript collection of William Thomson, Baron Kelvin in
GUL, 1977 (ULP 6); Some tools for scientific information search—
chemistry, 1977 (ULP 7); Some tools for scientific information
search and reference—zoology, 1977 (ULP 8); The catalogue hall—
what's in it for you? (A guide to the contents of the Catalogue
Hall and General Reference Division of GUL), 1977 (ULP 9);
Some tools for scientific information search—physics, 1977 (ULP
10); English language and literature: a selective guide to reference
material, 1978 (ULP 11); Psychiatry in Glasgow University Library,
1978 (ULP 12); Searching the literature—physiology, 1978 (ULP
13); Geography, a selective guide to reference material, 1978
(ULP 14); Glasgow University Library visitor's guide, 1978 (ULP
15); also exhibition catalogues, and a number of smaller subject
guides; Printed catalogues of the Hunterian books and the Hunterian mss

0) Medieval manuscripts other than Hunterian are fully described in
N R Ker, *Medieval manuscripts in British libraries* vol 2, 1977;
MacKenna, R O 'University of Glasgow Library' *Encyclopedia of
library and information science* vol 10 (New York, 1973), pp19-
26; MacKenna, R O 'Subject-divisional organization in a major
Scottish research library' *Of one accord: essays in honour of
W B Paton* (ed) P McAdams, Glasgow, 1977, pp99-109; Rodger,
E M 'University of Glasgow—information services and reader
instruction' *ISG news*: newsletter of the SCONUL Information
Services Group, no 2 (1976), pp7-9; Black, H M and Gaskell, P
'Special collections in Glasgow University Library' *The book
collector* vol 16 no 2 (1967), pp161-168; 'Building study: library
at Glasgow University'. *Architects' journal* vol 149 no 16 (16
April 1969), pp1043-1058; Baldwin, J 'Glasgow University Library's manuscripts: the non-Hunterian collections'; Black, H M
'The Stirling Maxwell collection of emblem books in Glasgow University Library'; Durkan, J 'The early history of Glasgow University Library 1475-1710' *The bibliotheck*, vol 8 nos 4-6 (1977),
pp102-147.

126 HERIOT-WATT UNIVERSITY LIBRARY Cameron Smail Library
1b) Heriot-Watt University
2a) Main Library Riccarton, Currie, Edinburgh EH14 4AS; Chambers
Street Library, Chambers Street, Edinburgh EH1 1HX; Mountbatten Library, Grassmarket, Edinburgh EH1 2HT (unstaffed
reference room, language dictionaries and electrical engineering
textbooks only); Ethicon Library, 79 Grassmarket, Edinburgh

126 HERIOT-WATT UNIVERSITY LIBRARY (continued)
EH1 2HJ (pharmacy only); 2b) 031-449-5111; Central Edinburgh libraries 031-225-8432

3) A Anderson MA FLA

4a) Heriot-Watt received its charter as a university in 1966, but was founded as a Mechanic's Institute in 1821 (Edinburgh School of Arts, Watt Institution) and became a higher technical institution in 1885 (Heriot-Watt College); 4b) Aims to be a service and reader oriented library, with maximum direct relevance to subjects taught and researched in university, but also to serve local industry (c100 firms use library), and cooperates with other local libraries informally and through Scottish (NLS) Cooperative Acquisitions Scheme; Two main libraries, both with reasonably full normal range of facilities, eg microform reader/printers, xerox, AV and TV equipment

5a) Science, engineering, social sciences, languages (for interpreters and translators); 5b) The main Riccarton Library covers mathematical and physical sciences. Other libraries are the Chambers Street Library (life sciences, brewing, building, civil and chemical engineering, electrical engineering, computer science, social sciences, languages); the Ethicon Library (pharmacy); Collection on History of Heriot-Watt College and University. Special interest in brewing

6a) c95,000 volumes. 1500 current periodicals; 6b) University historical collection, covering history of institution 1821 to date. Includes material relating to James Watt, Leonard Horner (founder of School of Arts, first warden of University College London, notable factory inspector). Other materials relating to people connection with institution; also institutional archives; Manuscript of/about Sir Robert Blair, 1st Chief Education Officer of London County Council (1904-1924). Strongest collections in chemistry, physics, biological sciences, especially marine biology, pharmacy, electrical engineering (fair historical collection), brewing (only undergraduate course in Britain; comprehensiveness intended, not yet achieved)

7a) Open-access; Dewey Decimal Classification; 7b) Author catalogue (Berghoeffer), classified catalogue, computer produced KWIC index (except literary texts);

8a) Members of university; others, for reference (borrowing in suitable cases), on written application; 8b) Riccarton, open Sat and Sun in term; all libraries closed Sat and Sun in vacations; 8c) Normal range of reader bibliographical information services: reader instruction using tape/slides, hand-outs and practical work where feasible

9) Library guide; Annual reports; Periodicals list; sundry instructional leaflets

10) Anderson, A 'Heriot-Watt University' in K W Neal *British academic libraries* 1973.

27 BRYNMOR JONES LIBRARY, HULL
1b) University of Hull
2a) Hull HU6 7RX; 2b) 0482-46311; 2c) 52530
3) P A Larkin CBE MA DLitt FRSL
4a) The university, formerly University College of Hull (founded in 1927), received charter in 1954. The east building of the Brynmor Jones Library was opened in 1959, and the west building, a 7-floor extension, in 1969
5a) General range of subjects; 5b) There are departmental collections in social sciences, chemistry, education and geography, primarily for undergraduate use
6a) 502,000 volumes; 6300 current periodicals; 6b) South-east Asian studies; British labour history; 20th century left-wing movements; emigration to America; German expression; medieval France; modern British and American poetry; European Documentation Centre; English printed background material scheme (1860-1869)
7a) Oepn-access; Library of Congress Classification; 7b) Name catalogue and classified catalogue (cards; entries for books, periodicals, NBM, theses, books on order; parliamentary papers are excluded); periodicals catalogue (current periodicals); South-east Asian studies catalogue
8a) Members of the university; members of the universities of Bradford, Leeds, Sheffield and York, for reference; others, for reference, on written application; 8b) Standard hours
9) Readers' guide; Reports for the session; Readers' handbooks
10) Crowther, P A 'Russian studies and library materials at the University of Hull' *Solanus* 10, 1975, pp4-9

28 UNIVERSITY LIBRARY, KEELE
1b) University of Keele
2a) Keele ST5 5BG; 2b) 0782-71371; 2c) 36113
3) S O Stewart MA ALA
4a) University College of North Staffordshire was founded in 1949, and became the University of Keele in 1962
5a) Humanities; social sciences; experimental science
6a) 359,000 volumes; 2000 current periodicals; 6b) Turner Collection (history of mathematics and allied subjects); William Blake; Izaak Walton; Private presses; Sneyd, Wedgwood and Spode papers; Arnold Bennett manuscripts; Department of Geography houses the National Air Photographic Library (mainly 1939-1945 material; access by prior arrangement)
7a) Library of Congress Classification; 7b) Author/title and subject catalogues
8a) Members of the university; others, for reference, on written application

135

129 UNIVERSITY OF KENT AT CANTERBURY LIBRARY
1b) University of Kent at Canterbury
2a) Canterbury CT2 7NU; 2b) 0227-66822; 2c) 965449
3)   W J Simpson BA Dip Lib ALA FRSA
4a) 1964; 4b) Library houses the Centre for the Study of Cartoons
5a) General, excluding engineering and medicine
6a) 350,000 volumes; 3500 current periodicals; 6b) John Crow Col-
     lection (early English literature); Frank Pettingell Collection (19th
     century plays, manuscripts and printed books); Lloyd George
     Collection; Cartoon Collection (originals of newspaper cartoons)
7a) Library of Congress Classification; 7b) Author and classified cata-
     logues; subject index
8a) Members of the university; others, for reference, on written appli-
     cation; 8b) Open on Sun afternoons in term
9)   Library handbook; Subject guides; Information sheets

130 UNIVERSITY OF LANCASTER LIBRARY
1b) University of Lancaster
2a) Bailrigg, Lancaster LA1 4YH; 2b) 0524-65201; 2c) 65111
     UNIVLIB LANCSTR
3)   A Davies BA ALA
4a) The university was granted its charter in 1964. The library was
     built in stages, 1964-70; 4b) To provide a library service (includ-
     ing audiovisual media) to an expanding and innovatory university.
5a) General range of subjects.
6a) 420,000 items (includes c 270,000 bound volumes); 3100 current
     periodicals; 6b) Arabic and Islamic Collection; Comenius Library
     (central and south-east Europe); Fell and Rock Climbing Club of
     the English Lake District; Ford Collection (railways); Hans Ferdin-
     and Redlich Collection (music); Quaker Collection
7a) Open-access (two-thirds), closed-access basement stack. Bliss
     Classification; 7b) Name catalogue; classified catalogue; computer
     print-out; subject index
8a) Members of the university; others, for reference, on written ap-
     plication; 8b) Closed on Sat and Sun in vacation; 8c) Information
     and bibliographical service founded on a corps of assistant (sub-
     ject) librarians.
9)   Reports of the librarian; Bibliographic guides; Occasional papers;
     Miscellaneous publications; Guide to the library.
10) Andrews, J S 'Some early Quaker material in the University of
     Lancaster Library' *Gutenberg-Jahrbuch* 1976, 333-339; Univer-
     sity of Lancaster Library *Catalogue of the Hans Ferdinand Red-
     lich Collection of musical books and scores* Lancaster, the Li-
     brary, 1976.

131 LEEDS UNIVERSITY LIBRARY
1b) University of Leeds
2a) Leeds LS2 9JT; 2b) 0532-31751
3)   D Cox BA ALA

(continued)

4a)   Founded as the Yorkshire College of Science in 1874, established
       as an independent university in 1904. Of the present main build-
       ings the Brotherton Library was opened in 1935, the South Library
       in 1975 and the Medical and Dental Library in 1977; 4b) Supports
       the teaching and research of parent institution. Principal facilities:
       loan and enquiry service (including inter-library loan), microform
       reading, photocopying and audiovisual services.

5a)   Virtually all academic subjects; 5b) The university library com-
       prises the Brotherton Library (humanities and social sciences);
       the South Library (sciences and general student collections); the
       Medical and Dental Library; the Education Library; the Law Li-
       brary; the Clothworkers' Library (textiles) and many departmental
       libraries;

6a)   1,340,000 volumes; 8000 current periodicals; 116,000 microforms;
       6b) Brotherton Collection (rare books and manuscripts, especially
       English 17th to 19th centuries; Yorkshire local history and top-
       ography; Romany literature); Icelandic and Scandinavian Collec-
       tion; Anglo-French Collection (books before 1805: translations
       into French of English books and French books about Britain);
       Harold Whitaker Collection (maps and atlases); All Souls Collec-
       tion (early science and theology); Leeds Philosophical and Literary
       Society Library; Chaston Chapman Library (chemistry); Blanche
       Leigh and John F Preston Collection (cookery); Holden Library
       (theology); Yorkshire Geological Society Library; Roth Collection
       (post-Biblical Judaica); European Documentation Centre; Canadian
       government publications

7a)   The greater part of the library's stock, with the exception of special
       collections, is on open access. Own classification scheme;
       7b) Union name catalogue; separate periodicals and classified cata-
       logues; COM catalogue (author and title sequences) of the student
       library collections

8a)   All staff and students of the university, members of other insti-
       tutions or bodies with which an agreement about admission has
       been concluded; others may be admitted on written application to
       the librarian; 8b) Term: M-F 0900-2200, Sat to 1300, Sun (South
       Library only) 1400-1900. Christmas and Easter vacations: M-F
       0900-2100, Sat to 1230; Summer vacation: M-F 0900-1700, Sat
       to 1230; 8c) General enquiry service, reinforced by subject con-
       sultants covering all subjects, is available to users. The Oncology
       Information Service serves Yorkshire and selected subscribers
       further afield

9)   Numerous brief guides, and the following printed publications.
       Annual reports of the Brotherton Collection Committee; Current
       periodicals in the university libraries; Offor, R 'A descriptive guide
       to the libraries of the University of Leeds' 1947; Whitaker, H
       'The Harold Whitaker collection of county atlases, road books and
       maps presented to the University of Leeds; a catalogue' 1947;
       The Brotherton Collection: a brief description, 1953; A catalogue
       of German literature printed in the 17th and 18th centuries, 1973;

131   LEEDS UNIVERSITY LIBRARY (continued)
      Supplement, 1976; A century of benefactors: an exhibition of
      manuscripts and printed books commemorating gifts made to the
      libraries of the University of Leeds 1874-1974, 1974; Annual report
10)   Cox, D 'University of Leeds Library' *Encyclopedia of library and
      information science* vol 14, (ed) A Kent, H Lancour and J Daily.
      New York, 1975, pp130-140; Page, B S and Masson, D I 'Brother-
      ton Collection University of Leeds' *Encyclopedia of library and
      information science* vol 3. New York, 1970. pp359-367;

132   LEICESTER UNIVERSITY LIBRARY
1b)   University of Leicester
2a)   University Road, Leicester LE1 7RH; 2b) 0533-50000; 2c) 341198
      LEICUL G
3)   D G F Walker MA LIB ALA
4a)   The University College of Leicester was founded in 1918; received
      its charter as a university in 1957; The library building was of-
      ficially opened in 1975
5a)   General; 5b) Separate School of Education Library
6a)   450,000 volumes; 4500 current periodicals; 6b) Robjohn Collec-
      tion (Bibles); works of Bunyan; Halton Library (topography);
      Transport History Collection; the Library of the Mathematical
      Association; European Documentation Centre; English local
      history (all localities)
7a)   Open-access; Dewey Decimal Classification; 7b) Name catalogue
      (on cards; contains title entries for post-1969 books, and some
      series entries); classified catalogue (on cards); subject index (to
      certain sections of science only); periodicals list
8a)   Members of the university; others, for reference, on written ap-
      plication; 8b) Closed Sat; 8c) Reference and Information Depart-
      ment responsible for the enquiry desk, the reference collection
      (including secondary services), and user instruction
9)   Guide to the library; Advisory leaflets
10)   Goodstein, R L 'The Mathematical Association Library at the
      University of Leicester' *British journal for the history of science*
      7, 1974, pp100-103

133   UNIVERSITY OF LIVERPOOL LIBRARY
1b)   University of Liverpool
2a)   Sydney Jones Library, PO Box 123, Liverpool L69 3DA;
      2b) 051-709-6022; 2c) 627095
3)   V E Knight MA
4a)   Liverpool University College was founded in 1881, becoming an
      independent university in 1903. The Harold Cohen Library
      opened in 1938, the Sydney Jones Library in 1976; 4b) Serves
      the university community in its teaching and research functions.
5a)   General; 5b) Sydney Jones Library (arts and social sciences)
      Harold Cohen Library (sciences) are the main libraries. Associated

133   UNIVERSITY OF LIVERPOOL LIBRARY (continued)
with them are a number of specialised branch libraries in university departments. All are administered by the university librarian
6a)   820,000 volumes; 7000 current serials subscriptions; 6b) Latin-American Collections (especially Brazil and Peru); R A Scott Macfie Collection (gypsy books); 19th century children's fiction and school texts; Thomas Glazebrook Rylands Collection (early geography, astronomy, mathematics; local history of Lancashire and Cheshire); William Noble Collection (finely printed books, 1880-1910); Knowsley Collection (early books and 17th to 19th century English pamphlets); John Fraser Collection (tobacco, positivism, secularism, and Scottish material); Peers Collection (Spanish Civil War); Rathbone, Blanco White, Brunner and Glasier papers; Blake Collection (works by and about William Blake); selected modern poets
7a)   Library of Congress Classification; Universal Decimal Classification (engineering); Coates (music); Povey (local scheme); Open access except for special collections and Liverpool University theses; 7b) Arts and social sciences union name catalogue in Sydney Jones Library. Science and engineering union name catalogue in Harold Cohen Library; Each departmental library has name catalogue for its own stock. Finding-list of periodicals
8a)   Members of the university; others, for reference, on written applications; 8b) Branch departmental libraries closed Sats; 8c) Reader enquiry points in Sydney Jones Library, Harold Cohen Library, Law Library, Arts Reading Room, Education Library; Assistance to readers in use of bibliographic tasks. On-line bibliographic search service available, for which a charge is made.
9)   Annual reports; General and specialised notes for readers; Current periodicals finding list.
10)   Varley, D H 'Liverpool: University of Liverpool Library' *Encyclopedia of library and information science* vol 16, New York, Dekker, 1975, pp251-258; Talbot, J C 'SCOLMA area specialisation scheme: the acquisition of library materials of Spanish-speaking Africa by Liverpool University Library' *African research and documentation* 7, 1975, pp7-8

UNIVERSITY OF LONDON
The University of London is a federal institution. The main library serving all constituent institutions is the University of London Library at the Senate House, containing predominantly research material;
      The colleges are the main undergraduate teaching institutions, although they are all involved to a greater or lesser degree in post-graduate work. Undergraduate teaching also takes place at the schools—the London School of Economics, School of Oriental and African Studies and the School of Slavonic and East European Studies.

A high proportion of postgraduate work is carried out in the schools, and the institutes are almost exclusively concerned with this area. The institutes and schools possess libraries which range in size and scope of collections. Taking a general view the majority of research material is held in the school and institute libraries, although there are exceptions, notably University College London and King's College London.

There are 28 medical schools and institutes in the University of London. Libraries in these institutions are not listed in this publication, and for details the reader is referred to the *Directory of medical libraries in the British Isles* 3rd ed, London, Library Association (Medical Section), 1969; and to the less detailed 4th edition of the same work (published 1976).

For a recent account of libraries in the colleges and institutes of the University of London see: Richnell, D T 'London: University of London libraries' in: Kent, A (ed) *Encyclopedia of library and information science*, vol 16 New York, Dekker, 1975, pp289-335.

A guide to admission policies is provided by the following publication: *Guide to admission to libraries in the University of London* 4th rev ed, London, Library Resources Coordinating Committee, 1977. It is pointed out that individual library policy and details may be subject to change, and that a statement advising conditions of admission does not necessarily constitute a right of entry for any visitors.

134 **UNIVERSITY OF LONDON LIBRARY**
1b) University of London
2a) Senate House, Malet Street, London WC1E 7HU; 2b) 01-636-4514; 2c) 269400 UNILIBSEN LDN
3) D J Foskett (Director of Central Library Services and Goldsmith's Librarian)
4a) First established 1838 with further development in the 1870s. In 1900 the library collection was established at South Kensington, moving to Senate House in 1937-1938; 4b) The Senate House library provides a major research collection to serve the needs of all University of London institutions. Bibliography and reference collections in Middlesex North and South reading rooms.
5a) General range of subjects, but with major emphasis on the social sciences and humanities; 5b) Open-access subject specialist libraries in European history, geography and geology, Latin-American studies, music, palaeography, philosophy, psychology, United States studies.
6a) Bookstock: c one million volumes (monographs and bound serials). Current serials received: c5500 titles; 6b) Goldsmiths' Library of Economic literature (given by Professor H S Foxwell in 1903 comprising some 60,000 items); Sir Edward Durning-Lawrence

134 UNIVERSITY OF LONDON LIBRARY (continued)
Collection (Shakespeare and Bacon editions); Sir Louis Sterling
Collection (rare books); Augustus de Morgan Library (mathe-
matics and astronomy); George Grote Collection (classical litera-
ture); Bishop Porteous Library (theology); Harry Price Library
(magical literature); Broomhead Library (material relating to
London); British Psychological Society Library; Family Welfare
Association Library; Eliot Phelips Collection (early Spanish books);
Elzevir Collection (Elzevir press books); Austin Dobson Collection
(works about the poet); Edwin Deller Memorial Library; Carlton
Collection (shorthand); Society for Theatre Research Library;
Plainsong and Mediaeval Music Society Library; Malcolm Morley
Collection; Gregynog Press Collection; Belgian Library (ex-Belgian
Embassy); slide collection (architecture and fine arts)

7a) Bliss Classification; Dewey Decimal Classification; 7b) Author/title
catalogue and subject catalogue; numerous special catalogues

8a) Available to members of University of London

9)   Introductory guide; Annual report of the University Library Board;
Catalogue of the Goldsmiths' Library of Economic Literature
vols 1-3 Cambridge, CUP, 1971- *Volume 1 Printed books to 1800*
(1971); *Volume 2 Printed books 1801-50* (1975); Volume 3 (in
preparation); *Literary manuscripts in the University of London
Library*; *The palaeography collection in the University of London
Library; an author and subject catalogue* 2 volumes. Boston, G K
Hall, 1968

10) Rye, R A *Student's guide to the libraries of London* London, Uni-
versity of London, 3rd ed 1928, pp185-194; Pafford, J H P in:
Irwin, R and Staveley, R *The libraries of London* 2nd ed London,
Library Association 1964, pp140-156

135 BEDFORD COLLEGE LIBRARY
1a) University of London
2a) Inner Circle, Regent's Park, London NW1 4NS; 2b) 01-486-4400
3)   G M Paterson BA ALA
4a) The present library dates from 1913 (Tate Library), although the
college was originally founded in 1849; 4b) The library serves as an
undergraduate, postgraduate and research collection
5a) Languages, history, philosophy, social sciences, pure sciences,
physiology, medical sociology; 5b) Departmental collections in
chemistry, zoology, Italian, history and classics. Seminar collections of English, mathematics and philosophy.
6a) Bookstock: 210,000 volumes (monographs and bound serials).
Current serials received: 850 titles. Serials retained: c1000 titles;
6b) Board of Dutch Studies Library; Library of the Remote Sens-
ing Society (deposited on loan); Social Research Unit (medical
sociology)
7a) Own classification being replaced by Dewey Decimal Classification
(18th edition); Mostly open-access; 7b) Author card catalogue;

135 BEDFORD COLLEGE LIBRARY (continued)
   classified card catalogue for Dewey sequence with typed shelf lists
   for old classification sequence; alphabetical index to Dewey sequence
8a) Open to genuine inquirers, for reference; 8c) Inquiry service during
   term time; computer based information services available through
   University of London Central Information Service
9) Library handbook; various leaflets on library procedures and collections
10) Tyke, M *A history of Bedford College for Women 1849-1937*
   Oxford, OUP, 1939

136 BIRKBECK COLLEGE LIBRARY
1b) University of London
2a) Malet Street, London WC1E 7HX; 2b) 01-580-6622
3) A P Howse MA FLA
4a) Founded as London Mechanic's Institution in 1823 by Dr George
   Birkbeck, became Birkbeck (Literary and Scientific) Institution
   in 1866, and Birkbeck College in 1907; Library almost totally
   destroyed in 1941; Moved to present building in 1951;
   4b) Specialises in meeting the needs of part-time students reading
   for first and higher degrees in arts, sciences and economics
5a) General collection and range of subjects, excluding engineering,
   theology, law and medicine; 5b) Main undergraduate and postgraduate collections at Malet Street. Mathematics and statistics
   at Ormond House departmental library. Economics, geography,
   geology and politics in Gresse Street departmental library
6a) Bookstock: 160,000 volumes. Current serials received: 1100
   titles. Serials retained: 1750; 6b) Working papers and manuscripts
   belonging to J D Bernal; Hansard Society Library (on deposit)
7a) Bliss Classification. Open-access; 7b) Author and classified card
   catalogues. From 1979 computer catalogue on microfiche for
   current accessions
8a) SCONUL or COPOL card holders on written application to the
   librarian
9) Library guide

137 BRITISH LIBRARY OF POLITICAL AND ECONOMIC SCIENCE
1b) University of London: London School of Economics and Political
   Science
2a) 10 Portugal Street, London WC2A 2HD; 2b) 01-405-7686;
   2c) 24655 BLPESG
3) D A Clarke MA ALA
4a) 1896; 4b) The library provides a working library for the school
   as well as serving as a major national and international collection in
   its field. Over the years these interdependent functions have grown
   together. The school has given the library wide contacts with the
   public and academic worlds, and a high standing. The library has
   assisted in attracting researchers to the school.

5a) The social sciences in the widest sense; 5b) Economics, commerce, public administration, business administration, transport, statistics, political science, international law; social, economic and international aspects of history

6a) Bookstock: c700,000 books and pamphlets. Current serials received: 7350 titles. Serials retained: 12,700 titles, excluding British parliamentary papers and US public documents; 6b) The library collections are described in some detail for the general use in the publication 'Outline of the resources of the library' 3rd edition 1976. This is a revised but very much abridged edition of the library's Guide to the collections published in 1948 and long out-of-print. The collections are described under the following headings: general reference collection; government publications; international organisations; statistics; economics, commerce and finance; transport; politics and public administration; law; international affairs; sociology and anthropology; geography; history; philosophy, psychology, religion and education; Russian and East European publications; special collections. Collections of note include the following: world wide collection of government publications; unique collections of local authority reports, and reports of banks and railways; collection of more than 200,000 controversial leaflets, pamphlets etc. Depository library for US federal documents, documents of the UN and its agencies, and the Organization of American States. The library collects material on South Africa under the SCOLMA scheme. Schuster Library (comparative law); Fry Library (International law).

Manuscript and documentary collections are extensive; special permission and advanced notice are usually required before consultation. A special reading room is available for consultation. The collections divide roughly into four groups: modern political history; economic and social history; history of economic thought; persons connected with the London School of Economics; in addition there are a number of miscellaneous categories and collections

7a) Library of Congress Classification. Much of the collection is on open-access; 7b) Author catalogue; subject catalogue, which also provides entries for *A London bibliography of the social sciences.* Current summary list of major manuscript collections

8a) Freely available to members of the London School of Economics. Other scholars and researchers may apply for reader tickets. Fees payable: normally waived in the case of academic research; 8b) The library is closed for 6 days at Christmas and 6 days at Easter and on all public holidays

9) Notes for readers; Outline of the resources of the library: *A London bibliography of the social sciences* (34 volumes); Classified catalogue of a collection of works on publishing and bookselling in the British Library of Political and Economic Science; Publications of Sidney and Beatrice Webb: an interim checklist

137　BRITISH LIBRARY OF POL. AND ECON. SCIENCE (continued)
10)　Allen, C G 'Manuscript collections in the British Library of Political and Economic Science' *Journal of the Society of Archivists* 2 (2), 1960, pp52-60; John, A *The British Library of Political and Economic Science: a brief history* London, London School of Economics, 1971; Woledge, G 'The British Library of Political and Economic Science' in: Irwin, R and Staveley, R *The libraries of London* London, Library Association, 1964; 'The British Library of Political and Economic Science Reference Services' *Aslib proceedings* 24, 1972, pp459-463

138　CHELSEA COLLEGE LIBRARY
1b)　University of London
2a)　Manresa Road, London SW3 6LX; 2b) 01-352-6421
3)　A G Quinsee BA ALA
4a)　College founded in 1891, becoming Chelsea Polytechnic in 1922 and a College of Advanced Technology in 1957. Full university status achieved between 1966 and 1971 as a member of the federal University of London; 4b) The library caters for the teaching and research needs of staff and students of the college by lending its own stock and operating inter-library loans and photocopying services.
5a)　General collection with a heavy bias towards the sciences; 5b) There are four annexe libraries, closely integrated with the main library at Manresa Road. Main subjects relate to courses in pharmacy, education, science, nursing studies, sociology, psychology, humanities, European studies, environmental sciences
6a)　Total of some 110,000 volumes. 800 current serials. About 2000 titles held; 6b) Very small collection of materials relating to Charles Darwin; a collection of material relating to the geology of South east Asia is being accumulated slowly.
7a)　Most of the stock is on open-access and arranged by Universal Decimal Classification; 7b) Classified catalogue in card form: author/title sequence, classified sequence, and subject index. Union catalogue held at the main library: each annexe library has similar catalogue for its own stock. Computer print-out now available of mini author/title index to most of the stock which will be placed in annexe libraries.
8a)　Open to registered members of the college for full library services. Open to members of other colleges and universities, and the general public for reference, on application to the librarian; 8b) Main library—Term: M-F 0900-2100, Sat to 1300. Vacations: M-F 0900-1800 Christmas and Easter, summer to 1700. Annexe libraries—normally M-F 0930-1730, but may vary; 8c) The usual reference and lending facilities are available. Assistance is given to staff and postgraduates who request computerised bibliographic searching; these requests are channelled through the Central Information Services of the University of London.

138   CHELSEA COLLEGE LIBRARY (continued)
9)   Library guide; A short guide to Chelsea College Library; Guides
for readers: 1 Abstracts and indexes; 2 Basic medical sciences;
3 Biological sciences; 4 Theses and dissertations; 5 Recording
references

139   GOLDSMITHS' COLLEGE LIBRARY
1b)   University of London: Goldsmiths' College
2a)   Main Library: Lewisham Way, New Cross, London SE14 6NW
(tel 01-692-0211); Rachel McMillan Site Library: Creek Road,
London SE8 3BU (tel 01-692-7454); St Gabriel's Site Library:
Cormont Road, London SE5 9RG (tel 01-735-2143)
3)   Miss E M Moys BA FLA
4a)   College founded 1891, becoming a London University Institution
in 1904; 4b) The library provides reference and lending facilities
to students and staff on all sites
5a)   General range of subjects; 5b) Art, education, music, psychology,
social sciences.
6a)   Bookstock: c200,000 volumes (monographs and bound serials).
Current serials received: c1300 titles. Over 50,000 audiovisual
items, including 30,000 art slides; 6b) No special collections, but
strengths as in 5b
7a)   Dewey Decimal Classification (mixed editions). Mostly open-
access; 7b) Author and classified catalogues
8a)   Open to all members of the college. Other students admitted as
readers (preferably during vacations). General public admitted on
proof of need; 8c) Photocopying. Access to University Central
Information Service
9)   Library guide; various booklists produced (women's studies,
Russian art of the Revolution, art deco, art nouveau, British music since 1950)

140   HEYTHROP COLLEGE LIBRARY
1b)   University of London
2a)   11-13 Cavendish Square, London W1M OAN; 2b) 01-580-6941
3)   M J Walsh MA ALA
4a)   Founded Louvain 1614, moved to Liège in 1626, to Stonyhurst
(Lancs) in 1794, Heythrop (Oxon) in 1926, and to London as a
constituent college of the university in 1970; 4b) Undergraduate
provision in philosophy, theology and related disciplines (including classical and semitic languages); and research provision in
selected areas
5a)   Special coverage of history and literature of English Roman
Catholicism, and of the Society of Jesus (Jesuits).
6a)   Bookstock: c200,000 volumes (monographs and bound serials).
Current serials received: 250 titles. Serials retained: c350 titles;
6b) Special collection strengths in canon law, medieval philosophy,
theology and ecclesiastical history, and in medical ethics (in

140 HEYTHROP COLLEGE LIBRARY (continued)
cooperation with the Linacre Centre for the study of the ethics
of medical care)

7a) Library of Congress Classification. Pre-1801 holdings closed-access.
Most holdings in philosophy, theology and related disciplines on
open-access; 7b) Author/title catalogue, subject catalogue (LC
subject headings). Pre-1801 catalogue in preparation, with chrono-
logical and imprint files.

8a) Open to members of the college, and to others with letter of
recommendation; 8c) Photocopying and microreading facilities

9) No publications generally available

141 IMPERIAL COLLEGE OF SCIENCE AND TECHNOLOGY Lyon
Playfair Library

1b) University of London

2a) South Kensington, London SW7 2AZ; 2b) 01-589-5111;
2c) 261503

3) A Whitworth MA

4a) 1907; 4b) The central library of Imperial College is the Lyon
Playfair Library. In addition there are thirteen major departmental libraries (aeronautics, atmospheric physics, biochemistry
and chemistry, chemical engineering and chemical technology,
civil engineering, electrical engineering, geology, mathematics,
mechanical engineering and management science, metallurgy and
materials science, mineral resources engineering, physics; The
Haldane Library, housed adjoining the Lyon Playfair Library, is a
non-curricular library with a general humanities collection)

5a) Science and technology, management, economics and sociology;
5b) Subject strengths are represented in the departmental libraries,
and these hold the bulk of research material in their areas. The
departmental collections of life sciences, and computing and
control are housed in the Lyon Playfair Library as distinct collections;

6a) (Lyon Playfair Library only) Bookstock: c200,000 volumes (monographs and bound serials). Current serials received: 1075 titles;
6b) Annan Collection (history of metals, mining and metallurgy);
London Natural History Society Library; Operational Research
Society Library; Tensor Society of Great Britain Library. College
archive collections consisting of records of Imperial College (including the Royal College of Chemistry, Royal School of Mines,
Royal College of Science, City and Guilds College); the collection
includes manuscript collections relating to T H Huxley

7a) Lyon Playfair Library—UDC classification (except for Computing
and control Collection); mostly open-access; 7b) Author catalogue
(union catalogue of Lyon Playfair Library and departmental libraries); classified catalogue (Lyon Playfair stock only)

8a) Reference use by bona fide enquirers; borrowing by members of
Imperial College only; 8c) Photocopying, microreading, videotape,

141 IMPERIAL COLLEGE Lyon Playfair Library (continued)
listening facilities. College archives can be consulted on previous
appointment with the archivist
9) Union list of periodical and serial holdings in Imperial College;
Series of brief guides to bibliographic guides and information
sources

142 KING'S COLLEGE LONDON LIBRARY
1b) University of London
2a) Strand, London WC2 2LS; 2b) 01-836-5454
3) I Angus MA DipLib
4a) 1829; 4b) The library serves the teaching needs of the college,
and houses a wide range of research material
5a) General range of subjects, but especially strong in ecclesiastical
history, imperial history, modern Greek, Portuguese and Brazilian
history and literature, Spanish and Spanish American literature,
war studies, theology; 5b) The collections are divided amongst the
following subject libraries: a) Modern languages (English, German,
Italian, Portuguese, Brazilian, Spanish and Spanish American collections, general language and literature; history, philosophy and
war studies libraries; the Enk classical library; French library;
Burrows library of Byzantine and Modern Greek studies); b) Education; c) Theology and ecclesiastical history, including the Box
library of Hebrew and Old Testament studies; d) Music; e) Laws;
f) Science libraries (including medicine); Wheatstone library
(history of science); Earth sciences library; Plant sciences library;
Biophysics library (the last two at outstations); g) Engineering
6a) Bookstock: c390,000 volumes (including 80,000 bound serial
volumes). Current serials received: c2000 titles. Sound recordings:
3500 items; 6b) Dr William Marsden Collection (philology, early
bibles, travel); Wheatstone Library (electricity and related subjects
up to 1875); Dr F J Furnivall Library (English); Professor W W
Skeat Library (English); Professor A W Reed Library (English);
Dr R M Burrows Library (modern Greek studies); Frida Mond
Collection (Goethe); Dr Ludwig Kantorowicz collection (German
material on literature, history, science and Judaica); C G James
Library (mathematics); Rev T R R Stebbing Collection (zoology);
Professor F D Maurice Library (moral and social theology); Rev
Professor G H Box Library (theology, Hebrew and Old Testament
studies); Rev Professor H M Relton Library (theology); Professor
E H Prestage Collection (Portuguese); Professor F J C Hearnshaw
Collection (history); Professor Louis Brandin Collection (French
literature); Professor Alexander Souter Collection (classical and
patristic literature); Professor P J Enk Collection (classics); Linetta
de Castelvecchio Richardson Collection (Dante and Italian Re-
naissance); Professor R Norman Collection (German literature);
Rev Professor E C Ratcliff Collection (liturgy); Professor E J Cohn
Collection (German law); Sir Basil Liddell Hart Collection (military
147

142 KING'S COLLEGE LONDON LIBRARY (continued)
     studies). Associated with the library is the Liddell Hart Centre
     for Military Archives (a depository for papers on British defence
     policy since 1900 and strategy in the two world wars)
7a) Mainly Library of Congress Classification, except four subject col-
     lections arranged by Garside Classification. About three quarters
     of the stock on open-access; some of the remaining stock is
     housed at the University of London Depository Library at Egham,
     Surrey; 7b) Author and subject (classified) catalogues. Additional
     local catalogues in individual sections of library and for some
     special collections
8a) Members of the college. British university staff admitted with any
     identification; British university students with SCONUL card or
     written introduction; other visitors with written introduction;
     8c) Photocopying and microreading facilities
9)   Guide to library facilities (annual); Exhibition of bibles
10) Irwin, R and Staveley, R (eds) *The libraries of London* 2nd rev ed,
     London, Library Association, 1964; Pound, R W 'Portuguese
     speaking Africa (King's College London holdings)' in SCOLMA
     *Conference on the acquisition of material from Africa . . . 1969:
     reports and papers, comp by Valerie Bloomfield* 1969, pp63-72;
     Shadrake, A A 'The War Studies Library at King's College, London
     University' *Aslib proceedings* 29(8), 1977, pp295-301; Elliott, M 'The
     Rainbow collection of hymn books at King's College' *Bulletin of the A
     sociation of British Theological and Philosophical Libraries* June 1977
     pp 5-7.

143 QUEEN ELIZABETH COLLEGE LIBRARY
1b) University of London
2a) Campden Hill Road, London W8 7AH; 2b) 01-937-5411
3)   P M A Stonham BA ALA
4a) The college originated in 1908 as a branch of King's College for
     Women and became an independent school of the university in
     1928; 4b) The library is housed in two separate buildings, the
     Sargeaunt Library and the Burton Library
5a) Pure and life sciences; 5b) Collections developed around the fol-
     lowing subjects; astrophysics, biochemistry, biology, biophysics,
     chemistry, food science, management, mathematics, microbiology,
     molecular physics, nutrition, physics, physiology
6a) Bookstock: c37,000 volumes (monographs and bound serials).
     Current serials received: 450 titles; 6b) Important collections in
     food science and nutrition.
8a) Available to members of the college. Members of the public and
     other students admitted for reference purposes on approval of
     librarian.

144 QUEEN MARY COLLEGE LIBRARY
1b) University of London
2a) Mile End Road, London E1 4NS; 2b 01-980-4811

144   QUEEN MARY COLLEGE LIBRARY (continued)
3)   T H Bowyer BSc FLA
4a)   Library founded in 1887 within the People's Palace Technical
       Schools. Became a school of London University in 1934; 4b) Main
       library; separate law library
5a)   General range of subjects
6a)   Bookstock: c200,000 volumes (monographs and bound serials);
       Current serials received: c1500 titles; 6b) European Documen-
       tation Centre
7a)   Library of Congress Classification. Mainly open-access; 7b) Author/
       title and classified catalogues
8c)   Open-access collections

145   ROYAL HOLLOWAY COLLEGE LIBRARY
1b)   University of London
2a)   Egham Hill, Egham, Surrey TW20 OEX; 2b) 07843-4455
3)   R J E Horrill BA
4a)   College founded 1883. Development of the library has been
       mainly since 1946 and especially between 1964 and 1966;
       4b) Serves the teaching needs of the college. Departmental collec-
       tions in chemistry, biochemistry, botany, zoology
5a)   General range of subjects
6a)   Bookstock: c140,000 volumes (monographs and bound serials);
       Current serials received: c800 titles

146   ROYAL VETERINARY COLLEGE LIBRARY
1b)   University of London
2a)   Royal College Street, London NW1 OTU; 2b) 01-387-2896 ext 231
3)   R Catton BA ALA
4a)   Established 1791; The collection of books presented by Granville
       Penn on the foundation of the college formed the nucleus of the
       library; 4b) Teaching and research material for the needs of the
       staff and students of the college
5a)   Veterinary sciences; 5b) Pre-clinical veterinary subjects are pro-
       vided for in the main library. Clinical subjects are provided for in
       the branch library at the college field station
6a)   Bookstock: 27,000 volumes (monographs and bound serials);
       Current serials received: c400 titles
7a)   Barnard Classification. Mostly open-access; 7b) Dictionary cata-
       logue at main library; author and alphabetical subject catalogues
       in branch library
8a)   Available for reference use to other members of the university,
       and to others who have special need; 8b) Opening hours for
       visitors, M-F 0930-1700

147   UNIVERSITY COLLEGE LIBRARY
1b)   University of London
2a)   Gower Street, London WC1E 6BT; 2b) 01-387-7050
3)   J W Scott BA ALA

147   UNIVERSITY COLLEGE LIBRARY (continued)
4a)   1829; 4b) The library serves the teaching, postgraduate and
      research work of the college
5a)   General range of subjects; 5b) The collections are dispersed amongst
      several locations: a) Arts libraries in the main building comprise
      those in ancient history, art, classical archaeology (Yates Library);
      classics; comparative philology; English; French; German; Hebrew;
      Italian; librarianship; literature; palaeography and archives; papyr-
      ology; philosophy; phonetics; political economy; Spanish;
      b) History (excluding ancient and American history) at 25 Gordon
      Square, WC1; c) D M S Watson Library: international relations;
      Scandinavia; botany; geography; geology; phychology; zoology;
      medicine; anthropology; d) Physical Sciences Library: science and
      engineering; e) Egyptology Library; f) Environmental Studies Library
6a)   Bookstock: c860,000 volumes (monographs and bound serials);
      Current serials received: 8000 titles; 6b) The college library is
      particularly strong in American history, Egyptology, Hebrew, Latin-
      American studies, London history and Scandinavian studies.
      Among the mss collections are those of Jeremy Bentham, Edwin
      Chadwick, Sir Francis Galton, Moses Gaster, Latin-American
      Business Archives, Karl Pearson, Sir William Ramsay, Routledge
      and Kegan Paul Archives, and the papers of the Society for the
      Diffusion of Useful Knowledge. Other special collections are the
      Graves Early Science Library, Barlow Dante Library, Whitley
      Stokes Celtic Library, Smith Woodward Palaeontological Library,
      C K Ogden Library, the George Orwell archive, the James Joyce
      centre, Little magazines.
         The libraries of the following learned societies are housed in
      the college library: British Society of Franciscan Studies; Folk-
      lore Society; Gaelic Society; Geologists' Association; Hertford-
      shire Natural History Society and Field Club; Huguenot Society;
      London Mathematical Society; Malacological Society; Mocatta
      Library of Anglo-Judaica; Philological Society; Royal Historical
      Society; Viking Society for Northern Research; Bibliographical
      Society.
7a)   Garside Classification. Open and closed access; 7b) Name cata-
      logue, periodicals catalogue, subject catalogue
8a)   Open to members of the college. Others by special permission
      on written application to the librarian; 8c) Subject specialists
      available; on-line information retrieval
9)   Library guide; Manuscript collections in the Library of University
      College London (occasional publications no 1); the Gaster papers
      (occasional publications no 2); The papers of Sir Edwin Chadwick
      1800-1890 (occasional publications no 3)
10)   Scott, J W 'The library of University College London' in: Irwin, R
      and Staveley, R *The libraries of London*. London, Library Associ-
      ation, 1964; Dorling, A R 'The Graves mathematical collection in
      University College London' *Annals of science* 33, 1976, pp307-310;

147 UNIVERSITY COLLEGE LIBRARY (continued)
Martin, R 'University College Library' *Library world* 65, 1964,
pp296-298; Scott, J W 'The Mocatta Library' in Shaftesley, J M
(ed) *Remember the days: Essays on Anglo-Jewish history presented
to Cecil Roth.* London, Jewish Historical Society, 1965.

148 WESTFIELD COLLEGE LIBRARY Caroline Skeel Library
1b) University of London
2a) Kidderpore Avenue, London NW3 7ST; 2b) 01-435-7141
3) P Revell MA PhD FLA
4a) 1882; 4b) Developed primarily to serve undergraduates in the subjects taught at the college and has retained this emphasis
5a) Classics, English, French, German, history, history of art, Spanish,
botany and biochemistry, chemistry, computer science, mathematics, physics, zoology; 5b) Drama, post-1945 German literature,
environmental science
6a) Bookstock: c125,000 volumes (including 20,000 volumes bound
serials). Current serials received: 665 titles; Serials retained: 1030
titles; 6b) Rare book collection; Lyttelton family mss (c3000
items letters and papers); Allen Lane archive
7a) Library of Congress Classification. Open-access except for rare
Book Collection; 7b) Author/title and classified catalogues (with
alphabetical subject index)
8a) The full facilities of the college library are available to members
of staff and students. Students from other colleges may apply for
limited borrowing rights. Members of the public may use the
library for reference purposes; 8c) Photocopying and photographic
service; microreading facilities
9) Library guide; various information guides
10) *New library buildings, 1974* (ed) Herbert Ward. London, Library
Association, 1974, pp122-123.

149 WYE COLLEGE LIBRARY
1b) University of London
2a) Wye College, Wye, Ashford, Kent TN25 5AH; 2b) 0233-812401
3) Helen Greer MA
4a) Wye College was founded as a secular institution in 1447, and included a grammar school which existed until 1893, when it was
reorganised as an agricultural college. Became a school of London
University in 1900, and is now the department of agriculture and
horticulture; 4b) The library serves the teaching and research needs
of the college, which houses also the Centre for European Agricultural Studies
5a) Agriculture, horticulture, rural environmental studies and related
subjects; 5b) Departmental library at Centre for European Agricultural Studies
6a) Bookstock: c26,000 monographs. Current serials received: c600
titles. Serials retained: c1000 titles; 6b) Collection of historical

149   WYE COLLEGE LIBRARY (continued)
       material on agriculture and horticulture 1543-1918; Crundale
       Rectorial Library; parish and manorial records on deposit
7a)   Universal Decimal Classification. Open-access (except for histori-
       cal collections); 7b) Author/title and subject catalogues;
8a)   Open to the general public by arrangement for reference;
       8c) Linked to University of London Central Information Service.
       On-line access to data bases
9)   Library guide (annual); Library bulletin (bi-monthly); Catalogue
       of agricultural and horticultural books 1543-1918 in Wye College
       Library

150   COURTAULD INSTITUTE OF ART BOOK LIBRARY
1b)   University of London
2a)   20 Portman Square, London W1H OBE; 2b) 01-935-9292
3)   P M Doran BA ALA
4a)   1933; 4b) The library serves postgraduate teaching and research,
       as well as undergraduate needs
5a)   History of European art and architecture; 5b) In addition to the
       library collections there are fine art collections and two collec-
       tions of reproductions (Witt and Conway libraries of reproduc-
       tions)
6a)   Bookstock: 80,000 volumes (monographs and bound serials).
       Current serials received: c190 titles; 6b) Garrison collection of
       photographs of Italian early medieval paintings
7a)   Library of Congress Classification. Mostly open-access;
       7b) Author and classified (shelf order) catalogues
8a)   Institute teaching staff and registered students. Other university
       staff and students (London and others) can use the collection
       for reference purposes on proof of identity; 8b) Closed through-
       out April, and at Christmas and Easter

151   INSTITUTE OF ADVANCED LEGAL STUDIES LIBRARY
1b)   University of London
2a)   17 Russell Square, London WC1B 5DR; 2b) 01-637-1731
3)   W A F P Steiner LLM MA ALA
4a)   1947. Concept based on the recommendations for an institute
       of legal research contained in the *Report of the Legal Education
       Committee* 1934, Cmd 4663 (Chairman: Lord Atkin). The
       institute was established as part of the University of London, on
       the pattern of the existing Institute of Historical Research, to
       provide a focal point for legal research in the UK; 4b) To provide
       a comprehensive legal research library (mainly reference) in co-
       operation with other legal research collections mainly within the
       University of London. To provide bibliographical information
       both on request and by means of bibliographical publications

151 INST. OF ADV. LEGAL STUDIES LIBRARY (continued)
5a) Law; 5b) Special emphasis on the law of the British Isles, the Commonwealth (excluding Bangladesh, India and Pakistan), the United States, Western Europe and international law. Special responsibility for South African law (SCOLMA scheme); Parry Centre for Latin American Studies (law).
6a) 129,777 volumes. 48,486 monographs and pamphlets. 81,291 serial volumes. 2172 titles (including 88 duplicated), No record of total number of serial titles retained;
7a) Mainly open-access. Less used/superseded material on closed access; 7b) Name catalogue (A-Z); subject catalogue (A-Z); the following supplementary catalogues: British Government command papers (in command series and number order); University of London legal theses (in order of acquisition); Theses from non-British universities (by country and sub-filed chronologically); Documents relating to cases heard by the Judicial Committee of the Privy Council (two alphabetical sequences—by name of parties; by country of origin of the appeal); Subject catalogue of small staff library of works about librarianship
8a) Available to law research students and academic law teachers. Other legal scholars admitted on application to the secretary; 8b) The library is closed during the second fortnight of September; 8c) Photocopying facilities
9) Library guide. The following bibliographical publications are produced: Union list of legal periodicals: a location guide to holdings of legal periodicals in libraries in the United Kingdom 3rd ed, 1968 (4th ed in preparation); Union list of Commonwealth and South African law, 1963 edition; a location guide to Commonwealth and South African legislation, law reports and digests held by libraries in the United Kingdom at May 1963; Union list of United States law literature in libraries of Oxford 2nd ed, 1967; Union list of air and space law literature in the libraries of Oxford, Cambridge and London 2nd ed, 1975; Union list of West European legal literature: publications held by libraries in Oxford, Cambridge and London 1966; A manual of legal citations: part 1 The British Isles 1959, part 11 The Commonwealth 1960; A bibliographical guide to the law of the United Kingdom, the Channel Islands and the Isle of Man 2nd ed, 1973. The institute publishes the *Index to foreign legal periodicals* (3 pa) with annual and three year cumulation (1960-), in cooperation with the American Association of Law Libraries
10) Moys, E M 'The Library of the Institute of Advanced Legal Studies, London *Law library journal* 49, 1956, p23; Drake, K H 'Symposium on law libraries' *Journal of the Society of Public Teachers of Law* 8, 1964-1965, p71

152 INSTITUTE OF ARCHAEOLOGY LIBRARY
1b) University of London
2a) 31-34 Gordon Square, London WC1H OPY; 2b) 01-387-6052
3) Miss H M Bell BA
4a) 1937. The institute was originally founded as a research institute for graduates reading for higher degrees. In 1968 a first degree in archaeology was instituted and this has necessarily modified the balance of the collection; 4b) Mainly for undergraduates and postgraduates working at the institute, but other members of the university and visiting scholars are served
5a) Archaeology; 5b) Mainly European and Near Eastern archaeology, but also material on other regions including Latin-America
6a) Bookstock: c34,000 volumes (monographs and bound serials). Pamphlets (less than 100 pages); c13,500. Maps: c1500 items; 6b) Small special collection on nautical archaeology
7a) Own classification based on Library of Congress. Mostly on open-access; 7b) Author and subject catalogues; index to sites (monograph and periodical material); index to conferences
8a) Staff and students of London University; others by permission of librarian; 8b) Closed Sats during summer vacation; 8c) Telephone enquiries answered (if time permits)

153 INSTITUTE OF COMMONWEALTH STUDIES LIBRARY
1b) University of London
2a) 27 Russell Square, London WC1B 5DS; 2b) 01-580-5876
3) Mrs P M Larby MA FLA
4a) 1949; 4b) Offers facilities to postgraduate research workers from British and overseas universities, in addition to meeting needs of those associated with the Institute
5a) Commonwealth history (from 1850), and economic, social studies and political aspects; 5b) Important collections of Commonwealth official papers and bibliographical material.
6a) Bookstock: c80,000 volumes (monographs and bound serials); Current serials received: c700 titles; 6b) Institute seminar papers (reference set); Commonwealth newscuttings; Collection of political party documents and ephemera; Library of the West India Committee (on deposit); collects items from and about Sierra Leone and the Gambia under the SCOLMA scheme; Archives include papers of the following: Richard Jebb; Sir Keith Hancock (Smuts papers and Buganda papers); African National Congress; Richard Hart; Industrial and Commercial Union (South Africa); J Van Velsen
7a) Library of Congress Classification. Open and closed access; 7b) Author, subject and area catalogues
8a) Resources available to staff and postgraduates of the university and other universities in the UK and abroad. Others by application and at the discretion of the director. Apply to the assistant secretary; 8c) No borrowing permitted. Bibliographical guidance and advice given to personal visitors and by post
9) · Accessions list (4 pa) with political parties supplement (annual); Theses in progress in Commonwealth studies (annual)

154 INSTITUTE OF EDUCATION LIBRARY
1b) University of London
2a) 11-13 Ridgmount Street, London WC1E 7AH; 2b) 01-637-0846
3) N W Beswick MA PhD FLA
4a) The institute was founded by the London County Council in 1902
and transferred to the university in 1932; 4b) The library serves
principally staff and registered students of the institute
5a) Education; 5b) The library is divided into a number of sections by
floor in the building these include lending library, resources centre,
advanced studies collection, comparative education library.
National Textbook Reference Collection is kept at 2 Taviton
Street, WC1
6a) Bookstock: c180,000 volumes (monographs and bound serials).
Current serials received: c1700 titles; 6b) World Education Fellow-
ship archives; German Education Reconstruction Group archives;
AMA archives (to 1960). Personal papers relating to Sir Fred
Clarke, and Dr Nicholas Hans
7a) Several classification schemes operating in different departments
developed by the library. Mostly open-access; 7b) Author and
classified subject union catalogues; departmental catalogues
8a) Full facilities for present and former members of the institute.
Reference facilities for others; 8c) Full information services provided to staff and higher degree students; seminars to groups on
request
9) Library guides (to all departments); *Education libraries bulletin*
and supplements; *Catalogue of the Comparative Education Library,
University of London Institute of Education* 6 volumes, Boston,
G K Hall, 1971. *First supplement* 3 volumes, 1974
10) Bristow, T 'The University of London research library for comparative education in the Institute of Education' *Comparative education
review* 9, 1965, pp213-218

155 INSTITUTE OF GERMANIC STUDIES LIBRARY
1b) University of London
2a) 29 Russell Square, London WC1B 5DP; 2b) 01-580-2711/3480
3) V J Riley MA ALA
4a) 1950; 4b) The purpose of the institute is to promote the advance-
ment and study of German language and literature. The library
has developed to provide a reference collection for postgraduate
research
5a) German language and literature; 5b) Bibliographical and lexico-
graphical material; critical editions of authors
6a) Bookstock: c 29,000 volumes. Pamphlets and offprints: c6000
items; Current serials received: c360 titles. Serials retained:
1500 titles; 6b) German and German-English dictionaries from the
sixteenth century onwards; collection of material on the Recht-
schreibreform; dialect dictionaries; comprehensive collection of
post-1945 German literary periodicals; Priebsch-Closs Collection
(c2000 volumes of first and early editions of 18th and early 19th
century authors); Shakespeare translations; comprehensive collection of material on George and the George circle; Material on the

155 INSTITUTE OF GERMANIC STUDIES LIBRARY (continued)
    history of German studies in the UK collected on behalf of the
    Conference of University Teachers of German; Library of the
    English Goethe Society (on permanent loan). Manuscript material
    (Friedrich Gundolf archive; Majut correspondence; Jethro Bithell
    correspondence; Karl Breul correspondence)
7a) Garside Classification (modified). Open-access, except for Priebsch
    Closs collection and manuscripts; 7b) Author/title and classified
    subject catalogue
8a) Membership of the institute is open to teachers and research
    students in the departments of Germanic languages and literature
    of London University, and to scholars in the Germanic field in
    other universities. Single or occasional visits to consult material
    not available elsewhere permitted without, or on temporary, mem-
    bership; 8c) Photocopying and microreading facilities
9) Periodical holdings 1970 with supplements 1971-1973; German
    language literary and political periodicals 1960-1974; 16th and
    17th century books in the library of the institute (1967)

156 INSTITUTE OF HISTORICAL RESEARCH
1b) University of London
2a) Senate House, Malet Street, London WC1E 7HU; 2b) 01-636-
    0272/3
3) W Kellaway MA FLA FSA (Secretary and Librarian)
4a) 1921; 4b) The institute is the University of London's centre for
    postgraduate work in history
5a) Sources and books about the sources for the history of the
    peoples of Western Europe and their expansion overseas;
    5b) Apart from bibliographies and sources, the library contains
    historical periodicals and a number of reference works.
6a) Bookstock: 120,000 volumes (monographs and bound serials).
    Current serials received: c600 titles. Serials retained: c600 titles;
    6b) School and college registers; printed parliamentary poll
    books; record society publications; Harvard and Yale English
    legal manuscripts (microform); Clarke papers (microform).
7a) Open access; special classification; 7b) General name catalogue;
    special room catalogues.
8a) University teachers of history, postgraduate students of history;
    bona fide historians and others by arrangement; 8b) M-F 0900-
    2100, Sat to 1700
9) *The Victoria history of the counties of England* is published by
    OUP for the Institute. The Institute itself publishes: Bulletin of
    the Institute of Historical Research (2 issues yearly); Bibliography
    of historical works issued in the United Kingdom 1971-5, comp
    R Taylor; History theses, 1901-70. comp P M Jacobs; Historical
    research for university degrees in the United Kingdom (2 pts yearly
    Fasti ecclesiae anglicanae (19 vols, in progress); Office-holders in
    modern Britain (7 vols, in progress); Teachers of history in the uni-
    versities of the United Kingdom (yearly); Writings on British
    history 1946- (in progress).

157 INSTITUTE OF LATIN AMERICAN STUDIES LIBRARY
1b)   University of London
2a)   31 Tavistock Square, London WC1H 9HA; 2b) 01-387-4055/6
3)   Mrs B M Harrington BA ALA
4a)   1965; 4b) Acts as a centre for the collection and distribution of
       information about Latin American studies in British universities.
       The activities of the institute range both within and outside the
       university world.
5a)   Latin America; 5b) Basic reference coverage (especially biblio-
       graphies and guides) to complement other Latin American collec-
       tions in the university
6a)   Bookstock: c2500 items. Current serials received: 96 titles.
       Serials retained: 199 titles; 6b) British Union Catalogue of Latin
       Americana (c100,000 titles recorded)
7a)   Almost entirely open access; 7b) Author/title catalogue with geo-
       graphical headings
8a)   Admission to the institute open to scholars, persons who have
       assisted in the development of the institute, teachers and post-
       graduates of London University, approved researchers from other
       universities; others admitted on inquiry to the secretary; 8c) Per-
       sonal bibliographical guidance
9)   New Latin-American titles (termly list of additions to the Union
       catalogue); Latin American periodicals (1970); Contributions to
       Naylor, B et al (eds) *Directory of libraries and special collections
       on Latin America and the West Indies* London, Athlone Press for
       Institute of Latin American Studies, 1975.

158 INSTITUTE OF UNITED STATES STUDIES LIBRARY
1b)   University of London
2a)   31 Tavistock Square, London WC1H 9EZ; 2b) 01-387-5534
3)   Mrs A Phillips BA ALA
4a)   1965; 4b) The institute acts as a bibliographic information centre
       for Americanists. Maintains a small collection of bibliographies
       and general reference works, and a union catalogue of American
       studies books in 21 libraries together with a comprehensive current
       American studies bibliography on microfiche. Details of special
       material and collections in other British libraries of all kinds.
5a)   Everything relevant to the study of the USA
6a)   Bookstock: 1500 volumes. Current serials received: 20 titles.
       Serials retained: 20 titles;
7a)   Library of Congress Classification. Open access; 7b) Dictionary
       catalogue
8a)   Open to staff, students and members of the institute, and to other
       Americanists at the librarian's discretion; 8c) Bibliographical in-
       formation service
9)   American Studies in Britain: areas of teaching and research (1975)
       new edition every 2-3 years; List of theses in progress and com-
       pleted (published biennially in the Journal of American Studies);
       American studies bibliography (published monthly with annual
       cumulations, on microfiche)

158 INSTITUTE OF US STUDIES LIBRARY (continued)
10) McCarthy, S *Report on a proposed union catalogue in the field of American Studies in Britain*; Institute of United States Studies, Computer Committee *Proposals for a machine readable catalogue of American studies material*

159 LIBRARY OF THE HELLENIC AND ROMAN SOCIETIES AND THE INSTITUTE OF CLASSICAL STUDIES
1b) (1) Hellenic Society, (2) Roman Society, (3) University of London
2a) 31-34 Gordon Square, London WC1H OPY (institute) WC1H OPP (societies); 2b) 01-387-7697
3) Miss A E Healey BA ALA
4a) Hellenic Society founded 1879; Roman Society founded 1911; Institute of Classical Studies founded 1953; 4b) The institute aims to provide primary reference facilities; the societies provide lending coverage; both in most subjects within the scope of the parent institutions
5a) Classical antiquity; 5b) The institute cooperates with the Byzantine Library Committee, specialising in hellenising Greek texts; maintains union catalogue of Byzantine acquisitions in certain London libraries from 1965
6a) Bookstock: c50,000 volumes (monographs and bound serials); Current serials received: c400 titles. Serials retained: c600 titles. Colour transparencies: c5000 items (societies' collection); 6b) Wood Donation; Leaf Collection (societies' collection)
7a) Own classification. Almost all open-access; 7b) Author and classified catalogues
8a) Available to institute members; others admitted on discretion; 8c) Photocopying. Information provided by phone and post. Borrowing by societies' members only
10) 'Survey of classical periodicals' *Bulletin of the Institute of Classical Studies*, supplement 13, 1962

160 SCHOOL OF ORIENTAL AND AFRICAN STUDIES LIBRARY
1b) University of London
2a) Malet Street, London WC1E 7HP; 2b) 01-637-2388
3) V T H Parry MA Dip Lib FLA
4a) 1917. In 1961 the Hayter Report recommended that the library should be regarded as the national lending library for Oriental and African Studies; the school accepted this recommendation; 4b) Primarily a working collection for the staff and students of the school. Although possessing some rare books and manuscripts it does not collect actively in these fields, preferring to aim at a wide current coverage.
5a) Oriental and African studies in the humanities and social sciences; 5b) The main divisions of the collection are as follows: Africa, Far East (China, Tibet, Mongolia, Japan, Korea); Near and

160 SCH. OF ORIEN. AND AFR. STUDIES LIBRARY (continued)
Middle East (Islamic and Caucasian countries, and non-Islamic
and Ancient Near East); South Asia; South-east Asia. The general
collections are strong in history, geography, economics, politics,
sociology, religion, law, linguistics, travel and non-oriental
languages

6a) Bookstock: c450,000 items (printed books and pamphlets).
Current serials received: c3000 titles. Manuscripts: c2000 items.
Maps: over 10,000 sheets. Slides and photographs: over
50,000 items; 6b) The regional collections are the special strength
of the library. African material: material on African languages;
Sir William Mackinnon papers (British East Africa Company); Fox-
Pitt papers (Federation of Rhodesia and Nyasaland). Far Eastern
material: The China Collections are especially important founded
on the Robert Morrison Collection (early 19th century private
library); manuscript collections include papers of Edward and
Cecil Bowra, and Sir Frederick Maze; Collection of classical Tibetan literature. Near and Middle East material: William Marsden
Oriental library; Martin Hartmann Library; Sir Thomas Arnold
Collection; Auboyneau Collection (European printed books on
Turkey and the Turks); Talbot Rice Collection (manuscript material on the Levant Company); C J Edmonds Collection (Kurdish
material); Hebrew, Akkadian and Hittite collections. South Asian
material: material from the William Marsden Collection; North-
brook Society Library (on permanent loan); Important holdings
on South Asian languages. South-east Asian and Pacific material:
important collection of material on Pacific and in Oceanic languages;
Sidney Herbert Ray papers (languages and ethnology of the Pacific
islands). Art materials: The Asian collection of the Courtauld
Institute of Art Library was deposited in 1957 on permanent loan;
this has formed the basis for further acquisitions on a wide regional
basis. Besides printed materials there are collections of photographs,
slides and paintings (Chinese Palace and Central Museums Collection, Taiwan; Hunt Collection of Indian archaeology and anthropology). American Indian languages collection; J Sampson Collection (Gypsies and Gypsy language)

7a) Own classification scheme with modifications for different categories of material. The majority of the collections are on open-
access; 7b) Author and titles catalogues. Subject catalogue arranged by six main area divisions, and then by language, country
and subject. Various special catalogues (art collection; various
periodical article catalogues; Chinese catalogue). Union Catalogue
of Asian Publications is maintained by the school library to provide a national bibliographic service for Asian studies

8a) Staff and students of the school have access to all facilities as full
members; other members of London University institutions may
be granted ordinary membership of the library. Others may use
the library on production of satisfactory references;

160 SCH. OF ORIEN. AND AFR. STUDIES LIBRARY (continued)
8c) Photographic, photocopying and microreading facilities. Expert
subject specialists available for consultation
9) Library guide 3rd rev ed (1976); *Library catalogue of the School
of Oriental and African Studies, University of London* 28 volumes,
Boston, G K Hall, 1963. *First supplement* 16 volumes (1968),
Second supplement 16 volumes (1973)
10) 'The history of the SOAS library' in Saunders, W L (ed) *University and research library studies* Oxford, Pergamon, 1968; *Journal
of Asian Studies* 17, 1957, pp183-188.

161 SCHOOL OF SLAVONIC AND EAST EUROPEAN STUDIES
LIBRARY
1b) University of London
2a) Senate House, Malet Street, London WC1E 7HU; 2b) 01-637-
4934/40
3) J E O Screen MA PhD ALA
4a) Founded 1915 as part of King's College, and became a university
institute in 1932; 4b) The library supports the teaching and
research at the school into the languages, literature, history and
social conditions of the USSR and Eastern Europe
5a) Material on Russia, the western Soviet republics, the countries of
Eastern and South-eastern Europe, and on Finland; 5b) Humanities and social science subjects
6a) Bookstock: c200,000 volumes (monographs and bound serials).
Current serials received: c1000 titles; 6b) Moses Gaster Collection
(Rumanian literature); Péla Iványi-Grünwald Collection (books
in English relating to Hungary); Russian Orthodox Church in
London Library (on deposit)
7a) Own classification, mostly open access; 7b) Author catalogue;
subject catalogue for post-1974 acquisitions
8a) Bona-fide scholars admitted on written application to the librarian;
8c) Information on library services provided by occasional news
sheets
9) Notes for readers (annual); Bibliographical guides 1977-
10) Bartkins, D 'The Library of the School of Slavonic and East
European Studies' *Solanus* 2, 1967, pp3-6; Deletant, D 'A survey
of the Gaster books in the School of Slavonic and East European
Studies Library' *Solanus* 10, 1975, pp14-23

162 WARBURG INSTITUTE LIBRARY
1b) University of London
2a) Woburn Square, London WC1H OAB; 2b) 01-580-9663
3) Professor J B Trapp (Director), Dr W F Ryan (Librarian)
4a) Established 1944; Collection has developed out of the library
of Professor A M Warburg (1866-1929) of Hamburg; 4b) The aim
of the library is not to cover one discipline exhaustively but to
bring as much and as diverse information as possible to bear on
specific problems in its wide field of interest

162   WARBURG INSTITUTE LIBRARY (continued)
5a)   Survival and influence of Greek and Roman civilisation; 5b) Theory
      of art, literature and symbolism; history of state pageantry; idea
      of empire; medieval and Renaissance Platonism; cosmological and
      astrological ideas and their pictorial expression; ritual and myth;
      history of religion; emergence of modern science; survival of
      ancient forms and motives in literature; humanism; the Reform-
      ation; emblematics; history of art, architecture and archaeology
      with special reference to Europe and the Near East
6a)   Bookstock: c202,000 volumes of monographs. Bound serials:
      c24,000 volumes. Current serials received: 800 titles; 6b) Photo-
      graphic collection (arranged by subject; much material on Christian
      and secular iconography, and on illustrated secular texts of the
      Middle Ages)
7a)   Own classification. Open-access; 7b) Author and subject cata-
      logues
8a)   Open to academic staff and postgraduates of London University,
      and to teachers and researchers from other universities; others at
      the discretion of the director
9)   The Warburg Institute (guide); *Catalog of the Warburg Institute
      Library* 2nd ed rev and enlarged 12 volumes, Boston, G K Hall,
      1967. *First supplement* 1971
10)   Gombrich, E H *Aby Warburg: an intellectual biography, with a
      memoir on the history of the library by Fritz Saxl* London, the
      Institute, 1970; Bing, G 'The Warburg Institute' *Library Association
      record* 36, 1934, pp262-266

163   LONDON GRADUATE SCHOOL OF BUSINESS STUDIES
      LIBRARY (LONDON BUSINESS SCHOOL LIBRARY)
1b)   London Graduate School of Business Studies
2a)   Sussex Place, Regents Park, London NW1 4SA; 2b) 01-262-5050;
      2c) 27461
3)   K D C Vernon FLA
4a)   1966. The Library was formed at the same time as the foundation
      of the London Business School; 4b) To support the teaching and
      research work of the LBS by the provision of library and infor-
      mation services, with adequate seating accommodation for post-
      graduate and research students and staff.
5a)   All aspects of management and business studies; 5b) The library is
      particularly strong on company information and financial data;
      information on industries; abstracting and indexing publications.
      Participates in a joint indexing scheme known as SCIMP with
      other European business schools.
6a)   27,000 volumes; 500 current periodicals. Information files on
      industries and countries; 6b) Company reports; financial data
      services; working papers issued by business schools; statistical
      publications
7a)   London Classification of Business Studies. Open-access; 7b) Author
      and classified subject catalogues

163   LGS OF BUSINESS STUDIES LIBRARY (continued)
8a)   Members of the school; staff and students from other colleges; others, for reference, on written application; 8b) Closed on Sat in vacations; 8c) Enquiry and loan service, inter-library loans
9)   Periodicals in the library of LBS; Sources of information; Contents of current journals; Accessions list; Information notes.
10)   Vernon, K D C and Lang, V *London classification of business studies* London Business School, 1971; Vernon, K D C *Use of management and business literature* London, Butterworths, 1975.

164   LOUGHBOROUGH UNIVERSITY OF TECHNOLOGY LIBRARY
1b)   Loughborough University of Technology
2a)   Main Library, Loughborough, Leics LE11 3TU (tel 0509-63171); Towers Library, Ashby Road, Loughborough, Leics LE11 3TN (tel 0509-215751); 2c) 34319 UNITEC G
3)   A J Evans BPharm PhD FLA MIInfSc
4a)   Leicestershire Technical Institute was founded in 1908, and received its charter as a university in 1966; 4b) Provision for teaching, research and related background subject needs of the whole university
5a)   General academic subjects; 5b) The university library comprises the Main Library (science, technology, social sciences), the Towers Library (education, literature and the arts), and the Schofield Library Annexe (pre-1971 serials volumes; little-used books)
6a)   185,000 volumes of books and pamphlets; 50,000 bound volumes of serials. 3000 current serials; total serials: 3500. Microforms equivalent to about 25,000 volumes; Some tape-slides.
7a)   Open-access. Dewey Decimal Classification for books; periodicals in broad subject order; 7b) Name catalogue (cards); classified catalogue (cards); alphabetical subject index (computer printout); serials holdings list (computer printout); subject guide to periodicals (computer printout); sponsoring bodies list (computer printout; list of periodicals arranged by institution); guides to the reference and short-loan collections (computer printout)
8a)   Members of the university; others, for reference, on written application; 8b) Open on Sundays in term; 8c) Enquiry desk; Information Section deals with subject enquiries, provision of data, and literature searches; user education programme
9)   Guide to the library

165   JOHN RYLANDS UNIVERSITY LIBRARY OF MANCHESTER
1b)   Victoria University of Manchester
2a)   Oxford Road, Manchester M13 9PP (tel 061-273-3333); Special Collections Division, Deansgate, Manchester (tel 061-834-5343); 2c) 668932
3)   F W Ratcliffe JP MA PhD
4a)   The university was founded in 1851. The library arises from the

165 JOHN RYLANDS UNIVERSITY LIBRARY (continued)
     merger of the John Ryland Library and the University Library in
     1972
5a) General; 5b) The library comprises the Main Building (arts), the
     Special Collections Division (early and rare books), the Christie
     Science Library, the Medical Faculty Library, the Education
     Library, the Economic and Social Studies Library
6a) 2,650,000 volumes; 8000 current periodicals; 6b) Prince Lee Li-
     brary (theology, history); David Forbes Library (science); Free-
     man Library (medieval history); Muirhead Library (law); Hager
     Memorial Library (Greek law; Teutonic history); Manchester
     Goethe Society Library; Schiller Anstalt Library; Manchester Geo-
     graphical Society Library; Library of Lord Morley; Bullock Col-
     lection (16th century Italian literature); Partington Collection
     (history of chemistry); Althorp Library (early books); Spencer
     Library; Manchester Bibliographical Society Library; Manchester
     Medical Society Library; Deaf Education Library; the Library of
     William Temple College (theology); the Library of the Institute of
     African Studies, London; Iranian materials; the Library of the
     International African Institute (North African countries); Man-
     chester Museum Library (history of science and technology)
7a) Dewey Decimal Classification for open-access collections; large
     closed-access collections; 7b) Author catalogue (cards) in each
     building; partial union catalogue in main building; classified sub-
     ject catalogue and subject index in main building; various supple-
     mentary catalogues (printed and cards)
8a) Members of the university; others, for reference, on written appli-
     cation; 8b) The main building is open on Sundays, except for
     Easter Sunday, the summer vacation and part of the Christmas
     vacation
9)   Bulletin of the John Rylands University Library; Pocket guide to
     facilities and resources; Guide to special collections; History of
     the library; Catalogue of medical books in Manchester University
     Library 1480-1700; The anti-slavery collection; The Hobill Collec-
     tion of Wesleyana
10   Ratcliffe, F W 'Manchester: the John Rylands University Library
     of Manchester' *Encyclopedia of library and information science*
     vol 17, New York, Dekker, 1976, pp107-113; Brady, D 'Orient-
     alist collections in the John Rylands University Library, Man-
     chester' in Standing Conference of National and University
     Libraries, Group of Orientalist Libraries *Report of the annual
     conference, 1976* the Group, 1976, pp6-8.

166 MANCHESTER BUSINESS SCHOOL LIBRARY
1b) Manchester Business School
2a) Booth Street West, Manchester M15 6PB; 2b) 061-273-8228;
     2c) 668354 MBSMNCHR
3)   J D Dews MA FLA

166   MANCHESTER BUSINESS SCHOOL LIBRARY (continued)
5a)   Management and business studies
6a)   30,000 volumes; 700 current periodicals; 6b) Company reports;
      working papers issued by business schools
8a   Members of the school; others, for reference, on written appli-
      cation; 8b) Standard hours
9)   Contents pages in management

167   UNIVERSITY LIBRARY, NEWCASTLE UPON TYNE
1b)   University of Newcastle upon Tyne
2a)   Queen Victoria Road, Newcastle upon Tyne NE1 7RU; 2b) 0632-
      28511; 2c) 53654
3)   B J Enright MA DPhil
4a)   1871; 4b) To support the teaching and research of the university
5a)   General; 5b) There is a separate Law Library
6a)   475,000 volumes; 3800 current periodicals; 6b) Gertrude Bell
      Collection (Middle East); Burman Collection (Alnwick); Charlton
      Collection (brass rubbings); Gilchrist Collection (agriculture);
      Heslop Collection (dictionaries); Hindson-Reid Collection
      (engraved wood blocks); Merz Collection (mathematics); Pybus
      Collection (history of medicine); Runciman and Trevelyan
      papers; Robert White Collection (English literature, ballads, chap-
      books); early Northern school libraries
7a)   Open-access except for special collections and some older stock
      for which advance notice is required. Dewey Decimal Classifi-
      cation; 7b) Name catalogue and classified catalogue with alpha-
      betical subject index
8a)   University staff and students. Others by special arrangement;
      8b) Standard hours; 8c) Standard professional services
9)   Reports of the librarian; Library and literature guides; Cox, N S M,
      J D Dews, and J L Dolby *The computer and the library* 1966;
      Donkin, Winifred C *Catalogue of the Gertrude Bell Collection*
      1960; Emmerson, Joan S *Medical works in translation* 1965;
      Isaac, P C G *The Burman Alnwick Collection* 1973; Raw, Barbara C
      Lives of the saints: a description of MS 1 1961; Thomson, F M
      Newcastle chapbooks . . . 1969. *Extra series (duplicated):*
      Catalogue of the library at Wallington Hall, Northumberland, 1968;
      The Charlton Collection of brass rubbings, 1967; An exhibition of
      fine bird books, 1966; A list of the letters and papers of Gertrude
      Bell, 1966; A list of the post-incunabula in the University Library,
      1965; Old maps of N E England, 1600-1865, 1967; Short title
      list of the Sandes Library, 1969; Special collections in the Univer-
      sity Library, 4th ed, 1973; W B Yeats (1865-1939): catalogue of
      an exhibition, 1965. King's College Library Publications:
      Bland, D S *Chapbooks and garlands in the Robert White Collec-
      tion* 1956; Mitchell, W S *British signed bindings in the Library of
      King's College* 1954; Mitchell, W S *Catalogue of the Heslop Col-
      lection of dictionaries* 1955; Mitchell, W S *One hundred medical
      works,* 1957.

10) Enright, B J 'Newcastle: University of Newcastle upon Tyne Library' in: *Encyclopedia of library and information science*, vol 19, New York: Dekker, 1976, pp457-465

168 NOTTINGHAM UNIVERSITY LIBRARY
1b) University of Nottingham
2a) Nottingham NG7 2RD (tel: 0602-56101); School of Agriculture Library, Sutton Bonington, Loughborough LE12 5RD (tel: 05097-2386); Medical Library, Queen's Medical Centre, Nottingham NG7 2UH (Tel: 0602-700111 ext 3644); 2c) 37346 (Science Library—covers Main Library also); 341788 (Agriculture Library)
3) P A Hoare MA ALA
4a) Founded 1928. 1881-1928 used the facilities of the Free Public Library in Shakespeare Street. 1928 library opened as part of new college building, University Park. 1948 School of Agriculture Library opened. 1973 new Main Library (arts, social sciences and education) opened; 1977 Medical Library opened in new Medical School complex; 4b) To meet the literature and information needs of members of the university
5a) General (the university has faculties of arts, education, law and social sciences, pure science, applied science, agricultural science and medicine); 5b) The university library comprises the Main Library (humanities, social sciences and education), and separate Agriculture, Law, Medical and Science Libraries; departmental libraries for architecture, chemistry and music
6a) Books and periodical volumes 530,000. Pamphlets and government publications 165,000. Microforms, tapes, films etc 107,000. Manuscripts 2 million. Current periodicals c4700; 6b) The Manuscripts Department contains some 2 million items, many of them of archival nature and deposited by local families. Collections of printed material in the Main Library include: Briggs Collection (early educational literature); D H Lawrence Collection; French Revolution; Cambridge Drama Centre Collection (English drama of the late 18th and early 19th centuries); East Midlands Collection; European Documentation Centre. Science Library: Porter Collection (ornithology); Medical Library: F H Jacob History of Medicine Collection; Nottingham Medico-Chirurgical Society Collection.
7a) Open-access, except for rare books and mss: Library of Congress Classification (Medical Library: National Library of Medicine Classification); 7b) Name catalogue, classified catalogue, subject index (on cards in Main, Law, Science and Agriculture Libraries); some special catalogues eg international organizations; stripdex and printed catalogues of periodicals. Medical Library has COM fiche catalogues for author, title, keyword and MeSH. Main Library Short Loan Collection catalogue and subject index on line-printer output
8a) Members of the university; graduates of the university, for

168   NOTTINGHAM UNIVERSITY LIBRARY (continued)
reference; others, for reference, on written application; borrowing to all outside the university only on special application; 8b) Standard hours (closed on August Sats), with reference-only periods in evenings, Sat afternoons and Sun in summer; variations in these times in some libraries, notably Medical Library which is fully staffed unti 1900; 8c) Reference and bibliographical assistance is available to readers in all libraries, principally through subject librarians.

9)   Guide to the university library; Guides to the Science, Medical, Agriculture and Law Libraries; East Midlands Collection; Special collections; Readers' information leaflets. Lists of the periodical holdings in the University, Science and Medical Libraries. University of Nottingham theses on East Midlands subjects. Guides to Slavonic Material in the University Library. Science Library guides to resources: translating dictionaries, report literature, abstracts and indexes, etc; Medical Library: reports and series

10)   'Nottingham University Library' *Architect's journal* 159(17), 1974, pp895-910; 'Interior design: Library, Nottingham University' *Architectural review* 156(931), 1974, pp153-158; 'University buildings, Nottingham' *Architect and building news* 227(33), 18 August 1965, pp299-306; Logan, R G 'Nottingham University Law Library' *The Law librarian* 6(2), 1975, pp19-21; Brook, M 'Nottingham University Library Local Collection' *Bulletin of local history* (East Midlands Region) 10, 1975, pp9-12.

169   OPEN UNIVERSITY LIBRARY
1b)   Open University
2a)   Walton Hall, Milton Keynes MK7 6AA; 2b) 0908-74066; 2c) 826739
3)   D J Simpson BSc(Econ) FLA
4a)   Proposed in a government white paper of 1966, the Open University received its charter in 1969. The library was founded in 1969; 4b) Serves the staff of the university; students are expected to use their local libraries
5a)   General
6a)   80,000 volumes; 2100 current periodicals; extensive collection of non-book materials; 6b) Educational technology
7a)   Mostly open-access. Dewey Decimal Classification; 7b) Books: name catalogue (cards), and short-title catalogue by author, title, classmark. Periodicals: title and classmark sequences. TV and radio programmes: by classmark, title, name, programme
8a)   Staff of the university; others, for reference, on written application; 8b) Closed Sats; 8c) General reference service; picture research for OU printed course units; literature guide preparation for OU courses; current awareness for OU course teams and senior staff; bibliography preparation; literature searches; technology cuttings service
9)   Literature guides for OU courses; Guides to use of OU Library and its stock for each faculty; Annual reports

UNIVERSITY OF OXFORD

The entries for the University of Oxford comprise the Bodleian Library and its associated departments, and a selection of departmental libraries (as with Cambridge, mainly those with larger or more important collections which permit a reasonable degree of access).

A full list of departmental libraries is given, but intending readers are advised to make contact with librarians before attempting to use the collections.

The constituent colleges of the university each possess libraries varying in range from undergraduate working collections to unique historical and research collections. Intending readers should make contact with librarians before attempting to use the collections.

A very full description of departmental and college libraries in Oxford is given in: Morgan, P *Oxford libraries outside the Bodleian: a guide* Oxford, Oxford Bibliographical Society and the Bodleian Library, 1973.

Further details of opening hours and other useful information concerning Oxford libraries is to be found in *Oxford libraries*, a leaflet issued by the University Registry. *The union list of serials in the science area, Oxford, stage 11,* Oxford, Bodleian Library, 1970 (and supplements, 1st, 1971) is a further source of information on scientific and medical libraries.

Departmental libraries and libraries associated with the Bodleian
ASHMOLEAN MUSEUM OF ART AND ARCHAEOLOGY
Ashmolean Library, Oxford OX1 2PH (Phone: 0865-57222/51117)
AGRICULTURAL SCIENCE
Department Library, Parks Road, Oxford (Phone: 0865-57245)
BODLEIAN LAW LIBRARY
St Cross Road, Oxford (Phone: 0865-49631)
BOTANY
Botany School Library, South Parks Road, Oxford OX1 3RA
(Phone: 0865-53391)
COMMONWEALTH STUDIES INSTITUTE
Library, 21 St Giles, Oxford OX1 3LA (Phone: 0865-52952/4)
EDUCATIONAL STUDIES
Department Library, 15 Norham Gardens, Oxford OX2 6PY
(Phone: 0865-54121)
ENGLISH FACULTY
English Faculty Library, St Cross Building, Manor Road, Oxford
OX1 3UQ (Phone: 0865-49631)
ENGINEERING SCIENCE
Department Library, Parks Road, Oxford OX1 3PJ (Phone: 0865-59988)
ENTOMOLOGY
Department Library (Phone: 0865-57527)
EXTERNAL STUDIES
Department Library, Rewley House, 3-7 Wellington Square,
Oxford OX1 2JA (Phone: 0865-52901)

UNIVERSITY OF OXFORD *Departmental libraries* (continued)
FORESTRY
Forestry Library, Commonwealth Forestry Institute, South Parks Road, Oxford OX1 3RB (Phone: 0865-57891)
GEOLOGY AND MINERALOGY
Department Library, Parks Road, Oxford (Phone: 0865-54511)
HISTORY FACULTY
History Faculty Library, Merton Street, Oxford OX1 4JG (Phone: 0865-43395)
HISTORY OF ART
Ashmolean Museum, Oxford (Phone: 0865-57522)
HOOKE LIBRARY
Radcliffe Science Library, South Parks Road, Oxford (Phone: 0865-54161)
INDIAN INSTITUTE
Indian Institute Library, New Bodleian, Parks Road, Oxford (Phone: 0865-44675)
INSTITUTE OF AGRICULTURAL ECONOMICS
Institute Library, Dartington House, Little Clarendon St, Oxford OX1 2HP (Phone: 0865-52921)
INSTITUTE OF ECONOMICS AND STATISTICS
Institute Library, St Cross Building, Manor Road, Oxford (Phone: 0865-49631)
INSTITUTE OF SOCIAL ANTHROPOLOGY
Institute Library, 51 Banbury Road, Oxford (Phone: 0865-55971)
MAISON FRANÇAISE
Library, Norham Road, Oxford OX2 6SE (Phone: 0865-54576/7)
MODERN LANGUAGES FACULTY
Faculty Library, Taylor Institution, Oxford OX1 3NA (Phone: 0865-56303)
MUSEUM OF THE HISTORY OF SCIENCE
Museum of the History of Science Library, Broad St, Oxford OX1 3AZ (Phone: 0865-43997)
MUSIC FACULTY
Faculty Library, 32 Holywell, Oxford OX1 3SL (Phone: 0865-47069)
ORIENTAL INSTITUTE
Institute Library, Pusey Lane, Oxford OX1 2LE (Phone: 0865-59272)
PHILOSOPHY
Sub-Faculty Library, 10 Merton Street, Oxford (Phone: 0865-40719)
PITT RIVERS MUSEUM
Balfour Library, Ethnology and Prehistory Department, Pitt Rivers Museum, Parks Road, Oxford, OX1 3PP (Phone: 0865-54979)
PUSEY HOUSE
Pusey House Library, St Giles, Oxford OX1 3LZ (Phone: 0865-59519)

UNIVERSITY OF OXFORD *Departmental libraries* (continued)
RADCLIFFE SCIENCE LIBRARY
South Parks Road, Oxford (Phone: 0865-54161)
RHODES HOUSE
Rhodes House Library, South Parks Road, Oxford (Phone: 0865-55762)
SCHOOL OF GEOGRAPHY
Geography Library, Mansfield Road, Oxford OX1 3TB (Phone: 0865-46134)
SOCIAL STUDIES
Social Studies Library, 45 Wellington Square, Oxford OX1 2JF (Phone: 0865-55935)
TAYLOR INSTITUTION
Taylor Institution Library, St Giles, Oxford OX1 3NA (Phone: 0865-57917)
THEOLOGY FACULTY
Faculty Library, Pusey House, St Giles, Oxford OX1 3LZ (Phone: 0865-57117)
UNIVERSITY OBSERVATORY
Department of Astrophysics, South Parks Road, Oxford (Phone: 0865-511336)
ZOOLOGY AND COMPARATIVE ANATOMY
Department Library, South Parks Road, Oxford (Phone: 0865-56789)
ZOOLOGY–EDWARD GREY INSTITUTE OF FIELD ORNITHOLOGY
Alexander Library, Edward Grey Institute of Field Ornithology, South Parks Road, Oxford OX1 3PS (Phone: 0865-56789)

College libraries:
ALL SOULS COLLEGE
Oxford OX1 4AL (Phone: 0865-22251)
BALLIOL COLLEGE
Oxford OX1 3BJ (Phone: 0865-49601)
BRASENOSE COLLEGE
Oxford OX1 4AJ (Phone: 0865-48641)
CHRIST CHURCH
Oxford OX1 1DP (Phone: 0865-42201)
CORPUS CHRISTI COLLEGE
Oxford OX1 4JF (Phone: 0865-49431)
EXETER COLLEGE
Oxford OX1 3DP (Phone: 0865-44681)
HERTFORD COLLEGE
Oxford OX1 3BW (Phone: 0865-41434)
JESUS COLLEGE
Oxford OX1 3DW (Phone: 0865-49511)
KEBLE COLLEGE
Oxford OX1 3PG (Phone: 0865-59201)

UNIVERSITY OF OXFORD *College libraries* (continued)
LADY MARGARET HALL
Oxford OX2 6QA (Phone: 0865-54353)
LINCOLN COLLEGE
Oxford OX1 3DR (Phone: 0865-42580)
MAGDALEN COLLEGE
Oxford OX1 4AU (Phone: 0865-41781)
MERTON COLLEGE
Oxford OX1 4JD (Phone: 0865-49651)
NEW COLLEGE
Oxford OX1 3BN (Phone: 0865-48451)
NUFFIELD COLLEGE
Oxford OX1 1NF (Phone: 0865-48014)
ORIEL COLLEGE
Oxford OX1 4EW (Phone: 0865-41651)
PEMBROKE COLLEGE
Oxford OX1 1DW (Phone: 0865-42271)
THE QUEEN'S COLLEGE
Oxford OX1 4AW (Phone: 0865-48411)
ST ANNE'S COLLEGE
Oxford OX2 6HS (Phone: 0865-57417)
ST ANTHONY'S COLLEGE
Oxford OX2 6JF (Phone: 0865-59651)
ST CATHERINE'S COLLEGE
Oxford OX1 3UJ (Phone: 0865-49541)
ST EDMUND HALL
Oxford OX1 4AR (Phone: 0865-45511)
ST HILDA'S COLLEGE
Oxford OX4 1DY (Phone: 0865-41821)
ST HUGH'S COLLEGE
Oxford OX2 6LE (Phone: 0865-57341)
ST JOHN'S COLLEGE
Oxford OX1 3JP (Phone: 0865-47671)
ST PETER'S COLLEGE
Oxford OX1 2DL (Phone: 0865-48436)
SOMERVILLE COLLEGE
Oxford OX2 6HD (Phone: 0865-57595)
TRINITY COLLEGE
Oxford OX1 3BH (Phone: 0865-41801)
UNIVERSITY COLLEGE
Oxford OX1 4BH (Phone: 0865-41661)
WADHAM COLLEGE
Oxford OX1 3PN (Phone: 0865-42564)
WORCESTER COLLEGE
Oxford OX1 2HB (Phone: 0865-47251)

170   BODLEIAN LIBRARY
1b)   University of Oxford
2a)   Bodleian Library, Oxford OX1 3BG; 2b) 0865-44675; 2c) 83656
3)   R Shackleton MA DLitt FBA FSA FRSL (Bodley's Librarian)

4a) The earliest university library at Oxford dates from the 14th century, but the Bodleian Library, the University Library as such, dates from 1602, owing its refoundation to Sir Thomas Bodley. The Bodleian is entitled to receive British publications under the provision of the various copyright acts, but the library had in fact secured copyright privileges from the Stationers' Company in 1610. Consequently its 17th and 18th century English holdings are very strong. The Bodleian is second in size only to the British Library Reference Division.

4b) The Bodleian Library is the main library of the University of Oxford. It is spread over several buildings in central Oxford. The Old Bodleian Library incorporates the Duke Humphrey's Library; the Radcliffe Camera was occupied in 1862; and the New Library dates from 1936-1939. Incorporation of the Radcliffe Science Library, the Indian Institute and Rhodes House in the 1930s helped to evolve a closely-knit central library system to serve the university. The Bodleian is a library of outstanding national and international importance

5a) The Bodleian Library as such is mainly devoted to the humanities and the social sciences. Law and science are catered for in the Bodleian Law Library and the Radcliffe Science Library respectively; both these collections are administered as part of the Bodleian.

6a) Bookstock: c3,400,000 volumes: 6b) Robert Burton Library; John Selden Library; Gough Collection (liturgy, topography, etc); Malone Collection (Elizabethan and Jacobean plays and literature); Oppenheimer Collection (Hebraica); Backhouse Collection (Chinese material); Mortara Italian Library; Shelley Collection; Bywater Collection (Aristotelian philosophy); Henry Ward Poole Collection (Mexican independence pamphlets); John Johnson Collection (ephemeral printing); Albert Ehrman Broxbourne Library (on deposit). The extensive manuscript collections include the following: Barocci Collection (Greek manuscripts); Laudian manuscripts; Edward Pococke manuscripts (Oriental); Dr Robert Huntingdon manuscripts (Oriental); Douce Collection (illuminated manuscripts and printed books); John Locke papers; T W Bourne Collection (Handel)

7a) Own classification scheme; 7b) Author catalogue in book form. Card catalogue of foreign dissertations.

8a) Available to members of Oxford University. Non-members of the university require a letter of recommendation; 8c) Photocopying facilities

9) Visitors guide; Bodleian Library record

10) Craster, E *History of the Bodleian Library 1845-1945* Oxford, 1952; University of Oxford 'Report of the Committee on University Libraries' Supplement no 1 to the *University gazette* 97, November 1966.

171   BODLEIAN LAW LIBRARY

1b)   University of Oxford.

2a)   St Cross Building, Manor Road, Oxford OX1 3UR; 2b) 0865-49631;
       2c) 83656

3)   E H Cordeaux (until August 30 1978. Post to be filled).

4a)   Opened 1964 as a dependent library of the Bodleian Library
       (founded 1602); 4b) The principal function of the library is to
       serve as reference library for members of the university studying
       law, both for research and for undergraduate studies. The library
       is also used by members of the legal profession and by visiting
       academics from other universities, while students from other uni-
       versities may be admitted as vacation readers.

5a)   Law; 5b) Includes criminology, but most works on forensic science
       and medicine are in the Radcliffe Science Library. Canon law,
       ancient law in oriental languages, and most books published before
       1800 are in the main Bodleian Library. The Bodleian is a deposi-
       tory library for publications of the Council of Europe, the Euro-
       pean Communities, the United Nations and other international
       organizations, and also receives doctoral dissertations (including
       law) from universities in France, Germany, the Netherlands,
       Switzerland and Scandinavian countries.

6a)   Total stock: c200,000 volumes (not counting law books in the
       main Bodleian). Current serials received: 2079. Non-book ma-
       terial: 147 microfilms, 740 microprint cards, 5344 microfiches;
       6b) Strength of the library's collections: Very substantial holdings
       in the following areas: international law, comparative law, ancient
       law, Roman law, philosophy of law, criminology, Great Britain
       and Ireland, British Commonwealth, United States of America,
       Western European countries, Russia (both pre- and post-1917),
       South Africa. Fairly good holdings in Eastern European countries
       (apart from Russia).

7a)   Entirely open access. Classified by own system; 7b) Author cata-
       logue, alphabetical subject catalogue

8a)   Members of the University of Oxford and members of the Society
       of Public Teachers of Law are admitted without recommendation.
       Graduates of other universities and other persons doing serious
       research may be admitted on recommendation from someone in
       a responsible position. Undergraduates of other universities may
       be admitted in vacations only, on recommendation or with a
       SCONUL vacation reading card; 8b) Full term: M-F 0930-2200,
       Sat (1st to 7th weeks) to 1700. Vacations: M-F 0930-1900, Sat
       to 1300. Closed on public holidays; Encaenia Day; August bank
       holiday week; between Christmas and New Year; 8c) General and
       bibliographical information, photocopying from library books,
       use of microform readers, borrowing of books from the main
       Bodleian Library for use in the Law Library, borrowing of books
       on inter-library loan for regular readers

172

171   BODLEIAN LAW LIBRARY (continued)
9)   Notes for readers (latest revision 1975); Legal literature of the
       United Kingdom (by E H Cordeaux) 1974.
10)   Carter, P B The new Bodleian Law Library at Oxford in *The Jour-
       nal of the Society of Public Teachers of Law* new series, vol 8,
       pp80-5 (1964); Lawson, F H *The Oxford law school 1850-1965*
       pp178-183 (1968); Lush, S A 'The Bodleian Law Library, Oxford'
       in *The law librarian* vol 7, pp19-21 (1976); Bodleian Library
       Annual report of the curators from 1964/65 (especially the reports
       for 1964/65 and 1973/74)

172   ASHMOLEAN LIBRARY
1b)   University of Oxford
2a)   Beaumont Street, Oxford; 2b) 0865-57522/51117
3)   C Currie BCL MA LLB FLA
4a)   Library collections to support the museum have been in existence
       since 1677 but the present collection largely dates from 1901
       when collections in art (Eldon library) and classical archaeology
       were brought together; 4b) Today the library is of far more than
       just local importance. It contains collections of international im-
       portance in the fields of classical studies and archaeology in close
       proximity to a major museum collection
5a)   Art and archaeology; 5b) Western art, Eastern art, antiquities,
       classical culture and literature, ancient history, numismatics, Near
       Eastern archaeology, papyrology
6b)   Fortnum Collection (art), Barnard Collection (numismatics),
       Leeds (British archaeology), Murray (classical literature), Taylor
       (Roman archaeology), Griffith Collections (Egyptology), Hunt Col-
       lection (papyrology), Hope Collection (topography), Tyas Cook
       and Wedderburn Collections (Ruskin), Library of the Oxford
       Architectural and Historical Society. Archive and manuscript col-
       lections chiefly of Sir Arthur Evans (Cretan archaeology), and
       F J Haverfield and Sir Ian Richmond (Romano-British archaeology).
       Archives and papers of Near Eastern archaeologists and Egypt-
       ologists kept in the Griffith Institute. There are extensive collec-
       tions of prints and illustrative material in the Department of West-
       ern Art (F W Hope Collection; Douce Collection, etc)
8a)   Members of the university and others by application, for reference
10)   There is a considerable bibliography about the museum and its
       collections and activities. For a summary see: University of Ox-
       ford, Report of the Committee on the Ashmolean Museum
       Gazette supplement 1 (98), 1967.

173   BALFOUR LIBRARY, DEPARTMENT OF ETHNOLOGY AND
       PREHISTORY Pitt Rivers Museum
1b)   University of Oxford.
2a)   Parks Road, Oxford; 2b) 0865-54979

173 BALFOUR LIBRARY (continued)
3)   H P G Unsworth (Librarian)
4a) The library, founded in 1939, is named after Henry Balfour
     (1863-1939), curator of the Pitt Rivers Museum from 1891 until
     his death. His personal collection forms the core of the Library.
     After 1939 first steps were taken towards cataloguing other col-
     lections given to the library and incorporating them with the
     Balfour Collection; 4b) The library has been built-up to service
     the museum collections, which consist mainly of archaeology and
     ethnology, and the full range of teaching interests of the Depart-
     ment of Ethnology and Prehistory.
5a) Archaeology, ethnology and anthropology; 5b) the categories in
     5a are broadly interpreted and the library contains collections
     over a wide range of related subjects including non-industrialised
     technologies of ancient and modern simpler societies, music, re-
     ligion, art, travels and social ecology.
6a) Bookstock: 20,000 volumes (monographs and bound serial vol-
     umes). Current serials received: 136 titles. Serials retained: 140
     titles; 6b) Collections of manuscripts relating to Henry Balfour,
     H G Beasley, Miss Beatrice Blackwood, Dr L H Dudley Buxton,
     Sir John Myres, Sir Baldwin Spencer, Sir Edward Burnett Tylor,
     and Capt Robert Powley Wild. Collection of c200,000 war-time
     air photographs of Western Europe. Collection of air photographs
     of Burma, Malaya and Siam.
7a) Most books and all periodicals on open-access; closed-access for
     rare books, pamphlet collection, photographic and manuscript
     archive. Classification by area/subject subdivisions; 7b) Card cata-
     logue of authors; typescript list of manuscripts; area/subject shelf
     index; periodicals index by title.
8a) The library is open to senior members and graduate students of
     the University of Oxford and undergraduates taught in the De-
     partment of Ethnology and Prehistory. Other persons may be
     admitted at the discretion of the librarian; 8b) M-F 0900-1230
     and 1400-1700. Vacation: 0900-1230 and 1400-1600. Closed
     at weekends, summer bank holiday and for 10 days over both
     Easter and Christmas.
9)   Occasional papers in technology (monograph series published
     through the Pitt Rivers Museum)

174 ENGLISH FACULTY LIBRARY
1b) University of Oxford
2a) St Cross Building, Manor Road, Oxford OX1 3UQ; 2b) 0865-
     49631
3)   Miss M J P Weedon BA MA
4a) 1914; 4b) Serves as an undergraduate library, but also contains
     much material of interest to researchers
5a) English language and literature

174   ENGLISH FACULTY LIBRARY (continued)
6a)   Bookstock: c60,000 volumes (monographs and bound serials).
      Current serials received: c165 titles; 6b) A few small special
      author or subject collections, usually from the libraries of former
      professors. Anglo-Saxon philology (A S Napier); Swift (H J Davis);
      'Somerville and Ross' (Nevill and Sir Patrick Coghill); E H W Meyer-
      stein's published books and manuscripts; manuscripts and other
      material connected with Wilfred Owen. Working papers used by
      S Roscoe in the compilation of his bibliography 'John Newbery
      and his successors' (1973); Old Norse and Icelandic collection;
      F York Powell collection (lent by Christ Church); W P Ker collec-
      tion (lent by All Souls College)
7a)   Own classification. Open and closed access; 7b) Author card cata-
      logue; classified shelf list
8a)   Members of the university in residence reading for an Oxford
      degree in English, or teaching English for the university or one of
      its colleges. Others admitted in special circumstances as specified
      in the library rules; 8b) Closed for 10 days at Christmas and Easter,
      on Encaenia Day, and for 6 weeks in August and September
9)   Notes for readers; Library rules

175   FORESTRY LIBRARY
1b)   University of Oxford, Department of Forestry
2a)   Commonwealth Forestry Institute, South Parks Road, Oxford;
      2b) 0865-511431
3)   E P Hemmings
4a)   The library originated in the Royal Indian Engineering College at
      Cooper's Hill near Windsor in 1886. The college became the
      School of Forestry at Oxford in 1905. The Imperial (Common-
      wealth) Forestry Bureau which has always been based on the li-
      brary was established in 1938. Present building occupied from
      1950; 4b) The library serves the needs of everyone seriously con-
      cerned with the study of forestry and forest products. One of the
      most, if not the most, comprehensive collections in the world in
      its field
5a)   Forestry and forestry products; 5b) Related fields especially in
      plant science
6a)   Bookstock: c12,000 monographs. Current serials received: c350
      titles. Serials retained: c900 titles. Microfilm: c300,000 feet;
      6b) The main strength of the collection is in its serial holdings.
      About one third of the collection has been put on microfilm.
      One outstanding feature of the microfilm project is the filming
      of the complete range of the *Catalogues of the world forestry
      literature* (1822-1975), containing 1.5 million references. All
      pre-1965 catalogues are retained only on microfilm. The catalogue
      is arranged by subject, species and country.
7a)   Oxford Decimal Classification for forestry. Mostly open-access;

175 FORESTRY LIBRARY (continued)
7b) Author and subject catalogues; Catalogue of the world forestry literature
8a) Generally available for reference; 8c) Forestry Information Service based on catalogues . . . (See Finlayson, W, Hemmings, E F et al 'Forestry Information Services from Oxford' *Journal of forestry* 76(2), 1978, pp97-99; Card Title Service to subscribers
9) Hemmings, E F *Basic library list for forestry* Oxford, Commonwealth Forestry Institute, 4th ed, 1967 pp60
10) Hemmings, E F 'The Commonwealth Forestry Institute microfilm project' in: *Proceedings 3rd World Congress of Agricultural Librarians and Documentalists* Washington, 1965, 1968, pp117-121; Hemmings, E F 'The Forestry Library' *Oxford University libraries bulletin* 6, 1977, pp4-6.

176 GEOGRAPHY LIBRARY—SCHOOL OF GEOGRAPHY LIBRARY
1b) University of Oxford
2a) Mansfield Road, Oxford OX1 3TB; 2b) 0865-46134
3) Miss E M Buxton MA FLA (Librarian and Map Curator)
4a) 1889; 4b) Serves as an undergraduate library but its comprehensive collections make it an important national collection
5a) Geography and allied subjects
6a) Bookstock: 32,000 volumes (monographs and bound serials). Current serials received: 217 titles. Serials retained: 507 titles. Slides: 5500. Aerial photographs: 3500. Maps: c54,000 items; 6b) Buxton collection (Isle of Wight); weather records; Old Dominion collection (books on Virginia)
7a) Own classification. Mostly open access; 7b) Author catalogues, subject catalogue of periodical articles, map catalogue
8a) Members of the School of Geography for loan and reference. Members of Oxford and other universities for reference; 8c) Information retrieval on optical coincidence cards
9) Book lists and bibliographies
10) Williams, J 'The first department' *Geographical magazine* January 1972; Bromley, H 'The School of Geography, Oxford' *Bulletin of the Society of University Cartographers* 8 (1), 1973.

177 HISTORY FACULTY LIBRARY
1b) University of Oxford
2a) Broad Street, Oxford OX1 3BQ; 2b) 0865-43395
3) Miss M A Abley
4a) Established 1908 as a graduate seminar library in medieval history. Lending library opened in 1958, and scope widened to cover syllabus of Honours School of Modern History; 4b) Primarily an undergraduate collection but with some material of interest to researchers.

177   HISTORY FACULTY LIBRARY (continued)
5a)   History; 5b) Economic and social history, British history, medieval
       history, legal history
6a)   Bookstock: c35,000 volumes (monographs and bound serials).
       Current serials received: 84 titles; 6b) F W Maitland Collection;
       some material from the Sir Paul Vinogradoff bequest (legal and
       social studies); Graduate seminar collection in the history of science
       now incorporated in the main collections, as is the Maitland and
       Vinogradoff material; palaeography and diplomatic teaching
       collection. Good collection of bibliographies. The library contains
       nearly all the printed sources for British medieval history. No
       manuscript or unpublished materials.
7a)   Own classification. Open-access; 7b) Author card catalogue
8a)   Open to resident members of the university; 8c) No lending what-
       soever to readers or on inter-library loan

178   INDIAN INSTITUTE LIBRARY
1b)   University of Oxford
2a)   New Bodleian, Parks Road, Oxford OX1 3BG; 2b) 0865-44675
3)   J B Katz MA
4a)   Founded 1883 by Sir Monier Monier-Williams; Taken over by the
       Bodleian Library in 1927 as one of its dependent libraries. In
       certain fields has become one of the finest libraries for South Asian
       materials; 4b) To foster the study of the languages, literatures,
       histories and cultures of the countries of South and South-east
       Asia.
5a)   Languages, literatures, history, religion etc of India, Pakistan,
       Burma, Afghanistan, Nepal, Ceylon (up to 1795), Thailand and
       Tibet; 5b) Participates in the inter-library loans scheme. Organis-
       ation is as a separate library within the administration of the Dept
       of Oriental Books and Manuscripts, Bodleian Library.
6a)   Altogether about 90,000 volumes. Large number of periodicals
       and South Asian government and official publications. Some
       microfilms and facilities for reading them; 6b) The Indian Institute
       Oriental Manuscript Collection, now housed with the other Oriental
       and Western Manuscripts but separately catalogued. All relevant
       copyright material is deposited in this library.
7a)   Mainly on open-access with the library's own classification system;
       7b) Author catalogue, with some title and subject cross-references.
8a)   Readers of the Bodleian Library may use the Indian Institute after
       registering separately; also others at the discretion of the librarian.
       8b) Term: M-F 0900-1900, Sat to 1300. Vacation to 1700.
       Sundays closed; 8c) An informed staff, a catalogue, and the books.
9)   Described in the university information booklets for prospective
       students; Guides available for readers; Article by H J Stooke in
       Indian archives, 1965; Oxford University libraries holding South
       Asian material (pamphlet).

179   MAISON FRANÇAISE
1b)   University of Oxford
2a)   Norham Road, Oxford OX2 6SE; 2b) 0865-54576/7
3)   Miss Marie-Laure Viala
4a)   Established 1946. The Oxford Maison Française is the only
      foreign institute to form an integral part of a British university.
      It is maintained by the Direction Générale des Relations Cultur-
      elles, Scientifiques et Techniques of the French Ministry of
      Foreign Affairs, and is sponsored by Oxford and Paris Univer-
      sities; 4b) The Maison's main role is to further the links between
      Oxford and French universities; the library supports the cultural
      work of the centre
5a)   French literature, fine arts and social sciences; 5b) Cinema, theatre
      music, sport, geography, archaeology
6a)   Bookstock: c30,000 volumes (monographs and bound serials).
      Current serials received: 91 titles. Serial titles retained: 108 titles.
      Record collection (discothèque): c2300 items. Collection of sets
      of slides: c170 sets; 6b) Main strength is in French history, and
      French literature of the twentieth century. All books in the collec-
      tion are in French
7a)   Own classification scheme. Mostly open access; 7b) Author/title/
      subject catalogue
8a)   Generally available to the public. There is a small admission
      charge and a charge for using the record and slide library; 8b) M-F
      1000-1300 and 1400-1830, Sat to 1200. Closed for 10 days
      each at Christmas and Easter, and for the whole of August;
      8c) Provides information service on France and Great Britain;
      photocopying facilities.
9)   Three-yearly list of periodical titles; Annual list of accessions;
      List of slides

180   MUSEUM OF THE HISTORY OF SCIENCE LIBRARY
1b)   University of Oxford
2a)   Broad Street, Oxford OX1 3AZ; 2b) 0865-43997
3)   Dr J L Speller
4a)   The library, which occupies the old Ashmolean Museum building
      constructed in 1679-1683, was opened in 1925; 4b) The library's
      holdings are primarily in subjects relating to instruments, etc, of
      which there are examples among the exhibits of the museum.
      There are some holdings of other aspects of the history of science.
5a)   History of science; 5b) Horology, sundials, microscopy and optics,
      photography, surveying, navigational and astronomical instru-
      ments, alchemy and chemistry, early electricity and electrostatic
      machines.
6a)   Bookstock: c9000 volumes. Current serials received: 42 titles;
      6b) There are several important ms collections including: Lewis
      Evans Collection (on sundials, navigational and astronomical in-
      struments); Radcliffe Collections (manuscripts and records from
      the former Radcliffe Observatory); Stapleton Collection (Islamic

180   MUSEUM OF THE HIST. OF SCIENCE LIBRARY (continued science and alchemy); Buxton Collection (mainly relating to Charles Babbage and his difference engine) Other collections on general history of science, particularly in Oxford. There are also a number of special collections of printed books, including the Lewis Evans Collection on sundials, navigational and astronomical instruments; the Stapleton Collection on alchemy and early chemistry and the Royal Microscopical Society Collection on microscopy and optics.

7a)   Books may be consulted in the library during its opening hours; 7b) There are catalogues of all the library's collections

8a)   Available to researchers on prior application to the curator; 8b) M-F 1030-1300 and 1430-1600

181   PUSEY HOUSE LIBRARY

1b)   University of Oxford

2a)   St Giles, Oxford OX1 3LZ; 2b) 0865-59519

3)   Rev P G Cobb (Custodian of the Library)

4a)   1884; 4b) Pusey House is an independent Anglican institution and place of worship and study for members of the university. It contains the library of the Faculty of Theology divided into two sections—an undergraduate library and a senior library. It is a working library of theology and an important research collection

5a)   Theology, philosophy, church history; 5b) Oxford Movement, and tractarians of the 19th and 20th centuries

6a)   Bookstock: c55,000 volumes; 6b) E B Pusey Collection (general works, Anglican church history, Hebrew studies); Jacomb Collection (general works); H P Liddon Collection; C C Balston Collection (early printed theological books); Robert Barrett Collection (general works); C H Turner Collection (canon law); W G F Phillimore Collection (ecclesiastical law); Darwell Stone Collection (general works and patristic literature). The pamphlet and tract collections are very extensive and include those of Archdeacon G A Denison, R W Church, William Ince, Thomas Keble, Richard Jenkyns, W Hayward Cox, A J Stephens, E M Ingram, the second Viscount Halifax, and material from Church House and the English Church Union libraries. The manuscript collections are almost all modern, dating from the mid-19th century and relate to the major figures of the high church movement, as well as to the main institutions connected with it. Hall Collection of photographs of 19th century clerics

7a)   Open access except for manuscript and pamphlet collection; 7b) Slip index to manuscripts; card catalogues to book and pamphlet collection

8a)   Available to members of the university and to others for reference on application to the custodian; 8b) Term: M-F 0900-1830, Sat 0900-1300. Vacation M-F 0900-1700

10)   Hugh, S S F *Nineteenth century pamphlets at Pusey House* Faith Press, 1961

182   RADCLIFFE SCIENCE LIBRARY

1b)   University of Oxford

2a)   Parks Road, Oxford OX1 3QP; 2b) 0865-44675 (Bodleian switch-
board), 0865-54161 (direct line); 2c) 83656 (Bodleian Library)

3)   Dr Dennis Shaw CBE (Keeper of Scientific Books)

4a/b) The Radcliffe Science Library is the scientific, medical and mathematics library of Oxford University and a department of the
Bodleian; The library was first housed in the Radcliffe Camera
(1749-1860) which was designed for the original Radcliffe Library
by James Gibbs. In 1861 it was transferred to the University Museum and then, in 1901, when the Jackson Building was completed
on South Parks Road, was brought to its present site on the south-
west corner of the Science Area. In 1927 the Radcliffe Trustees
presented the library and its collection of books and periodicals
to Oxford University. The Worthington Wing on Parks Road was
opened in 1934 and an underground extension was completed in
1975. The extension includes a new reading room for physical
sciences (Lankester Room) and a new, larger bookstack. The
adaptation and modernisation of the Jackson and Worthington
wings during 1976-77 was the last stage in a major programme to
extend the science library provision in the University. Oxford
scientists now have access to one of the finest independent scientific collections in Europe with facilities probably unrivalled in
any other European university;

5a)   Science including mathematics and medicine; 5b) Library divided
between life sciences and physical sciences. There is close liaison
with the 50 small departmental libraries in the Oxford University
scientific laboratories.

6a)   Approximately 600,000 volumes total, of which 275,000 are
monographs and 20,000 periodical runs. The library has a collection of Radcliffe records including photographs and plans of the
present and past library buildings, and a small growing stock of
microfiche. There is a collection of 222,000 scientific theses from
European universities 1884-1930 and 1971 to date; 6b) Acland
papers, Tylor papers.

7a)   150,000 selected volumes on open access in reading rooms,
remaining stock on closed access. Own classification; 7b) Author
catalogue

8a)   All members of Oxford University may be admitted to readership.
Others needing access to the library's collection may be admitted
on the recommendation of a responsible person; 8b) Full term:
M-F 0900-2200, Sat to 1900 during first seven weeks, to 1300 on
other Saturdays; vacation: 0900-1900 (Sat to 1700). The library
is closed Sun, from Good Friday to Easter Monday inclusive, for
the whole week of the autumn bank holiday; and from December
24 until the New Year bank holiday inclusive. Full information
on opening times is published in the *Oxford University gazette*
and displayed in the library; 8c) There is a Keyword Index to

182   RADCLIFFE SCIENCE LIBRARY (continued)
      symposia and a union catalogue of science serials in Oxford Uni-
      versity. A member of staff is allocated to the provision of biblio-
      graphic assistance to readers and another member of staff is
      trained in Information Science and offers advice on searching
      computer data bases
9)   Brief notes for readers is published annually. A comprehensive
      readers guide is in preparation. The history of the library is
      recorded in Bibliotheca radcliviana.
10)   The annual report of the library has been included in the Univer-
      sity of Oxford—Annual Report of the Curators of the Bodleian
      Library since—1927 (supplement to the *University gazette*). The
      library is listed in the major library directories, eg *Aslib directory*,
      The Libraries, Museums and Art Galleries Yearbook, *Library
      Association Directory*, etc

183   RHODES HOUSE LIBRARY
1b)   University of Oxford
2a)   South Parks Road, Oxford OX1 3RG; 2b) 0865-55762
3)   F E Leese BLitt MA
4a)   Established 1928, incorporating previous Bodleian Library stock;
      4b) The library is one of the major academic libraries in the UK
      in its field, and enjoys copyright privilege through the Bodleian.
      Microfilm readers and xerox facilities are available; other copying
      can be done through the Bodleian. It is a reference library, and the
      only individual lending is from a small collection of duplicates.
      The library is particularly strong in government publications of
      Commonwealth countries
5a)   History (political, economic and social) of the United States,
      British Commonwealth (excluding South Asia, except Sri Lanka)
      and sub-Saharan Africa
6a)   Present foot run c20,000 feet, monographs, c300 series, current
      serials 2450 (including governmental), total serials 5000. Some
      maps for historical reference. Microfilms of US and Common-
      wealth newspapers; 6b) Rhodes House is the depository for the
      2500-odd collections of papers of former colonial administrators
      collected by the Oxford Colonial Records Project from 1963-73.
      There is also a major collection of manuscripts of Cecil Rhodes,
      and the archives of the Anti-Slavery Society. Rhodes House con-
      tains one of the largest collections of books on Malta in the UK,
      thanks to the generosity of the father of a former Maltese Rhodes
      scholar
7a)   There is a selection of books on open shelf, primarily to meet
      undergraduate needs. Limited access to the stacks is allowed for
      research work. The classification is unique; 7b) There is an author
      catalogue, and a subject catalogue for most of the Commonwealth
      countries. The manuscripts appear in a special manuscript cata-
      logue, by author and territory

183   RHODES HOUSE LIBRARY (continued)
8a)   The library is open to members of the Oxford University, and to
      others on application or recommendation; 8b) Term: M-F 0900-
      1900, vacations: 0900-1700. Sats to 1300; 8c) There is an inter-
      library loan service through the Bodleian. (See also 4b)
9)   Manuscript collections of Africana, 1968, reprinted 1971; and
      Supplement 1971; Manuscript collections (excluding Africana)
      1970. These are available from the Bodleian Library. A new
      supplement with a cumulated index is in preparation.
10)   *Rhodes House Library, Oxford* (1976) available from Rhodes
      House.

184   TAYLOR INSTITUTION LIBRARY
1b)   University of Oxford
2a)   St Giles, Oxford OX1 3NA; 2b) 0865-57917
3)   G G Barber BLitt MA FSA
4a)   Established 1845. The institution was founded from the estate
      of Sir Robert Taylor (1714-1788), sculptor and architect;
      4b) The Taylor Institution is the centre for the teaching and study
      of modern European languages (excluding English) in Oxford,
      particularly with relevance to post-1800 material. The library has
      always followed a policy of maintaining an active research collec-
      tion in its field of interest. The collections complement those of
      the Bodleian.
5a)   Modern European languages; 5b) Comparative philology; social
      and cultural background to the languages studied. Especially rich
      collections in the language and literature of French, German,
      Spanish, Portuguese (including Latin American usage), Italian,
      Slavonic languages and modern Greek. Also Afrikaans, Albanian,
      Basque, Celtic, Dutch and modern Scandinavian languages
6a)   Bookstock: 282,000 volumes. Current serials received: 700 titles;
      6b) Robert Taylor Collection (architecture); Robert Finch Col-
      lection (16th to 18th century material); Fry Collection (general
      works and botany). Special collections in the language and liter-
      ature of the modern European languages eg Hasluck Collection
      (Albanian); E S Dodgson Collection (Basque); Gustave Rudler
      Collection (French literature); H G Fiedler Collection (German
      language and literature); Dawkins Collection (Modern Greek);
      Edward Moore Collection (Dante editions); Morfill and Nevill
      Forbes Collections (Slavonic); W M Martin and H Butler Clarke
      Collections (Spanish); Theodore Besterman Collection (Voltaire).
      There are twentieth century autograph collections from major
      European literary figures
7a)   Own classification. Open and closed-access; 7b) Guard book
      catalogue. A number of specialist catalogues to the principal
      special collections
8a)   Members of the university and others on application; 8c) Photo-
      copying facilities
9)   Readers' guide

185   READING UNIVERSITY LIBRARY
1b)   University of Reading
2a)   Whiteknights, Reading RG6 2AE (tel: 0734-84331); Education
     Library, London Road Site, Reading RG1 5AQ (tel: 0734-85234);
     Music Library, 35 Upper Redlands Road, Reading RG1 5JE
     (tel: 0734-83584); 2c) 847813
3)   J Thompson BA FLA
5a)   General; 5b) There are separate Earley Gate (agriculture), Education,
     Music, and Social Science Libraries; also library at Museum of English
     Rural Life associated with Institute of Agricultural History
6a)   550,000 volumes; 5400 current periodicals; 6b) Overstone Library
     (18th and 19th century economics, political and religious thought,
     travel, literature, history); Cole Library (early medicine, history
     of zoology); Stenton Library (medieval history); Finzi Poetry Col-
     lection; Henley Parish Library; Turner Collection (French Revol-
     ution); European Documentation Centre
7a)   Mainly open-access, but some closed collections. Dewey Decimal
     Classification; Bliss (Education Library); 7b) Author and subject
     catalogues, with classified shelf list
8a)   Members of the university; others, for reference, on written appli-
     cation; 8b) Open on Sun afternoons in term
9)   Reports of the Curators; *Historical farm records: a summary guide
     to manuscripts and other material in the university library col-
     lected by the Institute of Agricultural History and the Museum of
     English Rural Life.* Reading, University of Reading Library, 1973;
     brief guides for students; Abstracts and indexes; Initials of period-
     icals (list of journals); catalogue of the Cole Library, 1969-75, 2 vols

186   ROYAL COLLEGE OF ART LIBRARY
1b)   Royal College of Art
2a)   Kensington Gore, London SW7 2EU; 2b) 01-584-5020
3)   H H Brill
4a)   The college opened as the School of Design in 1837, and adopted
     its present title in 1896. A royal charter was granted to the college
     in 1967. The library opened in 1953; 4b) to meet the needs of
     staff and students of the college
5a)   Visual arts; design; the history and criticism of the other arts;
     English literature; foreign literature in translation; history; religion;
     philosophy; psychology; science
6a)   30,000 volumes; 260 periodicals, including 200 current periodicals;
     6b) Henry Wilson archive; the photographic archive of the *Am-
     bassador* magazine; collection of books on all aspects of colour
7a)   Open-access. Own classification scheme; 7b) Dictionary catalogue
     (on cards)
8a)   Members of the college; others, for reference, on written appli-
     cation; 8b) Closed Sats; 8c) Technical Information Office provides
     technical literature, technical catalogues and samples

187 UNIVERSITY LIBRARY, ST ANDREWS
1b) University of St Andrews
2a) North Street, St Andrews, Fife KY16 9TR; 2b) 033481-4333/4/5
2c) 76213 SAULIB G
3) A G Mackenzie MA ALA
4a) Founded 1611-1612, incorporating earlier college libraries. The library received material on copyright deposit during 1710-1837.
5b) Three sectional libraries for the physical sciences, and separate colle
tions in the Buchanan building (modern languages), St Mary's Colle
(divinity) and most other departments. Lesser-used material is
stored, available at 24 hours notice.
6a) 600,000 volumes; 3700 current periodicals; 6b) Religion; history;
classical languages and literatures. Named collections include:
Typographical (early printed books); Buchanan (early editions of
George Buchanan's works); Bible (early printed texts and commen-
taries); Royal (chiefly theology and classics); Buccleuch (armorial
bindings and bookstamps); Wedderburn (chiefly medical); Forbes
(classics, Alpine travel, history of science). The Manuscript Dept
contains over 100,000 western and oriental mss and documents, library archives, photographs and prints, (including records of, and
postcards by, Valentines of Dundee); the university muniments are
housed in the department.
7a) Library of Congress Classification; special scheme for pre-1600
books; 7b) Name catalogue; classified catalogue; series catalogue;
departmental union catalogue. Post-1976 imprints in main and
sectional libraries; name/title and classified COM fiche catalogue.
8a) Members of the university; others on written application; 8b)
Closed Sats in vacation
9) Annual reports; Current serials; Recent accessions bulletin; series of
pamphlet guides to the library; Catalogue of incunabula

188 SAINT DAVID'S UNIVERSITY LIBRARY, LAMPETER LIBRAR
1b) Saint David's University College, Lampeter
2a) University College, Lampeter, Dyfed SA48 7ED; 2b) 0507-422351
3) G P Lilley MA FLA
4a) The college was founded in 1822, and became a constituent institution of the University of Wales in 1971. Main building opened 196(
5a) Arts and humanities; 5b) Separate Old Library (pre-1821 material)
6a) 110,000 volumes; 600 current periodicals; 6b) Tracts Collection
(mostly 17th and 18th century); 15th century books of hours;
early Welsh material
8a) Members of the college; others, for reference, on written applicatio
8b) Closed Sats in summer vacation; 9) Notes for readers

189 UNIVERSITY OF SALFORD LIBRARY
1b) University of Salford
2a) Salford M5 4WT; 2b) 061-736-5843; 2c) 668680 SULIB
3) A C Bubb BA FLA
4a) Founded as the Royal Technical Institute in 1896, the university
received its charter in 1967. Library building opened in 1971

89   UNIVERSITY OF SALFORD LIBRARY (continued)
a)   Over 200,000 volumes; 2000 current periodicals; 6b) Walter
      Greenwood Collection (English literature); European Document-
      ation Centre
a)   Open-access; Universal Decimal Classification; 7b) Name catalogue
      (cards); classified catalogue (cards); subject index (cards); period-
      icals catalogue (cards); current periodicals catalogue (computer
      printout and annual printed list); various specialised catalogues
a)   Members of the university; others, for reference, at the discretion
      of the librarian; 8b) Standard hours; 8c) Readers' advisers on
      each floor
)   Guide to the library

90   SHEFFIELD UNIVERSITY LIBRARY
b)   University of Sheffield
a)   Western Bank, Sheffield S10 2TN; Applied Science Library, St
      George's Square, Sheffield S1 3JD; Hallamshire Hospital, Glossop
      Road, Sheffield; 2b) 0742-78555; 2c) 54348 ULSHEF
)   C K Balmforth MA FLA
a)   A number of colleges, including the Sheffield School of Medicine
      (founded in 1828), were united in 1897 to form University College
      Sheffield. In 1905 Sheffield received its charter as a university;
      4b) To provide research and teaching/study material, in all relevant
      media, for the members of the university; and a cooperative ser-
      vice to the Sheffield area within the limits of current resources.
a)   All academic subjects; 5b) There are 12 branch libraries, of which
      the chief are: Applied science, Medicine, Law/Economics, and the
      Institute of Education Libraries. Member of SINTO and of
      Sheffield cooperative scheme.
a)   700,000 volumes; 4700 current periodicals; non-book material;
      6b) Japanese Collection; librarianship; Firth Collection (Civil War
      pamphlets)
a)   Open-access for about 60 per cent of the stock (including branches).
      Dewey Decimal Classification; 7b) Union catalogue (author and
      subject) in main library. Branch catalogues. Supplementary cata-
      logues for Japanese material; official publications; periodicals.
      Current policy is to go over to COM fiche catalogue, which is
      already used for periodicals list, Medical Library, short-loan collec-
      tion.
a)   Members of the universities of Bradford, Hull, Leeds, Sheffield
      and York; others, for reference, on written application; 8b) Open
      Sun afternoons for six weeks in the examination period; 8c) Usual
      basic information desk service; information officers; subject
      specialisation scheme; extensive basic and advanced teaching in the
      use of library services, plus tape-slide presentations; on-line infor-
      mation retrieval services.
)   Students' guide to some libraries in Sheffield; Librarian's annual
      reports; Information Service publications, (including Readers' guide)
0)   Balmforth, C K 'Sheffield University Library' in *Encyclopedia of
      library and information science* (to appear)

191 SOUTHAMPTON UNIVERSITY LIBRARY
1b) University of Southampton
2a) University Road, Highfield, Southampton SO9 5NH; University
Branch, Wessex Medical Libraries, Medical and Biological Sciences
Building, Bassett Crescent East, Southampton SO9 3TU; General
Hospital, Tremona Road, Southampton SO9 4XY; 2b) 0703-
559122; 2c) 47661
3) B Naylor MA DipLib ALA
5a) General; 5b) There are separate Education and Wessex Medical
(biological sciences and medicine) Libraries, as well as department
collections for chemistry, biology, geography, geology, oceanography and physics
6a) 575,000 volumes; 6450 current periodicals; 6b) Cope Collection
(Hampshire materials); Perkins Library (pre-1901 agriculture book
Parkes Library (relations between the Jewish and non-Jewish worl
Hampshire Field Club Library; Ford Collection (parliamentary pap
Wellington Collection; history of science
7a) Predominantly open-access. Library of Congress classification;
Dewey (Education); National Library of Medicine; 7b) Main Libra
union card catalogue (except Medical Library) in name, classified
and subject index sequences; several specialised catalogues. Wesse
Medical Library: microfiche catalogue in name, title, classified and
subject heading sequences. Education Library: sheaf catalogue in
name, classified and subject index sequences.
8a) Members of the university; approved applicants, on payment; othe
for reference, on written application. Members of the Wessex Regional Health Authority may use the Medical Libraries and local
teachers the Education Library; 8b) Open Sunday pm
9) Introducing the Library; Guide to library services for university st
and postgraduate students; Introducing the Wessex Medical Librar
Annual reports of the Librarian and Curators; Catalogue of the Pe
Collection; User guides; Automation project reports
10) Turley, R V 'Sir William Cope and his remarkable collection'
Hampshire 16, 1976, pp45-7

192 UNIVERSITY LIBRARY, STIRLING
1b) University of Stirling
2a) Stirling FK9 4LA; 2b) 0786-3171; 2c) 778874
3) P G Peacock BA
4a) University received its charter in 1966
5a) General
6a) 275,000 volumes; 2400 current periodicals; 6b) Watson Collectio
(Labour history); Sir Walter Scott; Scottish authors contemporary
with Scott; English printed material background scheme.
7a) Own classification scheme; 7b) Author and classified catalogues
8a) Members of the university; others, for reference, on written application; 8b) Open Sun in term; closed Sat in vacation; 8c) On-line
information retrieval services; Hinman collater
9) Notes for readers; Annual reports; Occasional publications

93 ANDERSONIAN LIBRARY, STRATHCLYDE
b) University of Strathclyde
a) McCance Building, 16 Richmond Street, Glasgow G1 1XQ;
    2b) 041-552 4156/4400; 2c) 77472 STRATHLIB GLW
)   C G Wood MA FLA
a) 1796; 4b) To provide information and material tailored to needs
    of university population in appropriate subjects and at appropri-
    ate levels. To assist members in use of this material. To act as
    back-up source for other library users nationally and regionally
    within framework of library policy on assistance to outside
    bodies and individuals. Facilities include loan of material, profes-
    sional library advice, photocopying, provision of reading space,
    ILL services, translation handling
a) Science and technology; bioengineering; modern languages; English;
    history; geography; business studies; economics; politics; law; archi-
    tecture and urban planning; 5b) University library comprises the
    Andersonian Library, and the Fleck (chemistry), Weir (mechanical
    and chemical engineering), Stenhouse (law), Scottish Hotel School,
    and Strathclyde Business School Libraries. Older, little-used ma-
    terial held in store, available in 24 hours
a) 270,000 volumes; 3700 current periodicals; 6b) Sciences; librarian-
    ship; Anderson Collection (personal library of the founder, John
    Anderson); Young Collection (early alchemical, chemical and
    pharmaceutical books); Laing Collection (17th and 19th century
    mathematical books)
a) Universal Decimal Classification (pre-1974 books; serials); Dewey
    Decimal Classification (1974- books). Open shelves, except for
    theses, special collections and short loan material; 7b) Author cata-
    logue; classified catalogue; subject index
a) Members of the university; others, for reference, on written appli-
    cation; 8b) Standard hours; 8c) Medical information retrieval ser-
    vice; Seminars to undergraduate, post-graduate and research sec-
    tion.
)   Andersonian Library notes; Annual information folder; Annual
    report on research
0) Tse, S Y 'Radical Clydeside' *Library review* 26, 1977.

94 UNIVERSITY OF SURREY LIBRARY
b) University of Surrey
a) Guildford GU2 5XH; 2b) 0483-71281; 2c) 895331
)   R F Eatwell MA FLA
a) Founded in 1894 as Battersea Polytechnic; became a university in
    1966, and moved from Battersea to Guildford in 1968. The
    present library building was opened in 1972; 4b) To support the
    teaching and research of the university
a) Science; technology; social sciences. Especially strong in chem-
    istry, physics and the biological sciences
a) 210,000 volumes; 2200 current periodicals; 6b) Ehrenberg Collec-
    tion (Germanic and French studies, especially signed and first

194 UNIVERSITY OF SURREY LIBRARY (continued)
editions of German literary works); Shepard Collection; Transport
Trust Collection; European Documentation Centre
7a) Most stock on open-access. Universal Decimal Classification;
7b) 'Self-generated' mini-catalogue on microfiche: name, classified
title, KWOC, conference, periodicals, subject index
8a) Members of the university; non-members, on payment of an annual
fee; others, for reference; 8b) Open Sun afternoons in term;
closed Sats in summer and Christmas vacations; 8c) Subject librarians are responsible for reader enquiry, information, and teaching services in their areas of responsibility. Audiovisual facilities.
9) Annual reports; Library newsletter; Guides to the literature;
Alcock, D and Carr, R P 'The Ehrenberg donation', 1978
10) Burden, M and Lord, J A 'The new automated circulation system
for the University of Surrey Library' *Program* 11, 1977, pp101-11
Cowburn, L M 'University of Surrey Library automated issue
system' *Program* 5, 1971, pp70-88.

195 UNIVERSITY OF SUSSEX LIBRARY
1b) University of Sussex
2a) Falmer, Brighton BN1 9QL; Institute of Development Studies
Library, Falmer, Brighton BN1 9RE; 2b) 0273-606755;
2c) 87394 UOSLIB
3) P R Lewis MA FLA
5a) General; 5b) The Library of the Institute of Development Studies
is a separately financed and administered library on Third World
development; it offers facilities to research workers. It is a deposit
library for United Nations, including Unesco, material.
6a) 450,000 volumes; 2200 current periodicals; 6b) Paris Commune
(1871) Collection; East Africa Collection (SCOLMA Scheme:
Kenya, Tanzania, Uganda); European Documentation Centre;
Science Policy Research Unit Collection; 'Mass Observation' Archive (social research)
7a) Library of Congress Classification; 7b) Author/title and classified
8a) Members of the university; others, for reference, on written application; 8b) Open Sun in term; closed Sat in vacation; 8c) Readers'
Advisory Service; desk staffed during 'office hours'
9) Library guide

196 UNIVERSITY COLLEGE OF SWANSEA LIBRARY
1b) University College of Swansea
2a) Singleton Park, Swansea SA2 8PP; University College of Swansea
Education Library, Hendrefoilan, Gower Road, Swansea SA2 7NB
2b) 0792-25678; Education Library: 0792-21231; 2c) 48358
ULSWAN
3) F J W Harding MA BLitt ALA FSA
4a) The college was founded in 1920; the first permanent library building was erected in 1937. Major extensions added in 1964 and

UNIVERSITY COLLEGE OF SWANSEA LIBRARY (continued)
1974; 4b) To serve the curriculum of studies and programmes of
research by means of printed works and micro-records. Principal
facilities include reading and reference, as well as borrowing, to
members of the college. There are some 1200 readers places including about 140 individual research desks.

a) General subjects in the faculties of arts, economic and social
studies, pure science, applied science, and education. Major subjects not covered include law, medicine, agriculture, architecture;
5b) There are separate collections for chemical engineering, chemistry, education, mathematics (periodicals only), natural sciences,
and physics (periodicals only), and for the residue of the South
Wales Miners' Institute libraries.

a) 380,000 volumes; 3500 current periodicals; 60,000 pamphlets;
108,000 microforms; 6b) Celtic, primarily Welsh (books and periodicals including material in English about Wales); coalfields and
industries of South Wales (archives and printed works)

a) Predominantly open-access according to Library of Congress
Classification with some modifications. There is a closed store for
some 50,000 volumes. Other closed collections include archives,
rare books, theses, microforms; 7b) Separate author, alphabetical
subject, and periodicals card catalogues.

a) Members of the college; others, including extra-mural and Open
University students, external researchers, for reference on written
application; 8b) Main library open Sun afternoons in term; 8c) A
bibliographic and information service to readers, including instruction in the use of the library, is provided under the direction of
the Sub-librarian for Readers' Services. Borrowing on the inter-
library loans service is available, mainly to academic staff and
research students.

) Library handbook (annual); Union list of current periodicals in
the University of Wales, 1972; computer produced listings of
current periodicals holdings and locations; A guide to British and
international social statistics held by the library, 1972; A bibliographical handbook for research workers in British medieval
history, 1974; Audio-visual materials: a select list of items available in the Education Library, 1975; A catalogue of material in
microform held by the library, 1975; Developing areas studies:
current periodicals, 1975; Guide to Russian studies in the library,
1975; Italian language and literature in the library, 1975; Library
guide to history, 1975; Notes on the use of the library for students
of Russian, 1975; Palaeography and diplomatic for the research
student, 1975; The structure of the literature of politics, 1975;
UK statistics: a guide to sources in the library, 1975; University
College of Swansea: higher degree theses, 1920-70; Supplements,
1971-76; A bibliographical handbook for research workers in
classical studies, 1976; British Government publications: notes for
readers, 1976; Diploma dissertations and higher degree theses in

196 UNIVERSITY COLLEGE OF SWANSEA LIBRARY (continued)
education held in the library, 1976; A guide to German language
and literature in the library, 1976; Reference books on education:
a select list of items available in the Education Library, 1976;
Scientific and technical periodicals: a short title catalogue of holdings. 2nd ed, 1971; Supplement 3, 1976; A select list of reference
works in the humanities held by the library, 1976; Title and keyword listing of abstracting, indexing and current awareness periodicals currently received, 1976; Guide to the literature of mathematics, statistics, computer science and physics, 1977; International organisations publications, 1977; A select list of reference
works in economic and social studies, 1977; Engineering and meta-
lurgy: an introductory guide (in preparation); Scientific abstracts
and indexes (in preparation); Guide to the archive collection, 197
Guide to the archive collections relating to the South Wales coalfield, 1971; Guide to the Royal Institution of South Wales manuscripts in the library, 1972; South Wales Coalfield History Project:
list of library and archive deposits, 1973; Guide to the Swansea
Corporation manuscripts, 1975;

10) A short account of the 1964 extension to the library was published in the *Library Association record* December 1964, pp580-
584. Other accounts describing the library and its collections are
as follows: 'Swansea Arts Building and Library', in *Building* Dec
23, 1966, p26; 'Library extension, University College of Swansea'
in *Architect and building news* July 10, 1968, pp52-59; Swansea,
in *University libraries in Britain: a new look* by Harrison Bryan,
London, Bingley; Hamden (Conn), Linnet, 1976, p163.

197 NEW UNIVERSITY OF ULSTER LIBRARY
1b) New University of Ulster
2a) Coleraine BT52 1SA; Library, Magee University College, North-
land Road, Londonderry BT48 7JL; 2b) 0265-4141; Magee Library: 0504-65621
3) F J E Hurst MA ALA FLAI
4a) The university opened in 1968, as the result of recommendations
of the Lockwood Committee's report 'Higher education in Northern Ireland' (1965). Magee University College, Londonderry,
was incorporated in the New University in 1970; 4b) The library
service exists to support and encourage the teaching and research
of the education centre and the schools of physical sciences,
biological and environmental studies, social sciences and humanities at Coleraine, and the Institute of Continuing Education in
Londonderry.
5a) General; 5b) The library's stock at Coleraine is currently located
in the phase 1 and phase 2 buildings; the two are completely
integrated functionally, but phase 1 is concerned mainly with
stock on education.

97   NEW UNIVERSITY OF ULSTER LIBRARY (continued)
a)   175,000 volumes; 2500 current periodicals and newspapers; considerable holdings in microform. 85,000 volumes and over 200
current periodicals at Magee; 6b) Headlam-Morley Library
(printed works and manuscripts on World War I); Henry Morris
Collection (Irish Studies); Stelfox Collection (natural history);
Denis Johnston, Robert Lloyd Praeger and George Shiels mss;
Paul Ricard Collection (World War II); Galbraith Collection
(medieval studies); Henry Davis Gift (incunabula and rare books);
Yakut language; European Documentation Centre. Magee has the
Spalding Collection (Far East); long-established Irish Collection;
special collections on education.

a)   Almost entirely open-access; Library of Congress Classification;
some residual Dewey Decimal Classification at Magee; 7b) Conventional card catalogues (author and subject); Their replace-
ment by a computer-based microfiche catalogue is projected.

a)   Members and graduates of the university; others, for continuous
reference, on written application; available to casual callers subject to normal control; 8b) Closed Sat in vacation; 8c) Normal
readers' services, including inter-library loans and seminars for new
students. Subscriber to BLAISE.

)   Guide to the library; Serials catalogue

0)   Feisenberger, H A 'The Henry Davis Collection, II: the Ulster
Gift'. *Book collector* 21, 1972; McDowell, B and Hunter, D 'The
New University of Ulser'. *Vine* 19, 1977; *The new University of
Ulster: report on the development plan* Coleraine, New University
of Ulster, 1969; Vowles, M 'The Henry Davis Collection of the
New University of Ulster' *An Leabharlann: the Irish Library* 6,
1977; Wintour, B J C and McDowell, B 'Automation at the New
University of Ulster' *Program* 10, 1976.

98   UNIVERSITY OF MANCHESTER INSTITUTE OF SCIENCE
AND TECHNOLOGY LIBRARY (UMIST)
b)   University of Manchester Institute of Science and Technology
a)   PO Box 88, Sackville Street, Manchester M6O 1QD; 2b) 9061-
236-3311
)   E D G Robinson JP MA ALA
a)   The institute is a direct descendent of the Manchester Mechanics'
Institute, founded in 1824. The present title was adopted in 1966
a)   Science; technology; management; European studies
a)   112,000 volumes; 1700 current periodicals; 6b) Joule Collection
(books collected by J P Joule, 1818-1889)
a)   Members of the university; others, for reference, on written application; 8b) Closed Sats in the Christmas and summer vacations
)   Annual reports

199 UNIVERSITY OF WALES INSTITUTE OF SCIENCE AND TECH
    NOLOGY LIBRARY (UWIST)
1b) University of Wales Institute of Science and Technology
2a) King Edward VII Avenue, Cardiff CF1 3NU; Applied Psychology
    Library, Llwyn-y-Grant Road, Cardiff; Law Library and Arts and
    Social Sciences Library, Corbett Road, Cardiff
3) J K Roberts MSc ALA
4a) UWIST was incorporated into the University of Wales in 1967.
    The main library and the periodicals library are in the main build-
    ing, opened in 1916
5a) Science; technology; social sciences; 5b) The main collections are
    in the main library, the periodicals library, the arts and social
    sciences library, and Dominions House library; there are separate
    libraries for law and applied psychology
6a) 100,000 volumes; 1300 current periodicals; 6b) Architecture
8a) Members of the institute; staff and postgraduate students of Uni-
    versity College, Cardiff and the Welsh National School of Medicine
    others, for reference, on written application; 8b) Open Sun in
    term; closed Sat in vacation
9) Guide to the library; Special leaflets

200 UNIVERSITY OF WARWICK LIBRARY
1b) University of Warwick
2a) Gibbet Hill Road, Coventry CV4 7AL; 2b) 0203-24011; 2c) 31406
3) P E Tucker BLitt MA ALA
4a) The university opened in 1964; 4b) Main campus library, for
    centralised services; the Westwood Library, formerly the City of
    Coventry, College of Education; Together these provide for the
    academic departments of the university, including an institute of
    education.
5a) General; 5b) Courtaulds Library (chemistry and molecular science
    contains unique materials; other departments (biology, mathe-
    matics) duplicates only
6a) Monograph holdings 360,000. Bound serials 85,000. Current
    serials 6500 including statistics. Serials retained 15,000 approx
    including statistics. Modern records and statistics holdings 100,00
    equivalent. Maps 8000 sheets. Microcards 51,000. Microfilms
    rolls 4000. Microfiche 2000; 6b) Statistics Collection (trade,
    finance and industry statistics); Modern Records Centre (trade
    union and other labour history records); Economics Working
    Papers; contemporary German literature; pure mathematics; 18th
    and early 19th century French plays.
7a) Open access; 7b) Main Library: name catalogue, classified cata-
    logues (3 separate sequences for materials in arts, social studies,
    sciences)—each with its own subject index, main subject index to
    classified catalogues. Westwood: name, classified, subject index:
    2 sets, main and schools catalogues. Supplementary catalogues
    and lists include a computer-produced short title index.

(continued)

200 UNIVERSITY OF WARWICK LIBRARY (continued)
8a) Members of the university; others on payment; subscription
arrangements for industrial and business users of the Statistics
Collection; 8b) M-F 0900-2130, Sat to 1830, Sun 1000-2130;
8c) Enquiry desks in the subject areas
9) Occasional papers; Guide to the modern records centre, 1977
10) Building: *Architects' journal* 144 no 21; General: 'New University
Libraries' *British librarianship and information science 1966-70*
(1972)

201 WELSH NATIONAL SCHOOL OF MEDICINE LIBRARY
1b) Welsh National School of Medicine
2a) Heath Park, Cardiff CF4 4XN; Dental Library, Dental Hospital,
Heath Park, Cardiff CF4 4XY; 2b) 0222-755944
2c) 49696 UNIHOSPITAL CDF
3) R J Dannatt BA ALA
4a) Founded in 1893, the school received its charter in 1931 as a
constituent school of the University of Wales; 4b) The library
aims to satisfy the needs of **students** and staff of the school for
documents and for bibliographical information. Facilities include
several branch libraries and on-line information retrieval
5a) Medicine; dentistry; nursing; pharmacology; 5b) Branch libraries
are available at two other Cardiff teaching hospitals, the Royal
Infirmary and Llandough Hospital
6a) 45,000 volumes; 750 current periodicals; 6b) Historical collection
which includes Cardiff Medical Society Collection and Lloyd
Roberts Collection
7a) Older periodicals are stored in compactus shelving but are on open-
access; Historical Collection and other special material, eg theses,
on closed-access. Main Library Classification is Dewey; Dental
Library has its own; 7b) Main Library catalogue: cards plus computer printout (KWOC). Sequences: author, title, subject. Other
libraries card catalogue only.
8a) Access to the library is available to all medical and paramedical
personnel; membership is available to students and staff of the
school; certain staff of South Glamorgan Area Health Authority
and staff of UWIST and University College, Cardiff; 8b) Except
in July and August the Main Library is normally open from
0900-2100 on weekdays and 0900-1230 on Sat; 8c) Borrowing,
photocopying, on-line information retrieval, translation service,
computer based current awareness, inter-library borrowing, use of
study carrels, use of tape slide machines, enquiry service.
9) Library guide; Library bulletin (Dental); Library news bulletin;
Lists of periodicals by title, subject etc

202 J B MORRELL LIBRARY, YORK
1b) University of York
2a) Heslington, York YO1 5DD; Institute of Advanced Architectural
Studies Library, King's Manor, York YO1 2EP; Gurney Library,

202 J B MORRELL LIBRARY, YORK
Borthwick Institute of Historical Research, St Anthony's Hall,
Peasholme Green, York YO1 2PW; 2b) 0904-59861; 2c) 57933
YORKUL
3) H Fairhurst MA ALA
4a) Library building completed in 1966; library established in 1962;
4b) General university library
5a) General; 5b) There is a separate Institute of Advanced Architectural Studies and the Gurney Library; the latter is a small library
connected with the Borthwick Institute of Historical Research—
itself an archive repository established in 1953 and absorbed into
the university in 1963. The Institute of Social and Economic
Research also has a small specialist library.
6a) 225,000 volumes; 2100 current periodicals; 6b) Dyson Collection
(18th century English literature); the libraries of Seebohm Rown-
tree, Lord Beveridge, Professor Henry Carter Adams, and Professor
G N Garmonsway; Wormald Collection (medieval studies); Mir-
field Collection (pre-1800 books); Halifax and Slaithwaite Parish
Libraries; Gurney Library (church history, church administration,
canon law); Library of Professor Arnold Toynbee; Milnes Walker
Collection (early medicine)
7a) Open-access. Own scheme, based on Dewey Decimal Classification
7b) Author and classified catalogues with subject index to the
classified catalogue. Short-title catalogue in machine readable
form output onto COMfiche.
8a) Members of the universities of Bradford, Leeds, Sheffield and
York; others, for reference, on written application; 8b) Closed
Sats in vacation; 8c) Professional staff organised on a subject
responsibility basis. Separate Reader enquiry desk adjacent to
catalogues.
9) The University Library and the research reader; Library guides;
Periodicals catalogue
10) Articles on building in *Library world* vol 68, 1967, pp244-249;
Architects' journal vol 147 no 19, pp1023-1036; General article
in *Rub-off* vol 18, 1967.

POLYTECHNIC LIBRARIES
(ENGLAND AND WALES)

203 CITY OF BIRMINGHAM POLYTECHNIC LIBRARY
1b) City of Birmingham Polytechnic
2a) North Centre Library, Franchise Street, Perry Barr, Birmingham
B42 2SU; South Centre Library: Camp Hill, Birmingham B11 1AR;
Commerce Centre: Aston Street, Gosta Green, Birmingham B4 7HA;
Anstey Department of Physical Education: Chester Road, Sutton
Coldfield, West Midlands B73 5HY; Centre for Teacher Education
and Training: Westbourne Road, Edgbaston, Birmingham B15 3TN;
Centre for Teacher Education and Training: 625 Chester Road,
Birmingham B73 5HY; School of Music Library: Paradise Circus,
Birmingham B3 3JG; Art and Design Centre Library: Corporation
Street, Birmingham B4 7DX; Art and Design Centre Library:
Margaret Street, Birmingham B3 3BU; 2b) North Centre Library:
021-356-6911
3) M M Hadcroft MA ALA AIInfSci
4a) Polytechnic designated 1971, formed from the amalgamation of
two technical colleges, a school of music, college of art and college
of commerce; The library was therefore spread between several
sites from the beginning. A librarian was appointed in 1972 and
in 1974 a Central Processing Unit was established to centralise all
acquisitions and cataloguing work. In 1975 three former local colleges of education—each with its own library, joined the polytechnic. The Polytechnic plans to move most departments to its main
site at Perry Barr during the next decade and a central library building is planned. In 1977 a temporary accommodation of 2100 sq m
in a new building, F Block, was provided for the largest of the
centre libraries and this collection will develop as the main Polytechnic Library.
4b) The resources and facilities at each library are designed to provide
for the needs of polytechnic students and staff on the site and the
total collection is available to any member of the polytechnic. In
line with the development of the polytechnic, the library's administration is being reshaped to enable it to operate eventually as an
organisation largely concentrated at Perry Barr, but at the same
time care is taken to preserve individual characteristics and special
features of the various libraries. In addition to the basic library
services such as loans, enquiries, inter-library loans, facilities include library tuition, current awareness services, short term loan
collections, audiovisual services.
5b) Science; technology; librarianship (North Centre Library);
physical education (Anstey Department of Physical Education);
music (Music Library); Education and related fields (centres for
teacher education and training); social sciences; business and
management; language and literature; history; geography (Commerce Centre); social and political sciences; architecture; planning;
law; social work (South Centre Library). Members of B-LINK;
WESLINK; BLCMP.

197

203 BIRMINGHAM POLYTECHNIC LIBRARY (continued)
6a) 305,035 volumes; 2295 periodicals; total non-book materials:
106,077; 6b) Particular strengths in art, music and education.
7a) Mostly open access; Dewey Decimal Classification; 7b) Author,
classified, subject index. Microfiche and microform for material
added since 1974. Earlier items are being recatalogued.
8a) Full facilities are available to staff and students of the polytechnic
The general public may be admitted for reference purposes;
8b) North Centre Library—Term: M-Th 0900-2000, F to 1800;
Vacation: M-Th 0900-1700, F to 1600; 8c) Literature searches
and current awareness services in particular subjects; introduction
to the library; some library instruction is included in course work
9) Library guide (North Centre Library); Guides to the literature;
Guides to indexes and abstracts

204 BRIGHTON POLYTECHNIC LEARNING RESOURCE CENTRE
1b) Brighton Polytechnic
2a) Moulsecoomb, Brighton BN2 4GJ; Falmer Site Library; Grand
Parade Site Library; Sussex Square Site Library; 2b) 0273-67304
3) Miss C R Lutyens LLB FLA
4a) Brighton Polytechnic established 1970 by amalgamating Brighton
College of Art and Brighton College of Technology. Brighton
College of Education added in 1976;
5a) Architecture and management; engineering and environmental
studies (Moulsecoomb); art and design (Grand Parade); education;
natural and life sciences; social and cultural studies (Falmer)
6a) 167,000 volumes
8b) Moulsecoomb—Term: M-F 0900-2100, Sat to 1200

205 BRISTOL POLYTECHNIC LIBRARY
1b) Bristol Polytechnic
2a) Bolland Library: Coldharbour Lane, Frenchay, Bristol BS16 1QY;
Unity Street Library: 3 Unity Street, Bristol BS1 5HP; Ashley
Down Library: Ashley Down Road, Bristol B57 9BU; Bower
Ashton Library: Clanage Road, Bower Ashton, Bristol B53 2JU;
2b) Bolland Library: 0272-656261 ext 404
3) J C Hartas BCom ALA
4a) Polytechnic established 1969 on the amalgamation of colleges
of technology and commerce. Two colleges of education were
added in 1976.
5b) Business and professional studies, economics, social sciences,
computing, mathematics, science, (Bolland Library); Surveying,
town and country planning, (Unity Street Library); Engineering,
construction, humanities, (Ashley Down Library); Art and
design (Bower Ashton Library); Education (Redland Library)
6a) Bookstock: 200,000. Current periodicals: 2000; 6b) Bolland Collection (items of local interest), government publications, publications of societies, institutions and other bodies, company

205 BRISTOL POLYTECHNIC LIBRARY (continued)
reports, computer manuals, management case studies, children's
collection (Bolland Library)
7a) Open access. Dewey Decimal Classification; 7b) Name catalogue,
classified catalogue, subject index
8b) Bolland Library—Term:M-Th 0900-2000, Fri to 1800, Sat (Summer term only) to 1300; Vacation: M-F 0900-1700; 8c) Library
tuition on the structure and use of the literature of particular subjects, tracing information, using AV and microform equipment;
use of the libraries.
9) New services and acquisitions noted in Bristol Polytechnic News
or special lists of recent additions in each main group of subjects.
List of periodical holdings (annual); List of polytechnic membership of outside bodies; List of films held throughout the polytechnic.
10) Mathews, J 'The slide library of the Faculty of Art and Design of
Bristol Polytechnic' *Art libraries journal* 1 (4), winter 1976,
pp20-25.

206 HATFIELD POLYTECHNIC LIBRARY
1b) Hatfield Polytechnic
2a) PO Box 110, Hatfield, Herts AL10 9AD; Bayfordbury Library
(Polytechnic Field Station and Observatory); Birklands Library
(Polytechnic School of Management) St Albans; Balls Park (Polytechnic School of Social Science) near Hertford; 2b) Main library:
7072-68100; 2c) 262413
3) D E Bagley FLA
4a) 1952 Library of Hatfield Technical College; 1969 Library of Hatfield Polytechnic; developed after 1955 as the headquarters of a
network of libraries in the developing colleges of further education.
The network is known as HERTIS, Herts Technical Library and
Information Service, complementing the Public County Library
services; 4b) Centre for advanced and specialist edication in the
county, provides stock and information services to staff, students
and local industry.
5a) Humanities; science; social science, natural sciences; information
sciences, engineering; management; printing and packaging;
5b) Participation in LASER, the cooperative network of the
London and South Eastern Region;
6a) 105,000 volumes. 1600 periodicals, current titles; 6b) The
National Reprographic Centre for documentation (NRCd) is associated with the Polytechnic Library. Of especial interest is their
research into microforms. A printing and packaging information
centre has been developed at Watford College with specialist staff.
7a) Open access, Dewey Classification; 7b) Author catalogue; classified
catalogue; subject indexes (DDC); microform catalogues are produced via BLAISE/LOCAS
8a) Students and staff of the polytechnic and associated colleges.

206   HATFIELD POLYTECHNIC LIBRARY (continued)
Users from commerce, industry and public services in the county
can use reference facilities and loan facilities at the discretion of
the librarian. Postal loans and photocopies supplied to industrial
libraries; 8b) Term: M-Th 0845-2200, Fri to 2100, Sat 0930-1230;
Vacation: 0900-1700; 8c) Headquarters of HERTIS. Provides
information to local science-based industrial firms and research
organisations. Fifteen colleges in Hertfordshire constitute the
information resources of HERTIS. NRCd; access to BLAISE;
LOCKHEED: SDC: DIALTECH

9)   Library guide; Readers guides in particular subject areas or for
different types of material; Notes for visitors; A guide for industrial members of Hertis; pamphlet about the National Reprographic Centre for documentation; Hertis Information Review—
fortnightly current awareness service in fields of further and
higher education; pamphlet on Hertis on-line information services; HERTIS occasional papers; HERTIS bibliographies

10)   Bagley, D E 'Hatfield Polytechnic's new library' *New library
world* 13 (854), August 1971, pp50-52; Carey, R J P 'A systems
approach to exploitation' *New Library world* 73 (865), July 1972,
pp347-349.

207   HUDDERSFIELD POLYTECHNIC LIBRARY
1b)   Huddersfield Polytechnic
2a)   Central Library, Music Library, Chemistry Library (unstaffed):
The Polytechnic, Queensgate, Huddersfield HD1 3DH; Holly
Bank Library: The Polytechnic, Holly Bank Road, Huddersfield
HD3 3BP; Library, Bermerside Hall, Dept of Education Outpost,
Bermerside Hall, Skircoat Green, Halifax; Durham Outpost Library
(unstaffed); communications to Holly Bank Library
2b)   Central Library: 0484-22288 ext 2040 (after 5pm: 0484-21800)
3)   W A Price BA FLA
4a)   Formed from the libraries of Huddersfield College of Technology
(founded in 1841 as the Young Men's Mental Improvement Society
Oastler College of Education (founded 1963); and Huddersfield
College of Education (Technical) (founded 1949).
5b)   Arts (including art and design and music); business studies; education; engineering; law; sciences (Central Library, Chemistry
Library, Music Library); education; further education; vocational
and industrial training; curriculum studies; further education overseas (Holly Bank Library)
6a)   c225,000 volumes. c2000 periodicals—current titles. c1000 non-
book material; 6b) G H Wood Collection: books, papers and
tracts on 19th century social and monetary problems (Central
Library); Teaching Practice Collection, c8000 children's and class
text books (Central Library); Gramophone records; scores; sets
of vocal and instrumental music; reference books; music periodicals (Music Library); Audiovisual materials; Syllabuses and

207 HUDDERSFIELD POLYTECHNIC LIBRARY (continued)
examination papers of examining bodies relevant to further education (Holly Bank Library). The library has significant collections
in English literature, history, further education.
7a) Open access. Compact storage for pre-1946 periodicals and older
and less used books. UDC; 7b) Author catalogue; classified catalogue; subject index
8a) Central Library open to all for reference purposes; other libraries
by arrangement. Borrowing facilities available to members of the
polytechnic; 8b) Central Library—Term: M-F 0900-2100, Sat to
2345, Vacation: M-Th 0900-1715, Fri to 1700; 8c) Inter-library
loan; microform readers and reader-printer; photocopying; instruction in library and literature use; enquiry points; loan.
9) Guide to library services; Subject guides to catering, hotel management and tourism; geography and earth sciences; textiles; sociology;
mechanical engineering; psychology; business, management and
marketing; history. Information sheets giving information on the
library's audiovisual materials, the interlibrary loan service and the
citation of bibliographical references. Bibliographies (mainly for
internal use) on many aspects of further education and related
teaching methods and 'Library facilities and services' (Holly Bank
Campus).

208 KINGSTON POLYTECHNIC LIBRARY
1b) Kingston Polytechnic
2a) Penrhyn Road, Kingston upon Thames, Surrey KT1 2EE; Canbury
Park Library: Canbury Park Road, Kingston upon Thames, Surrey
KT2 6LQ; Gipsy Hill Library: Gipsy Hill Centre, Kingston Hill,
Kingston upon Thames, Surrey KT2 7LB; Knights Park Library:
Knights Park, Kingston upon Thames, Surrey KT1 2QJ; New
Malden Library: 40 Coombe Road, New Malden, Surrey KT3 4QF;
2b) Penrhyn Road Library: 01-549-1366; 2c) 928530
3) Mrs E Esteve-Coll BA
5b) Coombe Hurst Library: music; Knights Park Library: art, architecture, design, planning; New Malden Library: data processing,
management
6a) 210,000 volumes; 2000 periodicals (current titles). 100,000 slides.
15,000 illustrations; 6b) Government publications—all British
government publications taken since 1972 (New Malden Library,
Penryhn Road Library); Open University: complete set of course
units (Penryhn Road Library); Statistics Collection; all British
government series since 1972. Certain foreign countries and international organisations (Penryhn Road Library; Canbury Park Library)
7a) Largely open access, some special collections have restricted access;
7b) Author catalogue, card and microfiche; classified catalogue,
card and microfiche; (Microfiche catalogue—union catalogue);
Subject index, microfiche

208 KINGSTON POLYTECHNIC LIBRARY (continued)
8a) Reference facilities for all members of the polytechnic. Loan facilities for staff and students; 8b) Penryhn Road site—Term: M-Th 0900-2200, Fri to 2100, Sat 1000-1600 (Reference Library only), Vacation: M-F 0900-1700
9) Library guide and individual leaflets describing specific libraries and services in more detail

209 LANCHESTER POLYTECHNIC LIBRARY
1b) Lanchester Polytechnic
2a) Jordan Well (Main Library); Lanchester Polytechnic, Priory Street, Coventry CV1 5FB; Art and Design Library: Lanchester Polytechnic, Gosford Street, Coventry; Rugby Site Library (due to close summer 1979): Eastlands, Rugby, Warwicks; 2b) Main Library: 0203-24166; 2c) 31469
3) J Fletcher BA(Econ) MA ALA
4a) Polytechnic designated in 1970 from an amalgamation of Lanchester College of Technology, Coventry College of Art and Rugby College of Engineering Technology; 4b) To satisfy the study and information needs of the staff and students of the polytechnic. The catalogues and issue system are being automated. The information service and non-book media service are being rapidly developed.
5b) Engineering; education; applied science; social sciences; urban and regional planning (Main Library); art and design (Art and Design Library); engineering; applied sciences; computer sciences (Rugby site library)
6a) 170,000 volumes; 6b) Lanchester Collection, published works and private papers of Dr F W Lanchester (Main Library); European Documentation Centre (Main Library); parliamentary papers (Main Library)
7a) Open-access, except for small special collections. Dewey Classification; 7b) Author catalogue; classified catalogue; subject index—audiovisual material interfiled on coloured cards
8a) Bona-fide staff and students of the polytechnic and city council officers may use full facilities. Members of the Open University in the Coventry area may borrow material. Others may use reference facilities; 8b) Main Library—Term: M-F 0900-2100, Sat to 1200; Vacation: M-F 0900-1715; 8c) Information services: literature searches; SDI ; weekly list of periodical articles—*News on polytechnics and higher education*
9) Readers guide; Notes for students
10) 'New library buildings at Lanchester Polytechnic' *Times higher education supplement* October 29th 1971, p14.

210 LEEDS POLYTECHNIC LIBRARY
1b) Leeds Polytechnic
2a) Central Library: Calverley Street, Leeds LS1 3HE; Education Library: Beckett Park, Leeds, LS6 3DS; Town Planning, Architecture

210   LEEDS POLYTECHNIC LIBRARY (continued)
     and Landscape Library: Brunswick Terrace, Leeds LS2 8BU;
     Law Library: Vernon Road, Leeds LS1 3EQ; School of Librarian-
     ship Library: Park Place, Leeds LS1 2SY; 2b) Central Library:
     0532-462925

3)   J H Flint FLA

4a)   Polytechnic established in 1970 with the amalgamation of the
     colleges of art, education and home economics, commerce and
     technology. Two colleges of education were added in 1976;
     4b) To provide staff and students of the polytechnic with an
     extensive resource of books, journals, etc

5b)   Science and technology, social studies, economics, history,
     management, arts, foreign languages (Central Library); Education
     (Beckett Park Library); Town planning, architecture and land-
     scape Library; Law Library; Librarianship Library

5a)   300,000 volumes, including bound journals; 2000 periodicals
     (current titles). 73,000 slides; 6b) European Documentation
     Centre (Central Library); Carnegie Historical Collection—books
     on sport, health and physical recreation published before 1946
     (Beckett Park Library)

7a)   Open-access. Dewey Classification; 7b) Author catalogue;
     subject catalogue; subject index; audiovisual material in the Teach-
     ing Practice Collection is covered by a separate subject catalogue
     and subject index

8a)   Lending and reference facilities are available to all staff and
     students of the polytechnic. Members of the public are admitted
     for essential reference purposes; 8b) Central Library—Term:
     M-F 1000-2100, Vacation M-F 1000-1700; 8c) Staff are organised
     in five subject teams—science and technology; art; environment;
     education and the social sciences. They provide bibliographic in-
     formation, library instruction and readers' advice. Extel statistical
     service (Central Library)

9)   Library guide

10)   Flint, J H 'Some problems of planning for optimum efficiency'
     Library world 71 (839), May 1970, pp336-340.

211   LEICESTER POLYTECHNIC LIBRARY

1b)   Leicester Polytechnic

2a)   Kimberlin Library: P O Box 143, Leicester LE1 9BH; Scraptoft
     Campus Library: Scraptoft, Leicester LE7 9SU; 2b) City Campus:
     0533-50181; 2c) 34429

3)   S R Gadsden MLS ALA

4a)   Polytechnic established in 1969 with the amalgamation of the
     colleges of art and technology. The City of Leicester College of
     Education (including the National College for the Training of
     Youth Leaders, the Leicester School of Speech Therapy and the
     Knighton Fields Domestic Science College) was also amalgamated
     in September, 1976; 4b) The library provides an information and
     loan service to students and staff of the institution from a large

211 LEICESTER POLYTECHNIC LIBRARY (continued)
    4-storey purpose-built library on the City Campus, together with
    a 2-storey also purpose-built library 6 miles away on the Scraptoft
    Campus; The two libraries ultimately to be run as one provide
    some 900 study places of varying types. Qualified staff are avail-
    able for consultation and user education.
5a) City Campus: art and design, business studies, technology and
    construction, humanities, science and social science; Scraptoft
    Campus: education, sociology, psychology, services to the handi-
    capped, youth and community service, immigration and multi-
    racial society, linguistics and speech pathology, dance, drama,
    local history, American history, physical education; 5b) Separate
    Schools Services/Teaching Practice Resources Collection at Scrap-
    toft.
6a) 200,000 volumes. 2200 periodicals (current titles). 19,315 period-
    icals—(bound volumes); 5000 gramophone records. 101,000 non-
    book materials; 6b) Art and design, costume and textiles,
    children's literature
7a) Open-access bookstock; restricted access non-book media on the
    City Campus only. UDC City Campus; DDC Scraptoft Campus;
    7b) UDC card catalogues—classified name and subject index City
    Campus. Dewey Dictionary Catalogue Scraptoft. City Campus
    conversion to DDC in 1978. Conversion to COM microfiche union
    catalogue also commencing in 1978. Classified, name and subject
    index.
8a) Membership is available to all staff, academic and non-academic
    and to alls tudents of the polytechnic. Other persons may use the
    library on application and at the discretion of the librarian;
    8b) City Campus—Term: M-F 0845-2100, Sat 0900-1200; Vacation
    M-F 0900-1730. Scraptoft Campus: M-Th 0845-2000, Fri to 1700,
    Sun 1400-1700; Vacation M-F 0900-1700; 8c) Bibliographic
    searches; subject bibliographies; courses in library use and infor-
    mation studies integrated with many academic courses; current
    awareness services in education.
9) Library guide; Library newsletter; General and subject guides;
    reading lists (some in collaboration with Leicester University and
    materiographies School of Education Library)
10) Bradfield V J et al 'Librarians or academics? User education at
    Leicester Polytechnic' *Aslib proceedings* 29 (3), March 1977,
    pp133-142. Houghton, B 'Whatever happened to tutor librarian-
    ship?' *Art libraries journal* 1 (4) winter 1975, pp4-19.

212 LIVERPOOL POLYTECHNIC LIBRARY
1b) Liverpool Polytechnic
2a) Humanities Library: Walton House, Tithebarn Street, Liverpool
    L2 2NG; Art and Design Library: Hope Street, Liverpool; Con-
    struction Library: Clarence Street, Liverpool, and Victoria Street,
    Liverpool; Engineering and Science Library: Byrom Street,
    Liverpool; 2b) Humanities Library: 051-227-1781

212　LIVERPOOL POLYTECHNIC LIBRARY (continued)
3)　D H Revill BSc(Econ) FLA
4a)　Constituent parts go back to mid-19th century (eg School of Art,
　　School of Pharmacy, etc); 4b) Contained in book provision and
　　services policy statement and the library guide.
5a)　Engineering, science, art, construction, sociology, social work,
　　law, business, management, languages, accountancy, librarianship,
　　politics, economics, education, commerce, history, geography,
　　physical education; 5b) Humanities, social sciences, business and
　　management—(Humanities Library); Construction (Construction
　　Libraries); Art and Design (Art and Design Library); Engineering
　　and science (Engineering and Science Library)
6a)　140,000 volumes. 2000 periodicals (current titles); 6b) Art exhi-
　　bition catalogues (Art and Design Library); Construction industry
　　manufacturers literature (Construction Libraries); Fine and illus-
　　trated books (Art and Design Library); Illustrations collection
　　(Art and Design Library)
7a)　Open access; Dewey Classification; 7b) Alphabetic catalogue, in-
　　cludes keyword entries; subject catalogue; subject index; post-
　　1974 material is recorded in a computer produced microfiche
　　form for both alphabetic and subject catalogues. These are union
　　catalogues. Audiovisual material is included in the alphabetic
　　catalogue. Periodicals listed in main catalogues and as separate
　　fiche. Pre-1974 holdings available as separate alphabetical and
　　classified catalogues (no subject index)
8a)　All polytechnic students and employees. The libraries are avail-
　　able to the general public as reference libraries; 8b) Humanities
　　Library, Walton House Term: M-F 0900-2100, Sat to 1300 (for a
　　trial period), Vacation 0900-1630; 8c) Powder diffraction file—
　　card file containing over 20,000 crystalline substances (Engineer-
　　ing and Science Library); Technical Index Product Data—micro-
　　film information service in cassette form (Engineering and Science
　　Library); Subject listings of recent items of interest based on de-
　　partmental profiles. Art and Design listing of recent additions (all
　　formats). Current awareness services to Maritime Studies, Mathe-
　　matics and Physical Education Departments.
9)　Library guide, guides to bibliographies, audiovisual items, audio-
　　visual equipment, translations, computerised data bases
10)　Williams, G K et al Amy: Liverpool Polytechnic Library computer-
　　ised cataloguing system Liverpool Polytechnic, 1976; Revill, D H
　　'Computer out-put microfiche catalogues' Microdoc 17(1), 1978
　　pp14-26.

213　CITY OF LONDON POLYTECHNIC Library and Learning Re-
　　sources Centre
1b)　City of London Polytechnic
2a)　Calcutta House Library: Old Castle Street, London E1 7NT;
　　Moorgate Library: 84 Moorgate, London EC2M 6SQ; Central
　　House Library: Central House, Whitechapel High Street,

213 CITY OF LONDON POLYTECHNIC LIBRARY (continued)
London E1 7PF; Tower Hill Library: School of Navigation,
100 Minories, Tower Hill, London Ec3N 1JY; Waldburgh House
Library: Bigland Street, London E1; 2b) Calcutta House Library:
01-283-1030; 2c) 8812073

3) Mrs R Pankhurst MA ALA

4a) 1970 polytechnic designated with the amalgamation of the City of
London College Library, the Sir John Cass College Library and
the Edward VII Nautical School Library; 4b) To anticipate plan
and respond to the needs of the polytechnic. To provide learning,
teaching and research resources and to assist in the exploitation
of those resources and associated services.

5b) Accountancy, taxation, banking and finance, economcis, law,
insurance, marketing, management, transport, psychology, sociology of work (Moorgate); Biology, chemistry, data processing,
geography, languages, maths, physics, politics, government,
psychology, secretarial studies, sociology (Calcutta House);
Art, metallurgy, materials science (Central House); Marine and air
navigation, maritime studies, geology (Walburgh House)

6a) 95,000 volumes. 1750 periodicals (current titles). 27,385 periodicals (bound volumes). 16,741 non-book material; 6b) Fawcett
collection: 20,000 volumes, 18,000 pamphlets, periodicals,
letters, photographs of women especially the suffragette movement; United National Treaty Series, volumes 1-700 on microfilm

7a) Open-access; Dewey Decimal Classification

8a) The library is open for reference purposes during prescribed
hours to enrolled students and employees of the polytechnic.
Other persons may beadmitted at the discretion of the chief
librarian; 8b) Calcutta House Library—Term: M-F 0900-2100;
Vacation: M-F 0900-1715; 8c) Basic library skills multi-media
packages for new members of the library; instruction sessions in
literature searches in specific subject areas

9) LLRS guide 1976; Guide to media resources in specific subject
areas; Guides to the literature in specific subject areas; List of
journals in the polytechnic: autumn 1976; Pritchard, A and
Nobel, P *Computer assisted monitoring of technical processes*
summer 1976

10) See Publications in print, available from Calcutta House Library

214 NORTH EAST LONDON POLYTECHNIC LIBRARY

1b) North East London Polytechnic

2a) Waltham Forest Precinct: Forest Road, London E17 4JB;
Barking Main Library: Longbridge Road, Dagenham, Essex
RM8 2AS; Engineering and Science Annexe, Humanities Library,
Education and Languages Annexe (addresses as for Main Library);
Anglian Regional Management Centre: Asta House, 156/164 High
Road, Chadwell Heath, Romford, Essex RM6 6LX; ARMC:
Danbury Park, Danbury, Nr Chelmsford, Essex CM3 4AT; West

214 N E LONDON POLYTECHNIC LIBRARY (continued)
Ham Main Library: Maryland House, Manbey Park Road,
London E15 4LZ; Greengate House: Greengate Street, London
E13 OBG; Holbrook Centre: Holbrook Road, London, E15 3EA;
Livingstone House: Livingstone Road, London E15 2LJ; Three
Mills Annexe: Abbey Lane, London E15 2RP; 2b) Waltham Forest
Precinct: 01-527-2272
3)   P W Plumb JP FLA
4a)   Polytechnic established 1970
5b)   Architecture, civil engineering, surveying (Waltham Forest Main
Library); Social sciences, business studies, engineering, humanities,
education (Barking Precinct Libraries); Science, natural science,
art and design, social sciences (West Ham Precinct Libraries)
5a)   280,000 volumes (including bound journals). 3300 periodicals
(current titles).
8b)   Waltham Forest Precinct—Term: M-F 0900-2100, Sat 0930-1230.
Reading room, Sat/Sun 0900-2100. Vacation: M-F 0900-1700,
Reading room: Sat/Sun 0900-2100

215 POLYTECHNIC OF CENTRAL LONDON LONDON LIBRARY
1b)   Polytechnic of Central London
2a)   309 Regent Street, London W1R 8AL; 35 Marylebone Road,
London NW1 5LS; Languages Library: Red Lion Square,
London WC1R 4SR; Law Library: 235-238 High Holborn,
London WC1V 7DN; Media Studies Library: 18-22 Ridinghouse
Street, London W1P 7PD; Management Library: 35 Marylebone
Road, London NW1 5LS; Social Sciences and Business Studies
Library: 32/38 Wells Street, London W1P 3FG; 2b) 01-486-5811
3)   W Ashworth BSc FLA FIInfSc ARPS DipLib

216 POLYTECHNIC OF NORTH LONDON LIBRARY
1b)   Polytechnic of North London
2a)   Holloway Road, London N7 8DB; Prince of Wales Road, London
NW5 3LB; Ladbroke House, Highbury Grove, London N5 2AD;
207-225 Essex Road, Islington, London N1 3PN; 129-133 Camden
High Street, Camden Town, London NW1 7JR; Marlborough
Building: 383 Holloway Road, London N7 6PN
2c)   Holloway Road: 01-607-2789
3)   S Francis FLA
6a)   205,500 volumes. 2248 periodicals (current titles). 29,310
Periodicals (bound volumes).
8b)   Holloway Road—Term: M-F 0900-2100, Sat 1000-1300; Vacation:
M-F 0900-1700
10)   Thom, B *The library in the new polytechnic* North-West Polytechnic School of Librarianship, 1969

217 POLYTECHNIC OF THE SOUTH BANK LIBRARY
1b) Polytechnic of the South Bank
2a) Main Library: Borough Road, London SE1 OAA; New Kent Road
     Annexe: 83 New Kent Road, London SE1 6RD; Institute of
     Environmental Science and Technology Library: Borough Road,
     London SE1 OAA; Faculty of the Built Environment Library:
     Wandsworth Road, London SW8 2JZ; Manressa House Library:
     Holybourne Avenue, London SW15 4JF; Manor House Library:
     58 Clapham Common North Side, London SW4 9RZ; 2b) Main
     Library: 01-928-8989 ext 2456
3)   G J Broadis MA FLA FRSA
4a) Polytechnic designated in 1970. Four formerly separate colleges
     were then amalgamated; 4b) The library's role is to ensure com-
     prehensive provision of books and other media, the compilation
     of up-to-date bibliographies and other aids and library instruction
     for all students
5b) Administrative studies, education, human sciences, social sciences,
     science and engineering (Main Library); Education, human sciences
     social sciences, arts, humanities, education (New Kent Road
     Annexe Library); Environmental science and technology (Institute
     of Environmental Science and Technology Library); Built environ-
     ment (Faculty of the Built Environment Library); Education, hu-
     man sciences, social sciences, education, arts, humanities (Manresa
     House Library); Education, human sciences, social sciences, edu-
     cation, home economics (Manor House Library)
6a) 220,000 volumes. 2700 periodicals (current titles). 24,000
     periodicals (bound volumes).
7a) Open access. Dewey Classification; 7b) Author catalogue; subject
     catalogue, subject index
8a) Reference and loan facilities for all staff and students of the poly-
     technic. Members of other institutions and the general public
     may use the reference facilities upon application to the librarian
     in charge; 8b) Main Library—Term: M-F 0900-2100, Vacation:
     M-F 0930-1700. Hours of opening are extended towards the end
     of the Easter Vacation.
9)   Library guides

218 THAMES POLYTECHNIC LIBRARY
1b) Thames Polytechnic
2a) Main Library: Wellington Street, Woolwich, London SE18 6PF;
     Riverside House: Beresford Street, Woolwich, S18 6BU; Durford
     Library: Oakfield Lane, Dartford, Kent DA1 2SZ; 2b) Main
     Library: 01-854-2030
3)   R S Eagle MA DPA FLA
4a) Polytechnic designated 1970, formerly Woolwich Polytechnic.
     Dartford College of Education was added in 1976; 4b) To serve
     the staff and students of the polytechnic by providing books,
     periodicals and other media relevant to the polytechnic courses.

THAMES POLYTECHNIC LIBRARY (continued)

5b) Electrical, electronic, mechanical and civil engineering; business administration; law; geography; history; politics; sociology; economics; architecture; surveying; physics; biology; chemistry; materials science; computing; environmental science. Member of SEAL (South-East Area Libraries)

6a) 150,000 volumes. 1400 periodicals (current titles). 200 microfilms. 600 microfiche. 156 video cassettes. 74 audio cassettes. 12,000 architecture slides. 2000 gramophone records.

7a) Open-access apart from a small stack provision and undergraduate texts; 7b) Author catalogue (includes stock at Riverside House); subject catalogue (includes stock at Riverside House); subject index; periodicals catalogue (includes stock at Riverside House); Author and subject catalogue on microfiche; (BLCMP)

8a) All services are available to all staff and students of the polytechnic. Reference facilities are extended to others at the discretion of the librarian; 8b) Main Library—Term: M-Th 0900-2100 (2200 summer term), Fri to 1700, Sat to 1230 and 1330-1700; Vacation: M-F 0900-1700; 8c) Reference, enquiry and advisory service, microfilm and microfiche readers; video-tape and cassette players; audio cassette players; tape-slide viewers; calculator; photocopiers. Interlibrary loan service; reader induction and education programmes.

9) Users guide to the library includes specific subject guides.

219 MANCHESTER POLYTECHNIC LIBRARY

1b) Manchester Polytechnic

2a) Central Library: All Saint Building, Grosvenor Square, Oxford Road, Manchester M15 6BH; Didsbury Library: Manchester Polytechnic, 799 Wilmslow Road, Manchester M20 8RR; Hollings Library: Manchester Polytechnic, Old Hall Lane, Manchester M14 6HR; Aytoun Library: Manchester Polytechnic, 47-49 Chorlton Street, Manchester M1 3Eu; 2b) Central Library: 061-228-6171; 2c) 667915

3) I Rogerson ALA

4a) Polytechnic established in 1970 from the colleges of art and design technology and commerce. New Central Library building opened autumn 1977; 4b) To serve the needs of the polytechnic community.

5a) Comprehensive, except for civil, structural and marine engineering and some foreign languages; 5b) Art and design, humanities, science and technology, social sciences, psychology, librarianship (Central Library); Education (Didsbury Library)

6a) 363,553 volumes (includes bound volumes of periodicals). 3000 periodicals (current titles). 12,000 non-book materials; 6b) Book Design Collection, includes old and rare books, examples of fine printing and book illustration, private press books and examples of important publishers series and the work of particular publishers

219   MANCHESTER POLYTECHNIC LIBRARY (continued)
and printers; Children's Books Collection: extensive collection of
children's books published between 1850 and 1914; Penguin
Books: large holdings from their inception to 1955. Since 1974
there has been a standing order for these books; Detective stories
1918-1939: the chief interest in this collection is the design of
book jackets. Pre-war paperbacks, other than Penguin, supplement the collection; Literary journals: substantial holdings from
18th, 19th and early 20th centuries.

7a)   Chiefly open access, some compact mobile shelving. Dewey
Classification; 7b) Author catalogue; subject catalogue; subject
index; union COM catalogue with conversion of pre-1975 card
catalogues taking place. Interim microfile of pre-1975 Central
Library holdings with amendments at the Central Library. Holdings of pre-1975 items elsewhere on card catalogues

8a)   All members of the polytechnic. Reference facilities to students
of other polytechnics and universities through COPOL and
SCONUL schemes. Others by permission of the librarian;
8b) Central Library—Term: M-Th 0900-2100, Fri to 1700.
Vacation: M-F 0900-1630; 8c) Inter-library loan through NWRLS
and BLLD. Current awareness services to teaching departments.

9)   Brief general library guide supported by course and subject guides

10)   Smith, G 'Illumination: the art and design section of Manchester
Polytechnic Library' *Library Association record* 79 (6), June
1977, pp316-318.

220   MIDDLESEX POLYTECHNIC LIBRARY
1b)   Middlesex Polytechnic
2a)   Bounds Green site: Bounds Green Road, London N11 2NQ;
Enfield site: Queensway, Enfield, Middlesex EN3 4SF; Hendon
site: The Burroughs, London NW4 4BT; Ivy House site: North End
Road, London NE11 7HU; Hornsey sites: a) Crouch End Hill:
London N8 8DG; b) Alexandra Palace: Alexandra Park, Wood
Green, London N22 4BE; c) 47 Bowes Road: Palmers Green,
London N13 4BT; d) South Grove School: Tottenham, London
N15 5QE; Trent Park site: Cockfosters, Barnet, Hertfordshire;
College of All Saints: White Hart Lane, Tottenham, London N17;
2b) Bounds Green site: 01-368-1299
3)   J Cowley BA FLA
4a)   Polytechnic established in 1973 amalgamating colleges of technology and art. Colleges of education, and speech and drama were
added in 1974 and a second college of education in 1978/79;
4b) To provide services and resources designed to support the
learning, teaching and research activities in the polytechnic. These
services are provided on a multi-site basis, but with some attempt
made to create main subject collections at specified sites.
5a)   Most academic areas are covered, but no great strengths in the
sciences; 5b) Art and design (Hornsey site libraries); Business

220 MIDDLESEX POLYTECHNIC LIBRARY (continued)
studies and management (Enfield and Hendon site libraries);
Education and the performing arts (Trent Park and Ivy House
site libraries); Humanities (Enfield and Hendon site libraries);
Social science (Enfield and Hendon site libraries); Engineering
and mathematics (Enfield and Bounds Green sites);
6a) 350,000 volumes. 2500 periodicals (current titles). Non-book
material including 6000 gramophone records; 6b) Strong collections in the major areas of the social sciences: business studies
and management, education and the performing arts, Good collections in smaller fields such as microelectronics; dance and
ballet, film and television, social deviancy.
7a) Open access. Dewey Classification; 7b) Author catalogue; subject
catalogue; subject index
8a) Staff and students of the polytechnic can use library facilities at
all sites. Students of other institutions may use reference facilities.
COPOL and SCONUL vacation cards are accepted; 8b) Enfield
site—Term: M-Th 0900-2130, Fri to 2030, Sat to 1700. Vacation:
M, W 0900-2030, T, Th, Fri to 1700; 8c) Short introductory
sessions and advanced instruction in library use and information
searching.
9) Library guides. 'Learning resources bulletin' vol 1 (1), October
1977.

221 NEWCASTLE UPON TYNE POLYTECHNIC LIBRARY
1b) Newcastle upon Tyne Polytechnic
2a) Ellison Building, Ellison Place, Newcastle upon Tyne NE1 8ST;
Northern Counties Library, Newcastle upon Tyne Polytechnic;
Coach Lane, Newcastle upon Tyne; 2b) Main Library: 0632-26002
3) K G E Harris MA FLA
4a) Polytechnic designated in 1969, with the amalgamation of the
colleges of art, commerce and technology. Library facilities were
centralised at this time. In 1972 a temporary branch library was
created for science and technology. A second branch for education and the humanities was opened in 1974 when the City of
Newcastle College of Education was merged with the polytechnic;
A third branch was added in 1976 when the Northern Counties
College of Education was added. In 1977 the first two branches
were moved into an extension to the main library; 4b) The library
exists to serve the academic needs of the polytechnic staff and
students by providing the necessary material for taught courses,
background reading and research. Some 1200 seats are available,
including private and group study space, and there are lecture
rooms on both sites.
5b) Art and design, technology, science, humanities, community and
social studies, business and management studies, education,
librarianship (Central Library); education, health studies, home
economics (Northern Counties Library)

211

221 NEWCASTLE POLYTECHNIC LIBRARY (continued)
6a) 340,000 volumes. 4000 periodicals (current titles). 50,000 periodicals (bound volumes). 26,000 non-book material; 6b) Government publications (Central Library); European Documentation
Centre (Central Library)
7a) Open access; Dewey DC; UDC (science and technology);
7b) Author catalogue; subject catalogue; subject index
8a) Staff and students of the polytechnic; other persons under
reciprocal arrangements with Newcastle University Library,
Durham University Library, Sunderland Polytechnic Library, or
by permission of the polytechnic librarian; 8b) Main Library—
Term: M-Th 0900-2100, Fri to 1700, Sat 0930-1700; Vacation:
M-F 0900-1700; 8c) Loan of most items except journals. Photocopying, inter-library loan, short loan collection, full-time professional enquiry service, bibliographies, literature searches, (on-
line where appropriate), subject guides, library instruction.
9) Library guide; leaflets on the collections and facilities for each
faculty
10) Harris, K G E and Marsterson, W A J 'Inter-library book lending'
B L L review 3 (3), 1975, pp51-54; Marsterson, W A J 'Work
study in a polytechnic library' *Aslib proceedings* 28 (9), September 1976, pp288-304; Cox, J 'Self-renewal in the humanities'
New library world 78 (925), July 1977, pp126-127.

222 NORTH STAFFORDSHIRE POLYTECHNIC LIBRARY
1b) North Staffordshire Polytechnic
2a) College Road, Stoke on Trent; Beaconside, Stafford; Madeley,
Nr Crewe; 2b) Stoke Library: 0782-45531
3) E S Waterson MA FLA
4a) Polytechnic established in 1970, amalgamating two colleges of
technology and a college of art. The Madeley College of Education is expected to merge with the polytechnic in September
1978; 4b) The library supports the teaching and research of the
polytechnic by administering full services on all sites.
5b) Science, engineering, law, art, social science, management (Stoke
on Trent site); Engineering, computing, international relations,
politics, history, literature, geography (Stafford site); member
of LINOSCO; MISLIC; Regional Library Bureau
6a) 104,000 volumes (minus the College of Education). 1405 periodicals (current titles); 6b) Computing
7a) Open access; Dewey DC; 7b) Name catalogue; classified catalogue;
subject index (union catalogues). The name catalogue at each
site forms a union catalogue for material added since 1971. It is
expected that a substantial part of the catalogue will be transferred
to COM fiche or film during 1978
8a) The library is open to staff and students of the polytechnic and to
members of the public on application to the librarian; 8b) Stoke—
Term: M-F 0900-2100, Vacation: M-F 0900-1715; 8c) Information

222   NORTH STAFFS POLYTECHNIC LIBRARY (continued)
       is given on a selective basis to all staff. A computer based SDI
       service (POLCAS) given to computing staff. Selective biblio-
       graphies are compiled. Tape/slied teaching programmes are used
       to introduce students to the library and show methods of litera-
       ture searching, Photocopying and micro-reading facilities are
       provided at all libraries
9)   Introduction to the library for students; Bulletins on recently pub-
       lished journal articles; Guides to the classification of subject fields;
       Aids to literature searching

223   OXFORD POLYTECHNIC LIBRARY
1b)   Oxford Polytechnic
2a)   Headington Library: Headington, Oxford OX3 OBP; Wheatley
       Library: Oxford Polytechnic, Lady Spencer-Churchill College,
       Wheatley, Oxford OX9 1HX; 2b) Headington Library: 0865-64777
3)   P F Jackson ALA
4a)   Oxford Polytechnic designated 1970; Amalgamated with the Lady
       Spencer-Churchill College of Education, 1976; 4b) The library
       supports teaching and research in the polytechnic by providing a
       wide selection of literature in monograph and serial form.
5a)   All subjects covered by polytechnic courses; 5b) Mathematics,
       science, engineering, building, architecture and planning, social
       sciences, humanities, art and design (Headington Library); Edu-
       cation, business studies (Wheatley Library)
6a)   113,650 volumes; 1332 periodicals (current titles). 8551 period-
       icals (bound volumes). 34,770 non-book material; 6b) Reading
       centre containing children's reading schemes
7a)   Open access, small area of closed stacks. Dewey DC; 7b) Author
       catalogue; subject catalogue; subject index
8a)   Full lending and reference facilities to all full and part-time
       members of the polytechnic. Open to the general public for
       reference purposes. COPOL and SCONUL vacation reading
       scheme cards are accepted; 8b) Headington Library—Term: M-F
       0900-2200, Sat to 1300; Vacation M-F 0900-1700; 8c) Tape slide
       guide to the library for new students; Seminars on aspects of
       library use for groups of students at different levels and in differ-
       ent subjects—some are a formal part of the curriculum
9)   How to find out in Oxford Polytechnic Library; Brief guide to
       Oxford Polytechnic Library; Subject lists of periodicals and sub-
       ject guides

224   PLYMOUTH POLYTECHNIC Learning Resources Centre
1b)   Plymouth Polytechnic
2a)   Drake Circus, Plymouth PL4 8AA; 2b) 0752-21312 ext 219;
       2c) 45423
3)   Miss M Lattimore MA FLA

(continued)

224 PLYMOUTH POLYTECHNIC LIBRARY (continued)
4a) Established 1955 as the library of Plymouth College of Technology.
     Became the polytechnic library in 1971, which was the nucleus of
     the present learning resources centre, established in 1973.
4b) Aim is to promote effective learning in the polytechnic by providing
     library services, educational services and production services
5a) Engineering, science, behavioural sciences, management and business
     studies, architecture, maritime studies.
6a) 80,000 volumes. 1400 periodicals (current titles). 8500 periodicals
     (bound volumes). 6000 non-book material. 6b) Specialist
     holdings in maritime literature
7a) Open access. Dewey DC; 7b) Author catalogue; subject catalogue;
     subject index
8a) Staff and students of the polytechnic are entitled to full member-
     ship. Associate membership may be granted to members of staff
     of professional bodies and institutions associated with the poly-
     technic. On application to the head of the centre, members of
     the public may visit the library for reference only; 8b) Term:
     M-F 0830-2200; Sat 0900-1700; Sun 1000-1800. Vacation: M-F
     0830-1700; 8c) Maritime studies current awareness bulletin (weekly
     during term)
9)   A wide variety of publications are produced. They include guides
     to using the library, bibliographical series, bibliographical teach-
     ing handouts and various serial publications. A full list is con-
     tained in L R C Publications in Print, Series G 001
10) Lattimore, M 'Not so much a library—more a way of learning'
     Library Association record 79(3), March 1977, pp142-143.

225 PORTSMOUTH POLYTECHNIC LIBRARY
1b) Portsmouth Polytechnic
2a) Main Library: Hampshire Terrace, Portsmouth, Hants PO1 2EG;
     Faculty of Educational Studies: Locksway Road, Portsmouth,
     Hants; 2b) Main Library: 0705-27681
3)   W G Gale BA FLA
4a) 1969. College of Education added in 1976.
6a) 300,000 volumes (including bound periodicals). 3000 periodicals
     (current titles)
8b) Main library—Term: M-Th 0900-2200, Fri to 2100, Sat to 1730,
     Sun 1400-1800; Vacation: M-F 0900-1700

226 PRESTON POLYTECHNIC Library and Learning Resources Service
1b) Preston Polytechnic
2a) Preston Campus Library: Corporation Street, Preston, PR1 2TQ;
     Lancaster Annexe Library: Meeting House Lane, Lancaster;
     Chorley Campus Library: Union Street, Chorley PR7 1ED;
     Poulton Campus Library: Breck Road, Poulton-le-Fylde, Blackpool
     FY6 7AW; 2b) 0772-51831/7
3)   J R Edgar MA FLA
4a) Polytechnic established 1973. Two colleges of education were
     added in 1975. A new library building will be opened on the

226 PRESTON POLYTECHNIC Resources Centre (continued)
Preston Campus in October 1978; 4b) Aims to support actively the
wide range of teaching and research interests of the polytechnic
5b) Science, technology, business studies, law, art and design (Preston
Campus Library); fine art (Lancaster annexe library); education,
humanities (Chorley and Poulton Campus libraries)
6a) 170,000 volumes. 1500 periodicals (current titles); 6b) Preston
Incorporated Law Society Collection, c5000 volumes of reports,
texts and journals (Preston Campus Library)
7a) Open access. Dewey DC, UDC for material acquired before 1975
at the Preston Campus
8a) All staff and students of the polytechnic are entitled to full
membership. Membership may be extended to those organisations
approved by the Academic Board. Reference facilities may be
extended to students of other polytechnics and universities on
production of a COPOL or SCONUL vacation reading card, and
also to members of the public with the permission of the polytechnic librarian; 8b) Preston Campus—Term: M-Th 0900-2100,
Fri to 2000; Vacation M-Th 0900-1730, Fri to 1700
9) Information sheets on the stock, organisation and services of the
library system

227 SHEFFIELD CITY POLYTECHNIC LIBRARY
1b) Sheffield City Polytechnic
2a) Pond Street Site Library: Pond Street, Sheffield S1 1WB; Psalter
Lane Site Library: Psalter Lane, Sheffield S11 8UZ; Collegiate
Crescent Site Library: Collegiate Crescent, Sheffield S10 2BP;
Totley Site Library: Totley Hall Lane, Sheffield S17 4AB; Wentworth Woodhouse Site Library, Wentworth Woodhouse, Rother-
ham. 2b) Pond Street Site Library: 0742-20911 ext 276;
2c) 54680
3) D T Lewis, ALA DipAdEd CertEd
4a) The City Polytechnic was established in 1976, amalgamating
Sheffield Polytechnic and two Colleges of Education, and in 1977
a third College of Education was merged; 4b) To support learning,
teaching and research within the institution.
5a) Coverage of all subjects taught at the Polytechnic; 5b) Business,
management, engineering, humanities, science, social sciences (Pond
Street Site Library); Art and design (Psalter Lane Site Library); Education (Collegiate Crescent Site Library); Education (particularly
physical education) (Wentworth Woodhouse Site Library); Home
economics, humanities (Totley Site Library)
6a) 392,725 volumes (including bound journals and non-book material);
2311 periodicals (current titles); 6b) European Documentation
Centre (Pond Street Site Library); Statistical data collection—
covers a side range of economic and social statistics (Pond Street
Site Library); Exhibition catalogues on microfiche (Psalter Lane
Site Library); Antiquarian/rare books published before 1900
(Psalter Lane Site Library)
7a) Open-access; Dewey Decimal Classification; 7b) Author catalogue;

227 SHEFFIELD CITY POLYTECHNIC LIBRARY (continued)
classified catalogue; subject index; subject index to the European
Documentation Centre collection

8a) All members of the Polytechnic may use the full facilities of the
library system. Members of the public may use it for reference
purposes. Certain other groups of external readers (Open University students, past Polytechnic students, members of academic
staff in local colleges etc) may be given borrowing privileges;
8b) Pond Street Library—Term: M-F 0845-2100, Sat 0900-2100;
Vacation: M-F 0845-1700; 8c) Comprehensive user education
programme; On-line information retrieval services; On-line
circulation system in operation. Planned (later in 1978)
utilisation of BLAISE for centralised cataloguing records.

9) Series of leaflets describing the services and facilities available;
Subject book marks; 'Polybibs'—give guidance to special types of
material; Library news

10) COPOL news carries various articles on publications programme,
short-loan, part-time loan collections, inter-library loan service, etc.
Pickering, S *The special collection: a selective catalogue*, 1977.

228 SUNDERLAND POLYTECHNIC LIBRARY
1b) Sunderland Polytechnic
2a) Sunderland Polytechnic Library, Chester Road, Sunderland
SR1 3SD; Faculty of Art Library: Ryhope Road, Sunderland;
Faculty of Education Library: Langham Tower, Sunderland;
2b) Main library: 0783-52141
3) N J Hunter MA BSc(Econ) LLB ALA
4a) Founded 1939 as the Sir John Priestman Library in Sunderland
Technical College. 1969 polytechnic designated with the amalgamation of Sunderland Technical College and College of Art.
1975 Sunderland College of Education added; 4b) To provide
a library service appropriate to the educational objectives of
polytechnic teaching and research.

5a) Most academic disciplines; 5b) Science, engineering, humanities
(Polytechnic Library); social sciences, history, geography (Poly-
technic Library); fine art (Faculty of Art Library); education
(Faculty of Education Library)

6a) 150,000 volumes (including bound volumes of periodicals).
1350 periodicals (current titles)

7a) Open access, Dewey DC; 7b) Author catalogue, classified catalogue (both produced on COM)

8a) Full facilities available to members of the polytechnic. Reciprocal
borrowing arrangements with academic staff of other educational
institutions, Members of the general public may use reference
facilities; borrowing facilities may be allowed at the librarian's
discretion; 8b) Polytechnic Library—Term: M-F 0900-2200, Sat
to 1230; Vacation: M-F 0900-1730; 8c) Reference enquiries;
literature searches; inter-library loan; library instruction

9) Guide to the library; subject guides to the literature; subject bookmarks.

228 SUNDERLAND POLYTECHNIC LIBRARY (continued)
10) Lewis, D T 'Automation in a polytechnic library' *New library world* 75(887), May 1974, pp98-99; Haylock, J R 'Library automation at Sunderland Polytechnic' *Programme* 8 (4), October 1974, pp209-214

229 TEESSIDE POLYTECHNIC LIBRARY
1b) Teesside Polytechnic
2a) Borough Road, Middlesborough, Cleveland TS1 3BA;
     2b) 0642-244176 ext 37
3)   W R Moss BA FLA
4a) Polytechnic established 1970 from Constantine College of Technology. Teesside College of Education added in September 1978.
5b) Engineering, science, technology, mathematics, computer science, management, professional studies, arts, social studies
6a) 80,000 volumes. 1500 periodicals (current titles). 20,000 periodicals (bound volumes);
7a) Open-access except for older material; Dewey DC; 7b)Author catalogue; subject catalogue (card catalogues); subject index, mini-catalogue (computer print-out)
8a) Reference and loan facilities for staff and students of the polytechnic; COPOL and SCONUL vacation cards and letters of introduction are accepted for others who wish to use reference facilities; 8b) Term: M-F 0845-2100, Sat 0900-1200; Vacation: M-F 0900-1700; 8c) Senior staff have designated subject responsibilities. Computerised SDI service, lectures, seminars and literature searches are undertaken.
9)   Guides to readers: Computerised accession lists, Introduction for library users.
10) Moss, R 'Time factor classification' *Aslib proceedings* vol 27 (6), June 1975, pp273-277; Brophy, P 'Teesside Polytechnic library's acquisitions information system' *Program* vol 11 (3), July 1977, pp89-93.

230 TRENT POLYTECHNIC LIBRARY
2a) Newton Building, Burton Street, Nottingham, NG1 BU; Bonnington Building, Dryden Street, Nottingham; York House, Mansfield Road, Nottingham; Chaucer Building, Goldsmith Street, Nottingham; Clifton site, Clifton, Nottingham; 2b) Newton Building: 0602-48248
3)   D Daintree MA FLA
4a) Polytechnic established 1970. College of education added 1975.
5b) Engineering, life sciences, mining, physical sciences (Newton Building); art and design (Bonnington Building); education, social studies, economics, public administration (York House); business studies, law, town and country planning (Chaucer Building); education, humanities, professional studies (Clifton site)
6a) 220,000 volumes. 2200 periodicals (current titles).
8b) Newton Building–Term: M-F 0830-2100, Sat 0845-1200; Vacation: M-F 0830-1700

231 ULSTER POLYTECHNIC LIBRARY
1b) Ulster Polytechnic
2a) Shore Road, Newtownabbey, Co Antrim, BT37 0QB; The Art and Design Centre: York Street, Belfast; 2b) Main library: 0231-65131; 2c) 747493
3) B G Baggett BSc MIInfSc
4a) Polytechnic established 1971. A new library building was opened in 1974; 4b) To provide a complete library service to the polytechnic
5a) Most major disciplines are covered except medicine. Undergraduate courses in physiotherapy, special therapy and diploma courses in occupational therapy are supported; 5b) Humanities, art and design, accountancy, business, administration, computer science, social science, engineering, building, construction, education
6a) 167,000 volumes; 6b) American studies
7a) Open-access, Dewey DC; 7b) Author catalogue, subject catalogue, subject index (sheaf catalogues); non-book media catalogue, short-title file on COM, periodicals holdings list—line printer output, counter reserve collection—line printer output
8a) Reference and loan facilities to all members of the polytechnic. COPOL and SCONUL vacation cards are accepted. Reference facilities are available to others at the librarian's discretion; 8b) Term: M-Th 0900-2100, Fri to 1630, Sat 1000-1300; Vacation M-Th 0900-1700, Fri to 1630; 8c) Subject specialist staff catalogue and classify the stock and provide assistance to readers. On-line information searches are undertaken via DIALOC and DIALTECH.

232 POLYTECHNIC OF WALES LIBRARY
1b) Polytechnic of Wales
2a) Treforest site: Llantwit Road, Treforest, Pontypridd, Mid-Glamorgan; Barry site: College Road, Barry, Mid-Glamorgan; 2b) Treforest site: 0443-405133
3) G W F Ewins BSc(Econ) ALA
5b) Science, engineering, social science, arts (Treforest site); education, arts (Barry site)
6a) 160,000 volumes. 1600 periodicals (current titles); 6b) Official publications collections (Treforest site); Collection of Welsh literature (Barry site)
8a) Staff and students of the polytechnic are entitled to full membership. Non-polytechnic enquirers may register as external borrowers; 8b) Treforest site—Term: M-F 0900-2100, Sat to 1700; Vacation M-F 0900-1700; 8c) Tape slide guides on the use of certain reference works. Queries of a technical or commercial nature are welcomed from external organisations or individuals

233 WOLVERHAMPTON POLYTECHNIC LIBRARIES
1b) The Polytechnic, Wolverhampton
2a) Robert Scott Library: The Polytechnic, St Peters Square, Wolverhampton WV1 1RH; The Library, Faculty of Art and Design,

233 WOLVERHAMPTON POLYTECHNIC LIBRARIES (continued)
The Polytechnic, North Street, Wolverhampton WV1 1DT; Law
Library, Dept of Legal Studies, The Polytechnic, Stafford Street,
Wolverhampton; Himley Hall Management Centre Library, The
Library, Residential Centre, Himley Hall, Nr Dudley; Faculty of
Education Library, The Polytechnic, Castle View, Dudley DY1 3HR;
Faculty of Education Library, The Polytechnic, Compton Park,
Compton Road West, Wolverhampton WV3 9DX; 2b) Robert Scott
Library: 0902-27375 ext 121; 2c) 336301
3)   Mrs S G Ayerst BSc MIInfSci
4a)   Polytechnic established 1969. Three colleges of education were
added in 1977; A new Main Library building was opened in 1976;
4b) To support the academic work of the polytechnic; Facilities
include lending, inter-library lending, photocopying, reference
service; DIALTECH.
5b)   Humanities, social sciences, science and technology, engineering
(Robert Scott Library); art and design (Faculty of Art and Design
Library); law (Law Library); management, economics (Himley
Hall Management Centre Library); education (Faculty of Education
Libraries)
6a)   200,000 volumes. 3500 periodicals (current titles). 4700 periodicals (titles retained); 6b) European Documentation Centre (Robert
Scott Library); slides and illustrations collection (Art and Design
Library); statistical publications (Robert Scott Library)
7a)   Open-access, Dewey DC; 7b) Robert Scott Library has main card
catalogue: union catalogue, name catalogue, classified catalogue,
subject index (in printed format). Short-title catalogues, computer produced and in printed format cover the stock of the Robert
Scott Library and are available on each subject floor. All other
libraries have name and classified card catalogues of their own
stock;
8a)   Staff and students of the polytechnic are entitled to full membership of the libraries. Members of the public may use reference
facilities only; 8b) Robert Scott Library—Term: M-F 0900-2100,
Sat to 1230; Vacation: M-F 0900-1715; 8c) Library instruction is
incorporated in some courses. Library staff give personal guidance
for intensive subject enquiries. Literature searches may be undertaken for members of the academic staff. Current awareness services are offered to academic staff and research assistants in some
subject areas
9)   Library guides; Study guides; Subject guides

SCOTTISH CENTRAL INSTITUTIONS

234 DUNCAN OF JORDANSTONE COLLEGE OF ART LIBRARY
1b) Duncan of Jordanstone College of Art
2a) Perth Road, Dundee, DD1 4HT; 2b) 0382-23261
3) J Farish BA(Hons) ALA
4a) 1901
5a) Art, architecture, planning, design, home economics, institutional management and catering, interior design, printing
6a) 28,000 volumes. 185 periodicals (current titles). 92 periodicals (bound volumes). 40,350 non-book material; 6b) 18,000 trade catalogues
7a) Mainly open-access; modified UDC; 7b) Dictionary catalogue
8a) Reference and loan facilities to members or accredited persons only. Information given by post and phone to all enquirers; 8b) Term: 0900-2030; Vacation: 0900-1600; 8c) Inter-library loans through BLLD and the Scottish Central Lending Library.
9c) Accession lists; theses catalogue; guide to report and theses writing; guide to classification of slide and visual material

235 DUNDEE COLLEGE OF TECHNOLOGY LIBRARY
1b) Dundee College of Technology
2a) Bell Street, Dundee DD1 1HG; 2b) 0382-27225 ext 367; 2c) 76453 DUNCOTT G
3) N Craven MA FLA FSA(Scot)
4a) 1964; 4b) To collect, arrange and exploit all manner of educational materials for the benefit of staff and students of the college. To develop the library's facilities for use by local schools, industry and commerce.
5b) Accountancy, economics, business studies, civil engineering, electrical and electronic engineering, mathematics and computer studies, mechanical and industrial engineering, molecular and life sciences, physics, surveying and building, textile science
6a) 62,450 volumes. 750 periodicals (current titles). 10,550 periodicals (bound volumes, including abstracts). 600 periodical titles retained. 450 non-book materials; 6b) Company Information System. A collection of annual reports of over 3000 companies, mostly British, but with some from Europe, South Africa, North America and Australia. Acquired in 1976 and accessible to researchers, students or members of the public.
7a) Open-access; UDC; 7b) Author catalogue, subject catalogue
8a) Library services are available to all members of the college and to users from local schools, industry and commerce. Information given by post or phone to all enquirers; 8b) Term: M-F 0845-2100; Vacation: M-F 0845-1700; 8c) Loan and inter-library loan facilities. Advice on sources of information; literature searchers, preparation of bibliographies. Photocopying, micro-reading facilities.
9) Annual readers handbook, monthly accessions list, irregular journals list

236 EDINBURGH COLLEGE OF ART LIBRARY
1b) Edinburgh College of Art
2a) Lauriston Place, Edinburgh EH3 9DF; 2b) 031-229-9311
3) G Craig MA ALA
4a) Founded 1907 a year after the founding of the college which was
formerly the Edinburgh School of Applied Art within the Royal
Institution School. Libraries for architecture and town planning
have been established during the subsequent growth of the college;
4b) To provide a reference and learning facility to staff and
students of the college
5b) Art and design, architecture, town planning, humanities—literature
music, history. Contributes to the Union Catalogue of Art books
in Edinburgh libraries. Drawing, painting, sculpture, design, crafts,
humanities (Main Library); architecture, landscape design (Architecture Library); planning, law, sociology, maps (Town Planning
Library)
6a) 35,000 volumes. 290 periodicals (current titles). 38 periodicals
(bound volumes). 6000 reproductions and prints. 10,000 pamphlets. 1800 maps and plans. 71,000 slides. 1200 exhibition catalogues. 900 theses and dissertations;
7a) Open and closed access; UDC; 7b) Dictionary catalogue
8a) Access for reference purposes to all. Loan facilities to members
of the college or accredited persons only. Information given by
post and phone to all enquirers; 8b) Term: M-Th 0915-2030,
Fri to 1700; Vacation: M-F 0915-1600; 8c) Introductory talks;
library instruction and readers advice.
9) Guide to readers, bookmarks, subject bibliographies,

237 THE EDINBURGH SCHOOL OF AGRICULTURE LIBRARY
1b) A combined body including the East Scotland College of Agriculture and the Department of Agriculture, Edinburgh University
2a) West Mains Road, Edinburgh, EH9 3JG; 2b) 031-667-1041
3) Miss R M Johnson BA ALA
4a) 1945; 4b) To provide a comprehensive library service to the
advisory and teaching staff and to students at HND, BSc, and PhD
levels
5b) Agriculture, microbiology, veterinary medicine
6a) 8800 volumes. 450 periodicals (current titles). 800 periodicals
(volumes, current and non-current. 390 pamphlets.
7a) Open and closed access; UDC; 7b) Author catalogue, subject catalogue
8a) Access for reference purposes to all. Loan facilities to members
and accredited persons only. Information given by post and phone
to all enquirers; 8b) Term: M, T, Th: 0845-1700 and 1800-2100;
W, F: 0845-1700; 8c) Information retrieval service from 'popular'
journals provided for staff. Talks to all students on library use.
9) Monthly accessions list; annual list of college publications.

238 GLASGOW SCHOOL OR ART LIBRARY
1b) Glasgow School of Art
2a) 167 Renfrew Street, Glasgow G3 6RQ; 2b) 041-332-9797 ext 227
3) I C Monie MSc FLA
4a) Founded 1909. The original library is still used as a reference and
research library. The lending library was opened in 1977 in
studios designed by Charles Rennie Mackintosh for architecture
students; 4b) To support the work of the school, including undergraduate, post-graduate and evening recreational classes.
5a) Art and design, architecture, planning
6a) 27,000 volumes. 166 periodicals (current titles). 125 periodicals
(bound volumes). 19 films. 1400 slides. 138 microfiches. (V & A
Museum collection catalogue) 102 microfiches (Royal Commission
on Historical Monuments in Scotland); 6b) Material on Charles
Rennie Mackintosh. Press cuttings on the work of staff and
students of the school
7a) Open-access; UDC; 7b) Author catalogue, subject catalogue, subject index (including artists)
8a) Reference and loan facilities for members or accredited persons
only. Information by phone or post to all enquiries; 8b) Term:
M-Th 0930-2000, Fri to 1700; Vacation: M-F 0930-1700; 8c) Loan
service; subject specialists in art and design; architecture and planning provide bibliographic services.
9) Accession lists; guide to the library

239 LEITH NAUTICAL COLLEGE LIBRARY
1b) Leith Nautical College
2a) 24 Milton Road East, Edinburgh EH15 2PP; 2b) 031-669-8461
ext 209
3) Miss S McCullough BSc ALA
4a) 1969; 4b) Provides general library and audiovisual resource service
to staff and students of the college
5a) Maritime studies in general; 5b) Maritime engineering; navigation;
marine electronics; marine radio and radar; naval architecture;
maritime law
6a) 12,000 volumes. 150 periodicals (current titles). 80 periodicals
(bound volumes). Non-book material; 6b) 1000 trade catalogues
7a) Open-access; Dewey DC; 7b) Author catalogue; subject catalogue
8a) Reference facilities to all. Loan facilities to members or accredited
persons only. Information by phone and post to all enquirers;
8b) Term: M-Th 0900-2000, Fri to 1700; Vacation: M-F 0900-
1700
9) Accessions list; 'Index to M' notices

240 PAISLEY COLLEGE OF TECHNOLOGY LIBRARY
1b) Paisley College of Technology
2a) High Street, Paisley, Renfrewshire PA1 2BE; 2b) 041-887-1241;
2c) 778951

240   PAISLEY COL. OF TECHNOLOGY LIBRARY (continued)
3)   H C MacLachlan MA FLA
4a)   Founded 1965 as a central library with the amalgamation of the
      college and departmental collections. This was transferred to new
      accommodation in 1975; 4b) To meet both the educational needs
      of the students and teaching and research needs of the staff. Ma-
      terial related to courses is supplemented by a substantial number
      of works on West European civilisation.
5)   Social sciences, natural sciences, engineering
6a)   56,000 volumes (including bound periodicals). 835 periodicals
      (current titles). 8000 periodicals (bound volumes). 300 period-
      ical titles retained. c500 tape-slide units. 200 gramophone
      records. 1000 maps. 600 microforms; 6b) Scottish railway docu-
      ments and plans; Richardson Collection (printed copies of works
      written by, or annotated by, Dr Lewis Fry Richardson, FRS,
      former principal); Land economics with special reference to
      Scotland.
7a)   Mainly open-access. except for special collections: non-book ma-
      terial and unbound periodicals, UDC; 7b) Author catalogue;
      subject catalogue; periodicals catalogue; reserve books catalogue;
      calendar of Scottish railway documents
8a)   Full library facilities are available to staff and students of the
      college; persons nominated by local industrial concerns; local
      government organisations, local trades union branches and other
      qualified persons; Members of the public may use reference
      facilities; 8b) Term: M-F 0910-2100, Sat 0930-1230; Vacation:
      M-F 0910-1700; 8c) Subject assistance librarians assist with
      bibliographic problems. Bibliographies are compiled according
      to time available. Translations provided or arranged. A charge is
      made for these services to external users to accord with Scottish
      Education Department requirements. Facilities include 458 study
      places which includes study, audiovisual and sound-proofed
      carrels; microform readers, photocopier; microform printer; map
      enlarger—printer; light table; Farquhar celestial globe.
9)   Undergraduate guide; guide for staff and post-graduate students;
      special borrowers' guide; accessions list; periodical holdings;
      calendar of railway documents.

241   THE QUEEN'S COLLEGE GLASGOW LIBRARY
1b)   The Queen's College, Glasgow
2a)   1 Park Drive, Glasgow G3 6LP; 2b) 031-339-9211
3)   Miss H F Sommerville ALA
4a)   1962; 4b) Aims to support the teaching curricula of the college
5b)   Home economics, food and nutrition, design, fashion, textiles,
      hotel catering and institutional management, dietetics, physio-
      therapy, social welfare
6a)   22,000 volumes. 200 periodicals (current titles). 24 periodicals
      (bound volumes). Resources of non-book materials are to be

241 THE QUEEN'S COLLEGE LIBRARY (continued)
developed as from 1978. 6b) Small collection of historical material in the field of home economics.
7a) Dewey DC; 7b) Author catalogue; subject catalogue; subject index
8a) Loan and reference facilities to members and accredited persons only. Information by post and phone to all enquirers; 8b) Term: M-Th 0900-2000, Fri to 1700; Vacation: M-F 0900-1700; 8c) Inter-library loan and photocopying facilities are available. Inter-loans are supplied via BLLD or the Scottish Union Catalogue.
9) Monthly accessions list

242 QUEEN MARGARET COLLEGE Aileen King Library
1b) Queen Margaret College
2a) Clerwood Terrace, Edinburgh, EH12 8TS; 2b) 031-334-8111
3) Miss J K H Playfair MA DipLib
4a) 1970; 4b) To serve the teaching and research needs of staff and students of the college
5a) Drama, home economics, food and nutrition, design, nursing, management, sociology, speech therapy, physiotherapy
6a) 36,000 volumes. 450 periodicals (current titles). 400 periodicals (bound volumes).
7a) Open-access; Dewey DC; 7b) Author and title catalogue; subject catalogue, alphabetic (both card catalogues)
8a) Loan and reference facilities for college members and accredited persons only. Information by post and phone to all enquirers. 8b) Term: M-Th 0900-2100, Fri to 1700; Vacation: M-F 0900-1630; 8c) Photocopying and inter-library loan facilities are available.
9) Accessions list

243 ROBERT GORDON'S INSTITUTE OF TECHNOLOGY LIBRARY
1b) Robert Gordon's Institute of Technology
2a) Main Library: St Andrew Street, Aberdeen AB1 1HG; Gray's School of Art Library: Garthdee, Aberdeen; Scott Sutherland School of Architecture Library: Garthdee, Aberdeen; School of Health Visiting Library: Willowbank House, Aberdeen; King Street Library: Robert Gordon's Institute of Technology, 352 King Street, Aberdeen; Study and Demonstration Library: Robert Gordon's Institute of Technology, St Andrew Street, Aberdeen; 2b) Main Library: 0224-574511 ext 55/56
3) S R Latham MSc FLA FInstPet
4a) 1938; 4b) Provides library facilities for undergraduate and postgraduate teaching in a Scottish central institution offering a wide range of CNAA degree courses at ordinary and honours level. Facilities provided in support of research and consultancy work for industry. Wide range of books, journals with back runs, technical reports, bibliographical material, abstracts etc at graduate,

243 R GORDON'S INST. OF TECHNOLOGY LIBRARY (continued)
post-graduate and research level. Headquarters of ANSLICS—
Aberdeen and North of Scotland Library and Information Cooperative Service.

5a) Electronic, electrical, mechanical and off-shore engineering, chemistry, physics, mathematics, pharmacy, nutritional sciences, social
work, sociology, librarianship, art, architecture, quantity surveying, home economics, business management; 5b) Engineering,
science, social science, business, librarianship, health visiting,
nutritional science (Main Library); Nutritional sciences, home
economics, hotel and institutional administration (Kepplestone
premises); Business management, survival at sea (King Street Library); Library science (Study and Demonstration Library); Art
(Grays School of Art Library); Architecture, quantity surveying
(Scott Sutherland School of Architecture Library)

6a) 104,000 volumes. 1500 periodicals (current titles). 1000 periodicals (bound volumes). 2000 non-book materials; 6b) 2000 technical reports

7a) Open-access. Dewey DC and UDC; 7b) Author catalogue; subject catalogue

8a) Reference and loan facilities available to members and non-
members. Information by post or phone given to all enquirers;
8b) Term: M-F 0900-2200, Sat to 1700; Sun 1400-2200; Vacation
M-F 0900-1700; 8c) Reference, information and bibliographic
services provided on request. Regular distribution of accession
lists and information on new publications to academic staff. Computerised information retrieval service on off-shore oil using press
cuttings as data base. Available to all users.

9) Accessions lists; Library guides. ANSLICS *Oil: a bibliography*
3rd ed, 1977.

244 ROYAL SCOTTISH ACADEMY OF MUSIC AND DRAMA
LIBRARY
1b) Royal Scottish Academy of Music and Drama
2a) 58 St George's Place, Glasgow G2 1BS; 2b) 041-332-4101
3) K F Wilkins BA ALA
4a) Founded 1929
5a) Music and theatre arts
6a) 68,904 music. 8834 books. 55 periodicals (current titles).
52 periodicals(bound volumes). 3000 non-book material.
7a) Library of Congress Classification (modified); 7b) Author catalogue; subject catalogue
8a) Reference and loan facilities to members and accredited persons
only. Information given by post or phone to all enquirers;
8b) Term: M, W 0930-1800, T, Th 0930-1930, F 0930-1730;
Vacation: M-F 0930-1630

245 SCOTTISH COLLEGE OF TEXTILES LIBRARY
1b) Scottish College of Textiles
2a) Netherdale, Galashiels TD1 3HF; 2b) 0896-3351
3) U H Grant MA ALA
5a) Textile technology, textile design, management studies, clothing technology
6a) 10,237 volumes (including pamphlets). 190 periodicals (current volumes). 500 slides. Video cassettes, fabric samples, microfilms
7a) Dewey DC; UDC (modified); 7b) Dictionary catalogue
8a) Reference and loan facilities for members and non-members, information by post and telephone to all enquirers; 8b) Term: M-Th 0900-2030, Fri to 1700; Vacation M-F 0900-1645; 8c) SDI and retrospective mechanised information retrieval service for staff and students based on periodical articles
9) Accession lists

246 UNIVERSITY OF ABERDEEN SCHOOL OF AGRICULTURE LIBRARY
1b) University of Aberdeen
2a) 581 King Street, Aberdeen AB9 1UD; 2b) 0224-40241 ext OA 390; 2c) 73458
3) Mrs A A Park ALA
4a) Founded 1957 as the North of Scotland College of Agriculture Library. Became the School of Agriculture Library in 1968 when the college amalgamated with the University of Aberdeen (see entry 90); 4b) To provide a full library service to the staff and students of the school and related departments.
5a) Agriculture and allied subjects
6a) 7100 volumes (including pamphlets). 680 periodicals (current titles). 6160 periodicals (bound volumes). 1179 periodical titles retained.
7) Open-access; Dewey DC; 7b) Author catalogue; subject catalogue; subject index (all on microfiche)
8a) Loan and reference facilities to members and accredited persons only. Information given by post and phone to all enquirers; 8b) Term: M-F 0900-2300, Sat to 1700, Sun 1400-1700; Vacation: (Christmas and Easter) M-F 0900-2200, Sat to 1300; (summer) M-F 0900-1700, Sat to 1300; 8c) Advice given to staff and students of the university. Information is given to a limited extent to outposted members of academic staff.
9) Guides produced by readers advisors at the main university library which are circulated to branches.

247 WEST OF SCOTLAND COLLEGE OF AGRICULTURE
W J Thomson Library
1b) West of Scotland College of Agriculture
2a) Donald Hendrie Building, Auchincruive, Ayr KA16 5HW; 2b) 029-252-331

247 WEST OF SCOTLAND COLLEGE LIBRARY (continued)
3)   A J Brandram BSc ALA
4a) Founded 1938; 4b) Service to students, teaching and research
     staff and advisory staff
5b) Agriculture; horticulture; poultry; food technology; bee-keeping
6a) 13,200 volumes. 403 periodicals (current titles). 523 periodicals
     (bound volumes); 6b) 29,500 technical reports. 342 standard
     specifications. A small collection of 18th and 19th century agri-
     cultural books.
7a) UDC; 7b) Author catalogue; subject catalogue
8a) Loan and reference facilties for members and non-members. In-
     formation by post and phone to all enquirers; 8b) Term: M, T, Th
     0900-1700 and 1845-2045; W, F 0900-1700
9)   Monthly accessions list; Periodicals list.

INDEXES

All references in the following index relate to the entry numbers.

SUBJECT INDEX

235

238

Drawings–Collections 6, 9, 14, 40, 41, 59, 81, 107
Drawings–Collections. See also Prints–Collections
Durham–Local history 120
Durham, Palatinate 67
Drugs 86
Dutch language 184
Dutch literature 184
Dutch studies 135

Earth sciences 12
East 120. See also Far East
East Africa 73, 195
East Midlands. See names of counties
Eastern Europe 58, 125, 137, 161
Eastern Europe–Law 171
Eastern Gas Board 36
East India Company 41
Ecclesiastical history. See Church history
Ecclesiastical history. See also Fathers of the church
Ecclesiastical law 181, 202
Ecclesiastical libraries. See Parish libraries
Ecology 14, 31
Economic assistance 28, 65
Economic assistance. See also Underdeveloped areas
Economic conditions 177
Economic conditions. See also Natural resources
Economic conditions–19th century 207
Economic history. See Economic conditions
Economic thought 137
Economic zoology. See Zoology, economic
Economics 23, 28, 30, 122, 136, 137, 141, 147, 160, 202, 185
Economics–History 122
Economics–Research 200
Economics–Statistics 84, 91, 137, 163, 200, 227

Economists 202
Eden, Robert Anthony 96
Edinburgh–Local studies 26
Education 137, 138, 139, 142, 154, 168, 197, 203
Education. See also specific subjects
Education–Biography 126
Education–Further 207
Education, higher courses 208
Education–History 98
Educational technology 169
Edwardian studies 3
EEC. See European Economic Community
Egypt 73, 112
Egypt–Antiquities 120
Egyptology–Archives 172
Egyptology 147, 172
Ehret, G D 14
Elections; parliamentary 156
Elections–Great Britain 98
Electrical engineering 126, 141
Electricity 142, 180
Electronics 220
Emblem books 125
Emblematics 162
Emigration and immigration 127
Engineering 11, 142, 125, 147
Engineers. See Mechanical engineers
England–History 67, 68
England–History. See also Great Britain–History
England–Local studies 38
English artists 128, 133
English authors 96, 122, 123, 165, 189
English drama–Collections 49, 58, 96, 168, 170
English dramatists 197
English fiction 98
English language 5, 142, 147, 174
English language–Dialects 51
English language–Dictionaries 98
English language–Scholars 202

240

241

Milton, John 3
Mineralogy 14, 119
Mineral waters 98
Mines and mineral resources
45, 141. See also Coal mines
and mining
Mongolia 160
Mongol language 10
Mongol literature 10
Molecular physics 143
Montserrat 25, 153
Monumental brasses 167
More, Sir Thomas 38
Morley, John, Viscount
Morley of Blackburn 165
Morocco 74
Mountaineering 26, 47, 58
Murdoch, William 3
Music 3, 7, 19, 22, 25, 31
38, 49, 58, 59, 91, 95, 101,
107, 125, 130, 134, 139, 142,
173, 179, 203, 207
Music, history 38
Music, Irish 95
Music, manuscript 7, 9
Music, medieval 134
Music, oriental 125
Music, printed 7
Music, religious 7
Music, scores 7, 207
Music, Scottish 58
Music, Welsh 91
Musical theory 7
Mycology. See Fungi
Myres, Sir John—Archives 173
Mythology 162

National Register of Archives
72
National Socialism 51
Natural history 14, 88, 107,
197. See also Biology
Natural resources. See also
Fisheries; Forests and forestry;
Mines and mineral resources
Nauru 25, 153
Nautical archaeology 152
Naval architecture 60

Naval art and science 40, 60,
224
Naval history 60, 114
Navies 40, 60
Nazi movement. See National
Socialism
Near East 125, 160, 167
Near East—Ancient 160
Nematology 69
Nepal 115, 178
Nevis 25, 153
Newbery, John 174
New England Company—Records
38
New Hebrides 25, 153
New Jerusalem Church 3
Newspaper cuttings. See Press
cuttings
Newspapers 8, 30, 31, 49, 59,
129
Newspapers—British provincial
8
New Zealand 25, 153
Nigeria 25, 73, 153
Nightingale, Florence 89
Niue 25, 153
Nonconformity. See Conformity;
Dissent
Nonsuch Press 31
Norfolk Islands 25, 153
Norse languages 174
North Africa 165
North America. See under names
of countries
North Derbyshire—Local studies
83
Northamptonshire—Local studies
168
Northumberland—Local studies,
167
North Thames Gas Board 36
North west England—Local studies
22
Norway—History; Literature 187
Nottinghamshire—Local studies
168
Novelists, English 96, 128, 168
Novels. See Fiction

251

NAME INDEX

257

259

260

262

265

Modern Language Association
Library (Manchester Public
Libraries—Central Library) 51
Modern Poetry Collection
(University of Birmingham
Library) 96
Modern Records Centre
(University of Warwick
Library) 200
Moncrieff Mitchell Collection
(Glasgow Public Libraries—
Mitchell Library) 31
Mond (Freda) Collection (King's
College London Library) 142
Moodies cards 23
Moody Manners Collection
(Glasgow Public Libraries—
Mitchell Library) 31
Moore (Edward) Collection
(University of Oxford—Taylor
Institution Library) 184
Morfill Collection (University of
Oxford—Taylor Institution
Library) 184
Morison Collection (Glasgow
Public Libraries—Mitchell
Library) 31
Morrell (J B) Library 202
Morris (Henry) Collection (New
University of Ulster Library)
197
Morrison Collection (National
Library of Scotland) 58
Morrison (Robert) Collection
(School of Oriental and African
Studies Library) 160
Mortara Italian Library (Bodleian
Library) 170
Moses Gaster Collection
(School of Slavonic and East
European Studies Library) 161
Mountbatten Library 126
Muirhead Library (John Rylands
University Library of Man-
chester) 165
Munro (T K) Collection
(Glasgow University Library)
125

Murchison Pamphlet Collection
(Institute of Geological Sciences
Library—Reference Library of
Geology) 42
Murdoch (William) Collection
(Birmingham Reference Library)
3
Murray Collection (Edinburgh
University Library) 121
Murray Collection (University
of Oxford—Ashmolean
Library) 172
Murray (David) Collection
(Glasgow University Library)
125
Museum of English Rural Life
Library 185

Nathan collection on explosives
(Chemical Society Library)
21
National Air Photographic
Library (University Library,
Keele) 128
National Centre for Athletics
Literature (University of
Birmingham Library) 96
National College of Agricultural
Engineering Library 118
National Documentation
Centre for Sport, Physical
Education and Recreation
(University of Birmingham
Library) 96
National Farmers' Union
History Collection (National
Farmers' Union Library) 55
National Liberal Club archives
(University of Bristol Library)
98
National Reprographic Centre
for documentation (Hatfield
Polytechnic) 206
National Union of Women's
Suffrage Manchester Collection
(Manchester Public Libraries—
Central Library) 51

271

272

276

GEOGRAPHICAL INDEX

LIST OF LIBRARIES

National libraries, specialist libraries, and public libraries

1 Animal Breeding Library
2 Australian Reference Library
3 Birmingham Reference Library
4 British Architectural Library
  The British Library:
5 British Library Reference Division, Department of Printed Books
6 British Library Reference Division, Department of Printed Books
   Map Library
7 British Library Reference Division, Department of Printed Books
   Music Library
8 British Library Reference Division, Department of Printed Books
   Newspaper Library
9 British Library Reference Division, Department of Manuscripts
10 British Library Reference Division, Department of Oriental
   Manuscripts and Printed Books
11 British Library Science Reference Library, Holborn Branch
12 British Library Science Reference Library, Bayswater Branch
13 British Library Lending Division
14 British Museum (Natural History) Library
15 British Standards Institution Library
16 Business Statistics Office Library
17 Canada House Library
18 Central Asian Research Centre
19 Central Music Library
20 Centre for Environmental Studies Library
21 Chemical Society Library
22 Chetham's Library
23 City Business Library
24 Commonwealth Bureau of Horticulture and Plantation Crops
   Library
25 Commonwealth Institute Library and Resource Centre
26 Edinburgh Central Library
27 European Communities Information Office
28 Foreign and Commonwealth Office and Ministry of Overseas
   Development Library
29 General Register Office (Scotland) Library
30 Glasgow Public Libraries, Commercial Library
31 Glasgow Public Libraries, Mitchell Library
32 Goethe Institute Library (German Institute Library)
33 Grassland Research Institute Library
34 Greater London History Library
35 Greater London Record Office, London Section
36 Greater London Record Office, Middlesex Section
37 Greater London Record Office, Maps, Prints and Photographs
   Section

38 Guildhall Library
39 Hispanic and Luso-Brazilian Council, Canning House Library
40 Imperial War Museum, Department of Printed Books
41 India Office Library and Records
42 Institute of Geological Sciences Library, Reference Library of
      Geology
43 Institute of Oceanographic Sciences Library
44 Institut Francais (French Institute Library)
45 Institution of Mining and Metallurgy Library
46 Language Teaching Library
47 Leeds City Libraries
48 Library Association Library
49 Liverpool City Libraries
50 The London Library
51 Manchester Public Libraries, Central Library
52 Ministry of Agriculture, Fisheries and Food, Main Library
53 National Army Museum Library
54 National Book League, Mark Longman Library
55 National Farmers Union Library
56 National Institute for Research in Dairying, Stenhouse Williams
      Memorial Library
57 National Library for the Blind
58 National Library of Scotland
59 National Library of Wales/Llyfrgell Genedlaethol Cymru
60 National Maritime Museum Library
61 National Meteorological Library
62 National Monuments Record
63 National Monuments Record for Wales
64 Office of Population Censuses and Surveys Library
65 Overseas Development Institute Library
66 The Polish Library
67 Public Record Office
68 Public Record Office Library
69 Rothamstead Experimental Station Library
70 Royal Botanic Gardens Library (Edinburgh)
71 Royal Botanic Gardens Library (Kew)
72 Royal Commission on Historical Manuscripts
73 Royal Commonwealth Society Library
74 Royal Geographical Society Library
75 Royal Institute of International Affairs Library and Chatham
      House Press Library
76 Royal Institution of Chartered Surveyors Library
77 Royal Photographic Society Library
78 Royal Society of Medicine Library
79 Rutherford Laboratory Library
80 St Bride Printing Library
81 Science Museum Library
82 Scottish Record Office

284

213 London: City of London Polytechnic
214 London: North-east London Polytechnic
215 London: Polytechnic of Central London
216 London: Polytechnic of North London
217 London: Polytechnic of the South Bank
218 London: Thames Polytechnic
219 Manchester Polytechnic
220 Middlesex Polytechnic
221 Newcastle upon Tyne Polytechnic
222 North Staffordshire Polytechnic
223 Oxford Polytechnic
224 Plymouth Polytechnic
225 Portsmouth Polytechnic
226 Preston Polytechnic
227 Sheffield City Polytechnic
228 Sunderland Polytechnic
229 Teesside Polytechnic
230 Trent Polytechnic
231 Ulster Polytechnic
232 Polytechnic of Wales
233 The Polytechnic, Wolverhampton

Scottish central institution libraries
234 Duncan of Jordanstone College of Art
235 Dundee College of Technology
236 Edinburgh College of Art Library
237 Edinburgh School of Agriculture
238 Glasgow School of Art
239 Leith Nautical College
240 Paisley College of Technology
241 Queen's College, Glasgow
242 Queen Margaret College
243 Robert Gordon's Institute of Technology Library
244 Royal Scottish Academy of Music and Drama Library
245 Scottish College of Textiles Library
246 University of Aberdeen School of Agriculture Library
247 West of Scotland College of Agriculture